Explorer
Mallorca

Teresa Fisher

AA Publishing

Written by Teresa Fisher
Edited, designed and produced by AA Publishing
Maps © Automobile Association Developments Ltd 1998, 2001
Revised second edition 2001
First published 1998. Reprinted 1999, 2000

The contents of this publication are believed correct at the time of printing. Nevertheless, the publishers cannot be held responsible for any errors or omissions or for changes in the details given in this guide or for the consequences of any reliance on the information provided by the same. Assessments of attractions, hotels, restaurants and so forth are based upon the author's own experience and, therefore, descriptions given in this guide necessarily contain an element of subjective opinion which may not reflect the publishers' opinion or dictate a reader's own experiences on another occasion. We have tried to ensure accuracy in this guide, but things do change and we would be grateful if readers would advise us of any inaccuracies they may encounter. Some material in this book has been previously published by AA Publishing in various other publications.

A CIP catalogue record for this book is available from the British Library.

ISBN 0 7495 3036 7
Published by AA Publishing (a trading name of Automobile Association Developments Limited, whose registered office is Norfolk House, Priestley Road, Basingstoke, Hampshire RG24 9NY. Registered number 1878835).

Colour separation by Fotographics Ltd
Printed and bound in Italy by Printer Trento srl

Page 2: Botanicactus; working windmill
Page 3: Lluc-Alcari; near Deià
Page 4: Cap St Vincente
Page 5(a): Porto Cristo
Page 5(b): Santa Maria del Cami
Page 6–7: Magaluf
Page 6(b): Valldemossa
Page 7: Palma Nova
Page 8: North-west coast, near Deià
Page 192: Porrers market
Page 193: Fornalutx

Titles in the Explorer series:
Australia • Boston & New England • Britain • Brittany California • Canada • Caribbean • China • Costa Rica Crete • Cuba • Cyprus • Egypt • Florence & Tuscany Florida • France • Germany • Greek Islands • Hawaii India • Ireland • Israel • Italy • Japan • London Mallorca • Mexico • New York • New Zealand • Paris Portugal • Provence • Rome • San Francisco • Scotland South Africa • Spain • Tenerife • Thailand • Tunisia Turkey • Turkish Coast • Venice • Vietnam

AA World Travel Guides publish nearly 300 guidebooks to a full range of cities, countries and regions across the world. Find out more about AA Publishing and the wide range of services the AA provides by visiting our Web site at www.theAA.com

How to use this book

ORGANISATION

Mallorca Is, Mallorca Was
Discusses aspects of life and culture in contemporary Mallorca and explores significant periods in its history.

A to Z
Breaks down the island into regional chapters, and covers places to visit, including walks and drives. Within this section fall the Focus On articles, which consider a variety of subjects in greater detail.

Travel Facts
Contains the strictly practical information vital for a successful trip.

Hotels and Restaurants
Lists recommended establishments in Mallorca, giving a brief summary of their attractions.

KEY TO ADMISSION CHARGES
Standard admission charges are categorised in this book as follows:

Inexpensive	under 500ptas/EUR3
Moderate	500–1,000ptas/EUR3–6
Expensive	over 1,000ptas/EUR6

ABOUT THE RATINGS
Most places described in this book have been given a separate rating:

▶▶▶   **Do not miss**

▶▶   **Highly recommended**

▶   **Worth seeing**

MAP REFERENCES
To make each particular location easier to find, every main entry in this book has a map reference to the right of its name. This comprises a number, followed by a letter, followed by another number, such as 94A2. The first number (94) indicates the page on which the map can be found; the letter (A) and the second number (2) pinpoint the square in which the main entry is located. The maps on the inside front cover and inside back cover are referred to as IFC and IBC respectively.

Contents

How to use this book 4

Contents pages 5–7

My Mallorca 8

MALLORCA IS 9–26
The largest Balearic 10–11
Spectacular scenery 12–13
Flora and fauna 14–15
For bird lovers 16–17
Festivals and events 18–19
Entertainment 20–21
Beaches and coves 22–23
For the sporty 24–25
For the jet set 26

MALLORCA WAS 27–39
Talaiotic 28–29
Continually invaded 30–31
Seafaring and piracy 32–33
Creative 34–35
Artistic 36–37
A packaged paradise 38–39

A–Z 40–176

Palma 40–71
Focus on
Local heroes 50
Language 60–61

Walks
Historic Palma 53
Maritime Palma 56

West of Palma 72–91
Focus on
Activities for children 82–83
Gastronomic specialities 90–91
Walk
Sa Trapa 89

Drive
West of Palma 85

The North-West 92–121
Focus on
Island crafts 104–105
A Winter in Majorca 118–119
Walks
Badia de Sóller 112–113
Camí de S'Arxiduc 115
Drive
Serra de Tramuntana 120–121
Train ride
Palma to Port de Sóller 108–109

The North-East 122–151
Focus on
Spectator sports 128–129
Mallorcan mansions 138–139
The Plá de Mallorca 143
Walk
The Bóquer Valley 146
Drive
Badia d'Alcúdia 132–133

The South 152–176
Focus on
Caves 164–165
Watchtowers and windmills 170
Tapas 174–175
Walk
Serra de Llevant 169
Drive
The tranquil South 162–163

TRAVEL FACTS
Arriving 178–179
Essential facts 180–181
Getting around 182–183
Communications 184–185
Emergencies 186–187
Other information 188–191
Tourist offices 192

HOTELS AND RESTAURANTS
193–203

Index 204–207

Acknowledgements 208

Maps and Plans
Western Mallorca:
  three star sights IFC
Palma 42–43
Mallorca Locator 44
Historic Palma walk 53
West of Palma 74
Sa Trapa walk 89
The North-West 94
Badia de Sóller walk 112
The North-East 124
The Bóquer Valley walk 146
The South 154–155
Serra de Llevant walk 169
Eastern Mallorca:
  three star sights IBC

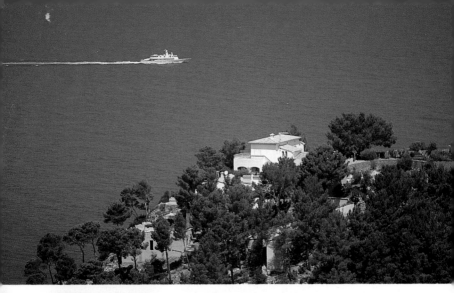

Freelance journalist and travel writer Teresa Fisher has travelled and worked widely in Europe. She contributes regularly to a variety of newspapers, magazines and guidebooks, both at home and abroad, and is the author of several recent AA publications, including *CityPack Munich*, *CityPack Amsterdam* and *Essential Provence & Côte d'Azur*. She has had a long-standing love affair with Mallorca and revisits the island whenever possible, drawn by *"la oltra Mallorca"* – away from the brash tourist resorts towards the more rural, traditional interior.

My Mallorca

What is "my Mallorca"? A cheap, cheerful, kiss-me-quick package holiday destination or "a golden island, full of light and colour; a land of dreams, a pearl enchanted, filled with splendour" (*Hymn of Mallorca* by Juan Alcover)? Essentially Mallorca is whatever you want it to be. Mass tourism is without doubt the island's lifeblood, and the main reason why 5 million tourists visit every year. But for those willing to leave the tourist-courting coastal resorts, it has so much more to offer than the hackneyed image of sun, sand, sex and sangria.

"Follow me to an island where calm reigns supreme", wrote the Catalan artist, Santiago Rusinyol in his famous poem *Mallorca – Isla de la Calma* (1911), a tempting invitation to discover *"la oltra Mallorca"* (the other Mallorca) – an island of tiny deserted coves and photogenic fishingharbours; of epic, eagle-haunted mountains plunging into transparent turquoise waters; of marshy wetlands famous for their rare birdlife; of twisting lanes that link sun-faded villages and bougainvillaea-drenched farmhouses; of terraced citrus groves with windmills whirling in the fragrant breeze.

Blessed by a perfect Mediterranean climate, Mallorca has long attracted outsiders, who have left their mark – prehistoric Talaiotic settlements, Roman amphitheatres, Arab baths, isolated hilltop monasteries, and Spain's finest gothic cathedral. Perhaps future historians will look back at the late 20th century and see the *turismo* invasion as just another phase in the island's rich history, and the strings of beach hotels fringing the coastline today as the monuments it has left behind?

It is these contrasts, combined with delicious local cuisine and friendly folk, which make the island such a fascinating holiday destination. It may well be an overused cliché, but there really are two sides to Mallorca: the sun-soaked, noisy beach holiday or the away-from-it-all break on the "Isla de la Calma". The choice is yours. I know which I prefer.
Teresa Fisher

Mallorca Is

Thanks to Mallorca's location in the Mediterranean, visitors find a unique blend of cultures here, with Europe to the north, North Africa to the south and mainland Spain, especially Catalunya, to the west. As George Sand wrote: "Simple, calm Majorca is a green Switzerland beneath a Calabrian sky, and with the silent solemnity of the Orient".

A shaded beach-side café at Can Picafort

THE ARCHIPELAGO Of all the islands in the Mediterranean Sea, none is more popular than the Balearic Islands, 82km east of the Spanish mainland. Mallorca is the largest island, roughly 100km from east to west. Menorca, only a fifth of Mallorca's size, lies 40km to its east, while the even smaller island of Ibiza, also known as Eivissa, is 85km to the south-west. Formentera, hanging close to Ibiza's southern coast, completes an archipelago attended by another 147 tiny uninhabited islands. Collectively, they form one of the 17 regions of Spain – the Comunitaónoma de les Illes Balears (the Autonomous Balearic Region).

In terms of population, this is Spain's fourth largest region, with 740,000 inhabitants. It is governed from Palma, the regional capital.

Each island has its own characteristics and a different atmosphere, with Mallorca as the longest established and most popular, Ibiza the most youth-orientated and trendiest and Menorca as the quiet, under-appreciated one with two surprising cities and spectacular unspoilt scenery. In recent years, frenetic Ibiza has become a summer mecca for ravers and clubbers, a popular holiday venue for rock and pop stars, and world famous for its nightlife. In stark contrast, the inhabitants of serene, little-visited Formentera have the longest life expectancy in the whole of Spain.

❏ The population of Mallorca is 630,000, of whom over half live in Palma. Every year around 6 million tourists visit the island, attracting an influx of seasonal staff to serve them. An idea of the lopsided effect of tourism can be gauged from the fact that the resort of Cales de Mallorca has a resident population of only 250, yet accommodation for 8,500 visitors. ❏

THE PEOPLE Most archipelagos have a collective name for their inhabitants, but not the Balearics. The people here are either Mallorquíns, Ibizencos, Menorquíns or Formenterans, and they do not always see eye to eye.

"Caution and reserve are the ruling trends of the Mallorcan character," George Sand declared in her notorious travel book, *A Winter in Majorca*. The pace of life tends to be lively in the tourist-courting coastal resorts, but slower inland where, as in Spain, *mañana* (tomorrow) is just as likely to mean the day after tomorrow, or next week, or even a month later. The population of the island has doubled since 1950, and includes a large number of expatriates – around 30,000 Germans and nearly as many from the UK.

The Catholic Church has held sway on Mallorca since the Reconquest in 1229, although, since the death of Franco in 1975, the influence of the church has declined. Nevertheless Mallorca remains a largely conformist society moulded by church, family and school. Every year some 50,000 islanders make a pilgrimage to the monastery at Lluc, home of Mallorca's patron saint, La Moreneta (see pages 95–96 and 103).

THE CLIMATE Mallorca enjoys a Mediterranean climate with mild winters and hot, dry summers. The mountains of the Serra de Tramuntana attract the greatest rainfall, and are sometimes capped with snow in winter. They act as a buffer against winds from the north, while sea breezes temper the heat of the summer months.

11

Rural Mallorca

"Here I am in the midst of palms and cedars and cactuses and olives and lemons and aloes and figs and pomegranates. The sky is turquoise blue, the sea is azure, the mountains are emerald green; the air is as pure as that of paradise." (Frédéric Chopin, 1838)

> ❏ "Sun, sea, mountains, spring water, shady trees, no politics." (Robert Graves, 1965) ❏

THE COAST Mallorca resembles a miniature continent with its hugely diverse landscape of beaches and bays, mountains, flat agricultural land and craggy cliffs. The 555km coastline is dominated by two massive bays, the Badia de Palma in the south-west and the Badia d'Alcúdia in the north-east.

The north coast is sheltered by sheer cliffs which fall abruptly to the sea while the jagged east coast is indented by hundreds of small *calas* (coves) and inlets. Two rocky islands just off the coast, Cabrera and Sa Dragonera, provide a haven for nesting seabirds.

Glass-bottomed boats allow an opportunity to observe the island's marine life, and some trips call in to beaches, coves and sea caves that would otherwise be impossible to reach – notably the 100m-long Cova Blava (Blue Grotto) on the island of Cabrera, where the reflections of the light create an intense blue.

The craggy Cap de Formentor

A MOUNTAINOUS LANDSCAPE The mountains of Mallorca are part of the Baetic Cordillera, a range of peaks that run south-west through Ibiza to southern Andalucía and Cádiz. Two mountain ranges stand guard to either side of a central plain. The limestone summits of the domineering Serra de Tramuntana (Mountains severe erosion has created deep canyons and extraordinary caves that have themselves become major tourist attractions.

HIDDEN CORNERS There is nowhere on Mallorca that is "undiscovered", but you can still find unspoilt and often deserted areas. The breezy

Mountain villages nestle in the foothills near Puigpunyent

of the North Wind) in the north-west march for 88km from Andratx to Pollença, with ten peaks over 1,000m and Mallorca's highest mountain, Puig Major (1,445m). Facing them in the south-east is the Serra de Llevant, a smaller range topped by the Puig de Sant Salvador (509m) near Felanitx. Between the two ranges lies the fertile valley known as Es Pla de Mallorca, a landscape of merrily twirling windmills and lush fields where apricots, almonds and melons are grown on a rich soil, coloured brick-red by iron oxide deposits. Here too, you will find patches of woodland, wetland, *maquis* and *garigue*, the last two habitats so characteristic of the Mediterranean region as a whole, and a magnet for wildlife.

Mallorca has no rivers, but there are numerous mountain torrents which swell after rain. The two reservoirs in the north-west, Cúber and Gorg Blau, are essential resources on an island frequently affected by drought. Mallorca is predominantly based on limestone, and in places

headland of Cap Blanc offers an invigorating walk above plunging white cliffs; the Parc Natural de Mondragó offers rich flora and fauna amid an attractive landscape of pines, shrubs, small lakes, dunes, and coves; the hairpinning coast road from Andratx to Sóller presents some of the most dramatic coastal scenery on the island. The 200-hectare protected headland of Punta de n'Amer also provides a welcome respite from the packed and noisy resorts on the east coast.

However, for many, the most scenic corner of the island is the long, narrow peninsula of Cap de Formentor. This exceptional area is reached by a winding, and often alarming, road from Port de Pollença, lined by barren rocks, lone pine trees and tall cliffs. On a clear day, the dazzling sea views from this far north-eastern tip of Mallorca stretch as far as Menorca.

A naturalist could happily spend a lifetime exploring the wilds of Mallorca and there is plenty of scope for observations throughout the year. Behind the façade of hotels, restaurants and tourist beaches lies an island rich in wildlife, and the range of Mediterranean flowers here has made Mallorca a mecca for botanists.

ISLAND OF FLOWERS One of the most memorable sights in Mallorca is the pinky-white haze of its almond trees in blossom. Come at the end of January or early in February and the fields of the central plain appear covered with snow.

In March and April wild flowers appear on the banks and verges – tiny orange field marigolds (*Calendula arvensis*), tall, white-flowered umbellifers and cow parsley known as Queen Anne's lace. On the roadsides you will see shepherd's purse (*Capsella bursapastoris*), common fennel (*Foeniculum vulgare*), bright yellow oxalis and spiky, white-flowered asphodel, alongside daisies, violets, primroses, gladioli, poppies and many species of orchid.

The natural terrain of Mallorca up to around 700m is *garigue*, a partly forested scrubland where the island's native trees – carob, holm oak, dwarf palms – are ubiquitous, as are silvery-leaved olive trees. Some of these are over 1,000 years old with

❑ The carob tree (*Ceratonia siliqua*) thrives in the hot arid soil of the Mediterranean region. It has thick shiny leaves, a gnarled trunk and long seedpods that turn from green to black as they ripen. The pods are primarily used as animal feed and the fruit is made into a chocolate substitute sold in health food stores. The word "carat", used today as a unit of weight for gold, derives from "carob". ❑

fantastically contorted trunks. Between 700m and 950m, the *garigue* is replaced by *maquis*, a scrubland illuminated by the blue-flowered rosemary, vivid yellow broom, laurel and myrtle interspersed with rich swathes of bracken. Higher still is a rocky terrain of hardy grasses and cacti.

Mallorca also has a wonderful variety of flowering shrubs. Look out for the many types of tree heather and rock-roses, the most common being the pink spring-flowering, velvety grey-leafed cistus. The shiny-leaved strawberry tree (*Arbutus unedo*) has fruits that turn red in October.

With such natural abundance, the Mallorcans are understandably fond of flowers. Take a walk through the flower stalls on Palma's

Colourful flowers abound in Mallorca

Pine marten and Moorish gecko

La Rambla and you can see the serious contemplation that invariably precedes a purchase. Like their Moorish predecessors, the islanders value gardens as places of beauty and refuge from the summer heat. Their balconies and patios are ablaze with carnations, geraniums and ferns while, in the resorts, garish modern architecture is softened by the presence of date palms, oleanders, hibiscus, honeysuckle and bougainvillaea.

GRASSHOPPERS, GOATS AND GECKOS The star performer of Mallorcan wildlife has long been extinct. Six million years ago *Myotragus* stalked the Balearic Islands, a peculiarly shaped antelope with eyes at the front of its head and buck teeth which functioned like a pickaxe. In comparison, the creatures currently scurrying around Mallorca appear unexciting – deer, mountain goats, wild sheep, pine martens, genets, weasels and rarely seen spotted civet cats, together with smaller mammals such as hedgehogs, rabbits, hares and shrews.

Warm summer nights are characterised by the strumming of grasshoppers, mole crickets and cicadas. There are over 200 species of moth and around 30 types of butterfly, including the unusual gold and bronze two-tailed pasha butterfly, found around strawberry trees.

This abundance of insects provides favourable conditions for lizards, snakes and other reptiles, including the poisonous horned viper and

Levantine viper. Look out also for the lowland-living wall gecko and the mountain-dwelling disc-fingered gecko basking in the sun. The island of Cabrera boasts the elusive, blue-bellied Lilford's wall lizard.

Mallorca's marshlands harbour frogs, and three types of toad: one, the rare Mallorcan midwife toad, is almost extinct. At S'Albufera, a chorus of croaking marsh frogs can be heard everywhere, whereas the Serra de Tramuntana mountains are uniquely the home of the ferreret, a small toad found nowhere else in the world.

Two-tailed pasha butterfly

In recent years, the Balearic Islands, and in particular Mallorca, have become established as one of Europe's finest birdwatching areas. Twitchers flock from all over the world to see such birds as Montagu's harriers, Eleonora's falcons, red kites, black vultures, booted eagles, Bonelli's eagles and other scarce birds of prey.

The rare hoopoe can be seen at S'Albufereta all year round

BIRD MIGRATION Mallorca occupies a geographical position of strategic importance. Not only does it enjoy a prime position in the Mediterranean where many migrating birds land each spring and winter, but it also offers a great diversity of habitat – marshes and reedbeds, freshwater lagoons and salt-pans, scrubland, fields, orchards and woods, rocky sea cliffs and wild mountains – attracting further varieties and luring bird-watchers to Mallorca from all over the world for the chance of seeing almost any European species of migrant bird.

Even if you are not a specialist, it is worth listening out for screeching and chirruping in the sky above, and gazing skywards from time to time to spot a flock of swifts, a rainbow-coloured swirl of bee-eaters, or maybe greenfinches and goldfinches, stonechats, tawny pipits, or even blue rock thrushes. On the coast, you may see black storks patrolling the shoreline, an osprey plunging down to snatch a huge fish or, in the northern corner of the island, black vultures with a wing-span of 3m, crag martins and Eleonora's falcons swooping round the Formentor lighthouse. Scan the sea far below and you may see Cory's shearwaters. Low bushes and scrub on the peninsula sometimes harbour skulking Marmora's warblers.

WETLAND BIRDS Keen twitchers should head straight to S'Albufera, the most important site for birdwatchers in the Balearics, with over 200 species of bird within a vast protected area of marshes, reed-beds and waterways. Here you will see wildfowl dozing in the creeks, herons and egrets concealed in the

❏ Hunting is a popular sport on the island with quail, turtle doves, wood pigeons, red-legged partridges, mallards and coots among the targets. The wholesale slaughter of migrating thrushes is also permitted using purpose-made nets known as *caças a coll*. The farmers consider these olive-loving birds a pest, while cooks see them as a country delicacy. Restrictions were recently introduced to promote responsible hunting – the fine for killing a black vulture is very large. ❏

reeds, and waders probing stealthily round the muddy lagoons. Look out also for black-winged stilts, Kentish plovers, marsh harriers, whiskered terns, water rail, purple heron and, at dusk, the elusive night heron. Although good throughout the year, S'Albufera has most to offer in spring, between March and June when resident birds are joined by migrants. If you are lucky, you may see stonechats, moustached warblers and the rare long-eared owl. Ospreys leave their breeding sites on the cliffs to fish here; peregrines and flamboyantly striped hoopoes live here all year round. A visitor centre provides a useful introduction, particularly the audio-visual display where you can listen to birdsong and learn about the programme devised to protect the white-headed duck.

The Salines de Llevant and S'Albufereta (a smaller version of S'Albufera) are two other magnets for wetland birds and visiting bird-watchers, keen to record egrets, warblers, black-winged stilts, Kentish plovers as well as numerous migrant waders and wildfowl. In winter, small groups of flamingos have been spotted at the Salines de Llevant. Near by, at the southernmost tip of Mallorca, Cap de ses Salines is an excellent area for seawatching with Cory's and Mediterranean shearwaters, and gulls being most in evidence during strong, onshore winds.

If you are lucky, you may see an osprey hunting off the coast

As in many parts of the Mediterranean, wildlife and the natural landscape are under threat from development. Fortunately, through the efforts of the environmental group GOB (Grupo Ornithologia Balear) and the local authorities, almost a third of the island is now protected in some way, ensuring its future as a paradise for birds and birdwatchers alike.

A black-winged stilt is a draw for keen birdwatchers at S'Albufera

Festivals are popular in Spain, and in Mallorca scarcely a week goes by without one. The inspiration for most festivities is religious, but rural traditions and historic events on the island make their mark too, with the celebration of animals, fish, grapes, sausages and even melons all excuses for a fiesta.

*Musicians entertain visitors to
La Granja*

FESTIVAL FROLICS One of the most popular fiestas on the island is the Moros i Cristianos, a mainland Spanish celebration of the Christian overthrowing of the Moors, which attracts equally large crowds in the villages of Mallorca. The grandest shows take place in Sóller and Pollença, where a villager representing a heroic figure from the past musters the people to defend the port. The ensuing mock battle is a noisy, colourful and dramatic affair.

Food is a popular theme for festivals, especially in villages on the agricultural plain. In Porreres, Lenten Carnival celebrations climax with a massive outdoor sardine feast. In Vilafranca de Bonany the second Saturday in September is dedicated to the melon, with competitions, and a free melon for every villager. On 4 September, Santa Barbara's Day, there is a *bunyols* (sweet fritters) feast in honour of their patron saint. But perhaps the most eccentric food fiesta is the Festa d'es Botifarró o de sa Torrada (the Sausage or Roast Feast) held at Sant Joan in October to mark the arrival of winter.

In contrast, the Cavellet fiesta of Felanitx during August is strictly religious, commencing with children dancing in the church then galloping around town on papier-mâché hobby-horses, followed by *cabezudos* (big heads – the traditional Spanish giants) and a small band of *xeremies* (Mallorquín bagpipe), *fabiol* (small flute) and *tamborí* (small drum).

Other dance festivals that are accompanied by these instruments include the famous Cossier dances, part of an ancient tradition which was documented in Mallorca as early as 1554. The dances are interpreted by three pairs of men, a devil and a lady; *cossier* means "to run ceremoniously". The men, dressed in colourful red, white and green costumes (resembling *siurells*, see page 104) and carrying bouquets of roses, pursue the lady, who carries little bows and bells. The Cossiers can be seen in Montuïri on 15, 23 and 24 August during the Saint Bartholomew fiesta and in Algaida on 16 January, in honour of the town's patron saint, Sant Honorat.

DEVILISH FUN! At one time the colourful and eye-catching *Dimonis* (devils) that dance through Mallorcan festivities were banned by the Church. Now they appear at many fiestas, hurling firecrackers and lewdly tempting saints and spectators alike. One of the island's oldest

rituals, played out annually at Montuïri, features a shabbily dressed devil with horns and a cow-bell being danced into submission by a Lady, who concludes her conquest by placing a triumphant foot on the defeated devil. In the fiesta at Santa Margalida – called Carro de la Beata (see page 150) – anarchic devils infiltrate a procession of villagers dressed in rural costume, snatching their *gerres* (pitchers) and smashing them at the feet of Mallorca's own saint, Santa Catalina Thomás.

Some fiestas begin on the eve (*revelta*) of a local saint's day, when ceremonial bonfires (*foguerons*) are lit. At Sa Pobla, the Revelta de Sant Antoni dates back to 1365; the celebrants tuck into specially made eel and spinach pie and dance to traditional music played on bagpipe, flute

and drum. In Pollença the local lads bring a pine tree down from the mountains; it is then made into a soapy pole for the townsfolk to climb.

The fiesta calendar is at its busiest between June and September. For the non-religious visitor, country fairs and the more theatrical fiestas are the most rewarding events to track down. Instead of standing around and waiting for the parade to begin (it's bound to be late), get into a bar, have a few drinks and ask the waiter where is the best place to stand – and when. Then have a devil of a good time.

Fiestas are an integral part of Mallorcan life

19

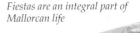

When it comes to entertainment Mallorca has something for everyone, whether it be a highbrow art exhibition, the latest Hollywood film release, a deafeningly loud disco or the opera. Indeed, in recent years, the island has become an important Mediterranean cultural centre, particularly renowned for its prestigious musical events.

Visitors are treated to a display of traditional dances at La Granja

ARTS EVENTS Concerts and music festivals are staged in Mallorca throughout the year, including a programme of musical and popular events in the resorts between November and April. Palma alone offers a festival of classical and light music for the Sant Sebastià fiesta in January, an international week of organ music in March, a spring opera season from March to June at the Teatre Principal, summer serenades in Castell de Bellver throughout July and August and a week of organ concerts in October.

Elsewhere on the island, of note are the international folk dancing festival at Sóller in July, the acclaimed international music festival in Pollença and Chopin festival at Valldemossa in July and August, various summer music festivals in Deià, Artà and Santuari de Cura on Puig de Randa, and an autumn festival of classical music in Bunyola in September and October. Exhibitions of traditional Mallorcan music and dance are staged regularly throughout the summer at La Granja and

❏ To find out what is happening on the entertainment front, pick up from any tourist office a free quarterly called *Events*, produced in English with an up-to-date listing of the main sporting and cultural activities in the Balearic Islands. Programmes and topical events are also advertised in local papers, the *Majorca Daily Bulletin* and other tourist-orientated publications (see page 184). ❏

Valldemossa and often coincide with coach excursions.

Mallorca has a buoyant art scene, and several art galleries have bars and bookshops attached – notably Fundació La Caixa (see page 51) and Sa Nostra (Carrer de Concepció 12, tel: 971 725210) in Palma.

Outside the capital, other major galleries include Maior (Plaça Major 4, Pollença, tel: 971 530095), Pedrona Torrens (Carrer de Sant Jaume 23, Alcúdia, tel: 971 548324) and a converted railway station arts centre called S'Estació (Carrer d'Estació, Sineu, tel: 971 520750). Look out for the free bi-monthly leaflet, issued by Associació Independent de Galeries d'Art de Balears, which gives details of some private exhibitions.

BARS, PUBS AND CLUBS All the resorts have a strip of wall-to-wall neon-lit pubs and bars. Some, such as Magaluf, S'Arenal and Can Pastilla, seem to offer little else. In Palma the greatest concentration is around Plaça Gomila in the seedy Es Terreno district. More upmarket and more central, Carrer dels Apuntadors to the west of the cathedral is always lively.

There are over 150 discothèques and nightclubs in Mallorca, providing sounds for everyone from teeny-boppers to the young at heart. Though the wilder scene is on the neighbouring island of Ibiza, home of the "Balearic beat", several establishments on Mallorca have earned a reputation for their extravagant décor and light shows. The best alternative discos tend to come and go, or at least change their names to suggest

they are moving with the times. To find out where is currently "in", you need to ask around in bars and trendy clothes shops, or chat up the beach Adonises handing out flyers. The island's top nightclubs include Palma's sophisticated Abacanto in the suburb of Indioteria, the open-air disco Menta at Port d'Alcúdia, and Dhraa, a designer disco with international sounds on the road from Porto Cristo to Cala Millor, and the riotous BCM in Magaluf (see page 84).

Night-time entertainment is widely available and varied

CINEMA AND SHOWS Many hotels and bars in the resorts screen English-language videos and TV programmes. Otherwise, programmes and times for cinemas are advertised in the local newspapers. Films are usually dubbed into Castilian Spanish. Other popular evening entertainment is provided by a variety of floorshows, barbecues, pirate adventures and medieval banquets which can be booked through your hotel.

Mallorca instantly conjures up visions of warm turquoise seas and sandy beaches shaded by pines and, with approximately 180 beaches and calas (coves) embracing the island, it really is a seaside paradise. Beaches range from tiny creeks to vast expanses of white icing-sugar sand, and there is always enough space to accommodate everyone, even at the peak of summer.

BEACHES One of the nicest jobs on Mallorca must be counting its beaches. The latest official tally of tourist beaches was 76, of which 25 were awarded Blue Flags by the European Union for being safe, clean and well kept.

Beaches are crucial to the success of tourism on the island, and the Mallorcans work hard to maintain high standards in the resorts – most notably in the recent facelifts given to the seafronts in Palma Nova, Magaluf and S'Arenal, with their new promenades, imported sand to widen the beaches and improved watersports facilities. What's more, the bathwater-warm shallow water and the exceptional cleanliness of so many beaches make them safe for children and ideal for family holidays.

If you come in the summer, don't waste time trying to find that undiscovered, blissfully deserted beach. Once Platja Es Trenc in the south of the island fulfilled most people's isolationist dreams, but now even that has a car park and a café-bar. There are no holiday developments here though, and as a result it is a popular spot for nude sunbathing and swimming. Nearer Palma, the tiny Platja Mago (off the road to Portals Vells) attracts a similar clothes-free crowd.

However, the majority of visitors are happy to join in with the seething, sun-worshipping masses in the resorts. The most popular beaches are those around Badia de Palma, Badia d'Alcúdia and Badia de Pollença. The nearest beaches to Palma are Can Pastilla and S'Arenal to the east and Cala Major to the south-west. On the east coast the tourist centres are Cala Bona, Cala d'Or, Cala Millor and Sa Coma. Although all these resort beaches are well equipped and have good sand, at the height of the season everyone is likely to be packed tightly together on towel-sized segments of sand.

❏ The best way to explore Mallorca's 555km coastline is by boat. Organised trips only run in the summer (except in the Badia de Palma). Scenic trips include Port d'Andratx to Sant Telm (tel: 971 246698), Port de Sóller westwards to Sant Telm or eastwards to Sa Calobra (tel: 971 630170) and Port de Pollença to Cap de Formentor (tel: 971 864014). ❏

CALAS A quieter and more enjoyable alternative to these well-known hot-spots are the many *calas* (coves) which indent the fjord-like coastline, especially in the south-east. High, deeply eroded cliffs often shelter tiny white ribbons of sand at the end of these small inlets, backed by shady pines.

The water tends to be invitingly blue and clear – ideal for snorkelling, diving from the rocks, and for strong swimmers who feel frustrated by the shallow waters of the larger bays. Try Cala Pi (south of Llucmajor), Cala Llombards and Cala Santanyí (both east of Santanyí), or the larger beaches at Cala Agulla and Cala Mesquida (both north of Capdepera).

Other hidden gems include Cala Tuent (a few kilometres away from tourist honeypot Sa Calobra, yet never crowded); pebbly Cala de Deià, with its ramshackle bar and icy, clear waters; and Playa Formentor, a classic palm-lined beach of fine white sand and crystal-clear turquoise waters. Then there's the little-known beach of Colònia de Sant Pere and, for something totally out-of-the-way, Cala Egos, best approached by boat. This 80m-long deserted beach of silken sand with no shop, bar or restaurant, no pedalos and no parasols, is perhaps the closest you come to paradise during your stay in Mallorca.

Away from the tourist resorts you will find hidden creeks like this one at Cala Pi

23

The range of sports available on Mallorca is wide and the facilities excellent. The main attractions for visitors are watersports and golf, while football, basketball and cycling appeal to many Mallorcans (see pages 128–129).

WATERSPORTS Of all sports in the Balearics, sailing must be the most pleasant and relaxing. Mallorca has for years been a proven favourite with the Mediterranean yachting fraternity because of its beautiful and varied coastline. A yacht also enables access to tiny, deserted coves

24

Mallorca offers a wide range of watersports, including sailing, waterskiing and windsurfing

and unspoilt beaches unapproachable by road. Several specialist holiday operators offer sailing packages and yachts can be chartered. The premier sailing event of the year is the Copa del Rey (King's Cup) in August, attended by King Juan Carlos.

Numerous hotels and beaches have small dinghies, canoes, kayaks and pedalos for hire on an hourly basis. Lessons in **dinghy sailing**, **waterskiing** and **windsurfing** are available in most marinas, and there are **scuba-diving** clubs in Palma, Port d'Andratx and Santa Ponça. For further details, contact the headquarters of the Escuela Nacional de Vela Calanova (National Sailing School) at

Avenida Joan Miró in
Palma (tel: 971 402512).

LANDLUBBER SPORTS

Most hotels and holiday
centres offer extensive
sports facilities. You will
find **tennis** courts in every
urbanización, and at many
hotels. The more exclusive
often have a resident coach
and insist that players wear
"whites". Many resorts also
have **horse-riding** facilities,
frequently offering special
instruction and mounts for
children. The best facilities and
terrain for trekking are around the
east and north-east coastal resorts.

*Cycling, a pleasurable and healthy way
to explore the island*

Cycling is one of Mallorca's most
popular sports and family activities.
July and August are usually too hot
to enjoy a major expedition, but you
can still have fun hiring a bike in a
resort for the day and pottering along
the coast. The Badia d'Alcúdia is
obligingly flat, and a pleasant *pista de
bicicletas* (cycle track) runs between
Port d'Alcúdia and Can Picafort. You
can cycle in the S'Albufera nature
reserve too (see page 148). Another
cycle track curls round the centre of
the Badia de Palma from Portixol
west to Sa Pedrera, passing along
Palma's seafront. For more of a challenge, ask for the Guia del Ciclista
map available from tourist offices,
detailing six itineraries ranging from
70km to 150km or, for real masochists,
there is always the 320km, 13-hour
round-island race every spring.

Thanks to the remarkable variety of
terrain, **walking** and **mountain climbing** have long been popular pastimes.
To scale the big peaks, it is best to
join a guided trek organised by the
Federacíon Española de Montanismo
in Palma (tel: 971 468807) or notify
the Guardia Civil of your intended
route. The most challenging climb is
the sheer Torrent de Pareis (see page
107), which should only be
attempted by experienced climbers.
Mallorca's highest mountain, Puig
Major (1,445m), has a military radar
station on its peak and can only be
scaled with special permission.

Mallorca is a popular destination
for **golfing** holidays, especially for
winter golfers fleeing the frosty
greens back home. The best of
Mallorca's 15 courses are near Palma,
including the oldest and most exclusive, Son Vida (tel: 971 791210) and
Real Golf de Bendinat (tel: 971
405200), with other scenic courses
dotted around the island at
Canyamel, Capdepera, Pollença,
Santa Ponça and Son Servera. Bring a
handicap certificate. For further
information ask the tourist office for
their golfing pamphlet or call the
Federació Balear de Golf in Palma
(tel: 971 722753).

*Mallorca is now a popular golfing
destination*

Mallorca's jet setters are no different from anywhere else in the world but, because of the island's size, they are more noticeable. Their presence is applauded by the proud locals, who see it as free publicity for their beloved island.

❏ You are certain to see members of the Spanish royal family at the following events in Mallorca: at Easter, Sunday Mass in Palma Cathedral and the "Princess Sofía Cup" sailing regatta in the bay; and in August, the Chopin Festival in Valldemossa, the HRH Princess Elena Horse Jumping Trophy in Bunyola and Palma's "King's Cup" sailing regatta. ❏

PRESTIGIOUS GUEST LIST Mallorca's reputation as an island of sun, sea and celebrities is well earned. Both the Spanish and British royal families frequently holiday here, heading a VIP guest list that has included Errol Flynn, Winston Churchill, Charlie Chaplin, Richard Nixon, Agatha Christie, Jack Nicholson, Joan Collins and Michael Schumacher. Some arrive in luxury yachts and cruisers, while others stay at top hotels like the Son Vida and La Residencia, or rent villas high up in the mountains.

The luxurious lifestyle enjoyed by the rich and famous

RESIDENTS A few celebrities have been so beguiled by the indefinable appeal of the island's countryside that they have bought property in Mallorca's interior. They include pop star Annie Lennox at Esporlas, model Claudia Schiffer at Camp de Mar, and actor Michael Douglas with his wife, actress Catherine Zeta-Jones, in S'Estaca near Deià. His residence, once owned by the island's favourite foreign aristocrat, known as S'Arxiduc (Archduke Ludwig Salvator of Austria, see page 114), was so expensive that local residents have since nicknamed him "Archdouglas".

Perhaps the next to join them will be British "Virgin" entrepreneur Richard Branson, whose interests on the island already include Deià's beautiful La Residencia, arguably the island's most exclusive hotel (see page 196), and two duty-free shops in Palma Airport. He has also bought a second estate at Banyalbufar (see page 85). The land covers a large region of vineyards, raising the question: is this going to be another luxury hotel, Branson's very own "Residencia", or is "Virgin vino" soon to be appearing on supermarket shelves?

Mallorca Was

"The Balearics can claim with justice to be a paradise for archaeologists. A professional archaeologist, or an amateur, would find a lifetime's occupation here, even if he confined himself to the stone memorials of prehistoric times – the monuments of the megalithic culture." (Luis Ripoll, Spanish writer)

Visitors will find well-preserved remains of the Talaiotic settlement at Ses Païsses

EARLY CIVILISATION The oldest traces of human life so far identified on Mallorca have been dated to around 4000 BC, the end of the neolithic period. Later discoveries of ancient stone dwellings, pottery and flint tools suggest a new era emerging, with the Balearic Islands settled by an industrious and well-organised people who left enigmatic visiting cards around Mallorca known as *talaiots*. These megalithic monuments get their name from *"atalaya"*, the Arab word for "watchtower", and have become eponymous symbols of the talented civilisation that flourished here during the Bronze Age. Pre-Talaiotic culture started around 2000 BC and was principally cave based. These people probably lived in peaceful communities dedicated to agriculture and hunting.

CHARACTERISTIC FEATURES By 1500 BC, new types of building were emerging. *Navetas*, burial chambers that resemble upturned boats, were being constructed and *talaiots*, tall, tower-shaped buildings with a central inner chamber, constructed using dry blocks of stone, without mortar. This most creative phase, the Talaiotic, lasted from 1300 BC until about 800 BC and coincided with the emergence of a more violent and hierarchical society.

Late Talaiotic is characterised by the construction of *taulas*, colossal table-like stone structures, well preserved in Menorca, although none remain in Mallorca. By the 6th century BC Talaiotic culture was on the wane as the islands came under

the influence of the Greeks and the Phoenicians.

Some 100 *talaiots* have been located in Mallorca. These towers were built to both circular and quadrangular plans, and were mostly constructed as observation posts and residences, perhaps for the settlement's leading clan. They often stood in the middle of surprisingly large settlements, sometimes surrounded by defensive walls some 2m high.

The best places to see structures like these on the island are at the well-preserved Talaiotic settlements of Capocorb Vell (see page 161) and Ses Païsses (see page 150). Archaeological finds from the period, including ceramics, weapons, tools and jewellery, can be seen in the Museu de Mallorca in Palma (see page 52) and the Museu Regional in Artà (see page 135).

TALAIOTIC LIFESTYLE Further research and comparison with similar cultures in Sardinia and Corsica suggest that life in Talaiotic times was surprisingly sophisticated. The islanders kept sheep, pigs and cattle, constructed ingenious wells and made

The outer wall at Capocorb Vell has stood since around 1000 BC

a delicate, decorated pottery. They also had bronze objects – dagger blades, arrowheads and coins. They were skilled in using a sling, and a number of sling stones have been recovered.

The questions raised by these prehistoric inhabitants are numerous and complex: why were the *talaiots* built, what was the significance of the *taulas*, and why were the burial chambers, the *navetas*, shaped like little boats? Whatever the answers, as Luis Ripoll said: "The archaeological richness of the islands is so impressive that all visitors – even those who have little interest in these problems – should make a point of seeing some of their prehistoric monuments."

Prehistoric pottery can be viewed at Palma's museums

29

For more than 2,000 years Mallorca has been the focus of strategic and economic interest because of its peculiar geographical situation in the centre of the western Mediterranean. All the nations of the ancient world have come here: Greeks, Carthaginians, Romans, Visigoths, Vandals, Byzantines and Arabs.

PHOENICIANS, GREEKS AND CARTHAGINIANS Following the Talaiotic period which reached its peak around 1000 BC (see pages 28–9), Mallorca suffered a period of great uncertainty, with constant invasions and conquests by sea-borne rulers and pirates. The Phoenicians were the first to arrive, maritime traders from the eastern Mediterranean. It is believed that they did not stay long, as few Phoenician artefacts have been discovered in the Balearics. However archaeologists have unearthed some remains at Alcúdia.

Around 800 BC the Phoenicians were displaced by the Greeks, who used the island mainly as a staging post for sea trade. The Greeks gave the Balearics their name, derived from *ballein*, meaning "to throw from a sling". Texts from this time refer to Balearic slingshot throwers from Mallorca fighting as mercenaries in the Punic Wars. During the 6th century BC the Balearic Islands were conquered by the Carthaginians, who used the islands' favourable position to develop their piracy and to

The statue of a slingthrower (hondero) *in Palma*

work as mercenaries. The islands remained firmly under the control of the Carthaginians for several centuries. Little is known of their occupation except that they established several new settlements in Menorca, and it is also claimed that Hannibal, the famous Carthaginian general, was born on Mallorca, although Ibiza and Malta claim this honour too.

ROMANS, VANDALS AND BYZANTINES After the collapse of the Carthaginian empire, Mallorca was annexed and subdued in 123 BC by the Romans, under Quintus Caecilius Metellus. Over the succeeding centuries a prolonged "Romanisation" of the island took place. The Romans called it Balearis Major, a forerunner of today's name. They introduced olive and vineyard cultivation, and they built paved roads, improved ports and fortresses and established cities at Pollentia (now Alcúdia) and Palmaria, close to modern-day Palma. The island's economy boomed, cultural development reached its height and, by the 2nd century AD, Christianity had taken hold. However, this stable situation changed suddenly. A Vandal invasion in 426 led to vast devastation and religious persecution until the Byzantine conquest in 534 restored

Christianity and introduced an element of self-government.

THE MOORS AND THE CHRISTIANS
The brief spell under Byzantine rule restored prosperity and stability to Mallorca. Then followed a period of devastating attack from the Moors. The islanders put up a fierce struggle, but the Moors retaliated and, with an armada of 300 ships, they finally conquered Mallorca in 902. This brought the island into the Caliphate of Córdoba and began a period when Mallorca was the envy of Europe. Moorish culture prevailed and flourished. Oranges, almonds and apricots were introduced, along with windmills and irrigation techniques, and Palma, known as Medina Mayurqa, enjoyed a level of civilisation only dreamed of elsewhere, with heated baths, street lights and covered sewers.

This luxurious lifestyle attracted the attention of potential conquerors, and in 1229 the young Catalan king, Jaume I of Aragón, set sail to capture

The remains of the smallest Roman amphitheatre in Spain can be seen at Alcúdia

the island. For most Mallorcans, history did not really begin until this date, when he landed at Santa Ponça in September to retake the island from the Moors. He entered Palma, "the most beautiful city I have set eyes upon", on New Year's Eve. He replaced the mosques with churches, converted the old Arab palace into Gothic style, and built the imposing Castell de Bellver as a sign that the Christians were here to stay. His reign (1229–1276) is still seen as Mallorca's golden age of independence.

Over the centuries, Mallorca's economy and social history has been strongly influenced by the sea. Despite repeated invasions and corsair raids, this tiny island was once world famous for its oceanographers, leading the way in maritime trade and exploration.

THE KINGDOM OF MALLORCA It was in the early 13th century that young King Jaume I, under political and economic pressure from the states of Aragón and Catalunya, decided to

get rid of the "unbelievers" (the Moors) and to conquer the "pirate's nest of Mallorca". His expedition of 150 ships, 16,000 men and 1,500 horses set sail for Pollença in September 1229. However, a strong *mistral* forced them to turn to the south of the island. Avoiding the heavily fortified harbour of Palma, they finally landed at the bay of Santa Ponça. Following a surprise attack on Palma, the Moors capitulated, Christianity spread throughout the island and the Kingdom of Mallorca soon gained power and importance beyond its immediate borders.

Following centuries of relentless invasions and conquests, Mallorca remained a "nest of pirates". Even Moorish corsairs still based in Mallorca continued to operate more or less undisturbed in the western Mediterranean.

By the start of the 14th century, the island was considered to have one of the most dynamic and economically successful societies in Christendom, in the forefront of the quest for new colonies and maritime trade. Mallorcan *cogs* were the best ships on the sea, leading the way in Atlantic exploration, and the island became famous for its cartographers, whose nautical charts were known for their accuracy throughout the world.

In the 16th century, there followed a period of political and economic uncertainty. New shipping routes had been discovered around the Cape of Good Hope to the Indies and to the Americas and the focus of European trade moved from the Mediterranean to the Atlantic seaboard. Mallorca lacked foreign currency and its merchants began to leave.

From Moorish to Christian – the 1229 conquest of Mallorca

Jaume I's reign brought great prosperity

At this time, the island once again became subject to large-scale maritime raids from North Africa, hence the watchtowers still seen around the coast today (see page 170). As the Moorish pirates increased the number and ferocity of their attacks, so the Mallorcans took precautionary measures, building their towns and villages well inland from their harbours.

Sea trade started to flourish again in the 18th and 19th centuries. Fast sailing ships sailed to the Caribbean and rounded the Cape of Good Hope. In 1833 a regular ferry service commenced between Palma and mainland Spain. Steamers built in Palma became important in the shipping business and trade relations overseas flourished.

20TH-CENTURY SEAFARING The
Austrian Archduke Ludwig Salvator ("Luis Salvator" in Mallorca), unknowingly laid the foundations for the development of tourism in Mallorca (see pages 35 and 114). His extensive writings on Mallorca's culture, flora and fauna drew the first tourists to the Balearics. During the Spanish Civil War (1936–1239), the island's development faltered once again. Later, during the Second World War, German submarines used the protected bays with their hideouts to attack the allies' ships.

The end of the war brought more security to the island, but no peace as mass tourism emerged. In 1935, only about 50,000 tourists arrived either by yacht or on cruise ships. Although nowadays most visitors arrive by air, the tradition of seafaring continues, as each year more and more yachts and sailing craft arrive to make Mallorca their permanent mooring, in some of the most prestigious marinas in the Mediterranean.

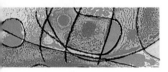

Over the centuries, Mallorca has stimulated the creativity of many of the writers, musicians and artists who have visited the island, lived here or were brought up amidst its glowing colours.

CHOPIN George Sand was convinced that the sublimity of Polish composer Frédéric Chopin's Preludes, composed or completed during their stay at Valldemossa (see page 116) in 1838–1839, was a direct response to an environment enriched by

Chopin's bust on display at Valldemossa's monastery

FRÉDÉRIC CHOPIN
1810 1849
J. BORRELL-Nic...fecit

"deceased monks, birds singing in trees, and the "twang" of far-off guitars". To her mind, raindrops falling on the Charterhouse roof were transformed by Chopin's "imagination and singing gift into tears falling on the heart" in his "Raindrop" Prelude. Chopin denied that his art was achieved by a puerile imitation of the external, but critics agree that he emerged from his Mallorcan sojourn a more mature composer.

MIRO The painter and sculptor Joan Miró, whose mother and wife came from Mallorca, was more candid about the direct influence of the island on his vibrantly coloured work. "As a child," he recalled, "I loved to watch the always changing Mallorcan sky. At night I would get carried away by the writing in the sky of the shooting stars, and the lights of the fireflies…It was here that I received the first creative seeds which became my work." It was here also that he moved away from traditional painting and experiments in Cubism to develop his own characteristically bold style of vigorous lines and intense primary colours. Miró's studio on the outskirts of Palma (see page 80) is a testimony to the way the artist found inspiration in nature – a piece of driftwood, an almond stone, a drystone wall. As his friend Joan Prats put it: "When I pick up a rock, it's a rock; when Miró picks it up, it's a Miró."

GRAVES The minutiae of island life also absorbed English poet, novelist and long-term Deià resident Robert Graves, whose *Mallorcan Stories* chronicle the tragicomic vicissitudes befalling both

34

locals and visitors, such as the theft of a bicycle or a farcical christening. He is best known for his bestsellers, *Goodbye to All That*, an autobiographical account of his experiences in World War I, and *I, Claudius*, a historical novel that brings to life ancient Rome. With money made from the first book he was able to move to Mallorca between the wars with his mistress and fellow poet Laura Riding. After World War II, he settled permanently on the island in the mountain village of Deià (see page 101).

❏ For further reading on Mallorca try:
• *The Doll's Room*, Llorenç Villalonga. A novel portraying life in 19th-century Mallorca, by a local writer.
• *A Winter in Majorca*, George Sand. Highly critical recollections of the island by Chopin's lover (see pages 118–119).
• *Jogging round Majorca*, Gordon West. A gentle, light-hearted account of travels round pre-touristic Mallorca in the 1920s.
• *Problem at Pollensa Bay*, Agatha Christie. A romantic short story set in pre-war Mallorca, with a twist to the tale (see page 144).
• *Our Man in Majorca*, Tom Crichton. A comical, disaster-filled account of life as a tour rep in the early 1960s.
• *Not Part of the Package*, Paul Richardson. Highly entertaining insight into mass tourism in the Balearics (set in Ibiza).
• *Wild Olives*, William Graves. An account of his experiences of Deia and its people from the 1940s to the 1970s, and also his troubled family life. ❏

Robert Graves working at his desk in Deià

THE ARCHDUKE The greatest and most diligent creative response to Mallorca, however, must be the work of the indefatigable Archduke Luis Salvador (see page 114). Arriving on the island in 1867, at the age of 19, he immersed himself in all things Mallorquín. He sank his entire fortune into researching his beloved island, sponsoring many investigations, particularly of its caves and archaeological sites, and producing *Die Balearen* (or *Las Baleares*), a comprehensive seven-volume study of the topography, archaeology, history and folklore of the Balearic Islands.

Mallorca's location as a Mediterranean cross-roads, its exotic mix of European and Arab culture, its sunny climate and natural beauty have made it an artists' haven for centuries.

MODERN ART Since the turn of the 20th century art has flourished on the island, thanks initially to the "Pollença School" of landscape artists between 1900 and 1930 and then to the great Catalan surrealist, Joan Miró (see page 34) who really put Mallorca on the map by moving here in 1940. Mallorca's art scene profited considerably from Miró's presence, assisted by the financier Juan March, founder of the Fundación J March, whose collection of contemporary Spanish art at the Museu d'Art Espanyol Contemporani (see page 51) includes works by Dali, Miró, Picasso and two Mallorquín artists, Sevilla and Barceló (see page 168). Artists' colonies sprang up on the island, especially in mountain villages like Fornalutx and Deià, favourite subjects for landscape artists.

A Miró carpet design

Today the island hosts perhaps 100 professional artists, another 1,000 serious amateurs and legions of *domingueros*, Sunday painters of seascapes and olive groves. There is a strong art market, with over 50 private galleries in Palma alone, specialising in the work of local artists.

MODERNISM Ironically, it was the failure of agriculture which brought Modernism to Mallorca at the start of the 20th century. Following an orange blight in Sóller in the 1860s, villagers were forced to emigrate to mainland Europe in search of work. When they returned, very prosperous, they contracted well-known Catalan architects who brought with them the latest European fashion – Modernista (Spanish art nouveau), known to some as *la época de mal gusto* (the epoch of bad taste).

The first Modernist building was begun in Palma in 1902 with the construction of the ornamental Gran Hotel by the Catalan architect Lluis Domènech i Montaner, today magnificently restored as the Fundació La Caixa (see page 51).

At the same time, a local bishop, having seen Gaudí's Sagrada Familia church in Barcelona, invited the famous Catalan architect to restore Palma's cathedral. Gaudí arrived in 1902, together with his student Joan Rubió. They were soon joined by two young locals, Gaspar Bennazar Moner and Francesc Roca Simó, both of whom had studied in Madrid.

Rubió set to work in Sóller, producing some of the finest examples of Modernista architecture on the island – the parish church and the Banco de Sóller, with its ornate twisted grilles. His mansion, Can Prunera (Carrer Sa Lluna 104) is particularly striking, with an external stone spiral staircase (see page 111).

GAUDÍ In the meantime, Gaudí spent the next ten years working intermittently on the cathedral, making some radical changes to the interior, introducing electric lighting, wrought-iron railings inspired by Mallorcan window grilles, ceramic inlays, and a highly controversial canopy of cardboard, cork, brocade and nails

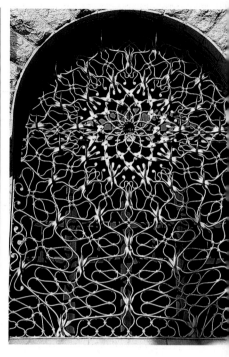

Modernista grille at Banco de Sóller designed by Joan Rubió

suspended above the altar, symbolising the Crown of Thorns.

He also worked on the church at Lluc (see page 103), and constructed a series of five sculptures on the mountain behind the monastery to represent the Mysteries of the Rosary, before suddenly abandoning the island for unknown reasons in 1914, leaving several projects unfinished.

Gaudí's influence can be seen in many of Palma's commercial and residential buildings of the early 20th century, including two vivacious buildings in Plaça del Mercat – Pensió Menorquina and Can Casasayas, rippling masterpieces decorated with butterfly and fern motifs.

However, surprisingly, it was not Gaudí, nor even an architect, but a silversmith, Lluis Forteza Rei whose Can Rei (Carrer Bolseria), with its lavish mosaic façade and ornate wrought-ironwork, leaves the most memorable legacy of Modernism on Mallorca. No visitor should leave Palma without admiring it.

It is hard to believe that Mallorca was a sleepy backwater and a refined winter sunshine resort until the latter half of the 20th century and the birth of package tourism. Almost overnight, the island was converted into one of Europe's most popular holiday destinations.

Magaluf – sun-lovers enjoy the widened beach

MASS TOURISM Mallorca's phenomenal development as a tourist island is now the stuff of textbooks, and the Mallorcan model has been copied in coastal resorts from North Africa to the Caribbean. Today tourism is taught as a subject in the island's state-run university and, in Palma, a private Escuela de Turismo (School of Tourism) draws hundreds of students from around the world.

Yet as recently as 1911, a friend told the British writer Mary Stuart Boyd, author of *The Fortunate Isles*: "You won't enjoy the Balearic islands. There are no tourists. Not a soul understands a word of English and there's nothing whatever to do. If you take my advice you won't go." – "So we went," she adds, and millions have followed in her wake. In 1931

Mallorca welcomed 43,000 tourists; by 1950, with the arrival of the first British and German charter flights, there were 127,000; by 1962, over a million arrived and by the late 1980s numbers had stabilised at around 5 million a year.

This sudden influx was chronicled with alarm by resident sage, Robert Graves. "Around 1951," he wrote, "British, French and American travellers accepted the fantasy of Mallorca as the Isle of Love, the Isle of Tranquillity, the Paradise where the sun always shines and where one can live like a fighting cock on a dollar a day, drinks included."

PARADISE LOST The Mallorcans were quick to catch on to the enormous economic potential of their 179 beaches. Greedy developers rushed in, bulldozing their way along the coast around Palma, creating

hideous, characterless mega-resorts in an uncontrolled building boom that was to change not only the landscape but the whole economic and social structure of the island. Tourism suddenly accounted for 75 per cent of the island's income, with the islanders earning the highest per capita income in Spain.

The growth of mass tourism also changed the traditional aspect of towns and coastal regions. S'Arenal and Can Pastilla in the Bay of Palma, both former fishing villages, fused together to form the island's largest resort, a massive tourist enclave of over 250 hotels along a 5km stretch of coast, invaded by tens of thousands of holiday-makers daily during the summer.

PARADISE REFOUND? In the late 1990s people started to question the pile-'em-high-and-sell-it-cheap philosophy. Environmental groups have campaigned against new hotels; local people have grown tired of the lager-fuelled *gamberros Ingleses* (English hooligans) and their Continental equivalents, who only want to get sunburnt and drunk as inexpensively as possible. Ironically, the island which was the first to experience the uncontrolled growth of mass tourism is now leading the way in looking beyond it, by examining its recent past for guidance to its future.

Talk today is of "green" or "sustainable" tourism – fewer hotels, more walking, cycling and golf, a new image based on quality.

The "Drunken Duck", popular with British visitors

Legislation has been passed to restrict new coastal developments. Smart new marinas, beach promenades and convention centres have sprung up; ugly high-rise hotels are being torn down and replaced with more traditional architecture, much as it was prior to the first holiday invasions of the 1950s. The package holiday continues to thrive here, albeit in a new guise, and another chapter in Mallorcan tourism is about to open.

British football by satellite is still popular at the British Bar in Alcúdia

A-Z Palma

▶▶▶ CITY HIGHLIGHTS

Basílica de Sant Francesc *pages 48–49*

Castell de Bellver *page 49*

Fundació La Caixa *page 51*

Museu d'Art Espanyol Contemporani (Fundación Juan March) *page 51*

Museu de Mallorca *page 52*

Old Town *page 54*

Palau de l'Almudaina *pages 54–55*

Passeig des Born *page 57*

Sant Miquel *page 58*

La Seu *pages 58–59*

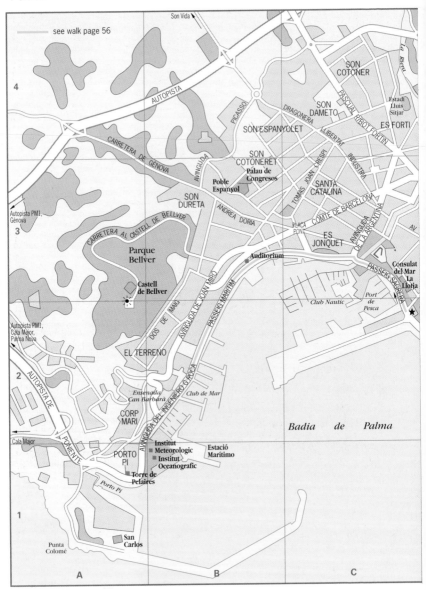

*Pages 40–41
Night-time view from
Castell de Bellver*

PALMA Palma is the key to Mallorca. To unlock it, stroll down its leafy promenades and behold the triumphant cathedral, savour the severe façades of its churches and the *joie de vivre* in its Modernista buildings and you will appreciate the richness of an island that has always been far more than a developers' playground.

ANCIENT AND MODERN Magnificently situated on the broad, beautiful Badia de Palma (Bay of Palma), Mallorca's capital city not only offers the island's best choice of hotels and restaurants, the most sophisticated shopping and the widest range of entertainment, but it is

also the economic centre, the main cultural hub and the capital of all the Balearic Islands.

Despite having become a vibrant and cosmopolitan city, Palma has kept a careful balance between the traditional and the present day, and, as a result, it is still easy to imagine what Palma was like 150 years ago when Frédéric Chopin and his mistress George Sand sailed into the bay to spend "a winter in Majorca". In her infamous book of that title, Sand prophesied "The day will come when those seeking rest, and even beautiful women, will be able to go to Palma with no greater fatigue and trouble than that with which they go now to Geneva". Indeed, the

thousands of flights that land at Palma's airport each year are the fulfilment of Sand's prophecy, for Palma has since shed its dusty provincialism and become one of Spain's most popular all-year-round holiday destinations – a paradise for sun-hungry visitors, and a summer haunt for the rich and famous.

MAIN SIGHTS There is no better way to approach Palma than by sea. Over a thousand years of history are etched along the waterfront – the Royal Palace of Almudaina, built by Muslim rulers and remodelled by Christian kings, the medieval merchants' stock exchange (La Llonja) and the 17th-century Renaissance Sea Tribunal (Consulat Del Mar). Standing sentry above the port on a hill is the circular 14th-century Castle of Bellver, and elsewhere the spires of Palma's ancient churches pierce the skyline. But the cathedral is undoubtedly the jewel in Palma's crown. One of the world's largest and finest Gothic cathedrals, it dominates the waterfront – living proof of Palma's history as a refined and sophisticated city, more in the mainstream of European thought and culture than most of Spain in medieval times.

Fanning out around the cathedral, the Old Town is a maze of narrow rambling lanes, stepped alleyways and stately, hidden squares, flanked by ageing mansions

Above: Castell de Bellver
Opposite: La Seu

PASSEIG IN PALMA
For a true taste of Palma, join the locals in the evening *passeig* (a ritual evening walkabout when all the family show off their best clothes) along the Passeig Marítim as the sun sets over the sea and the cathedral lights up for the night. To walk from La Llotja to the Club de Mar takes about an hour. You can then return on a no 1 bus.

The tranquil cloisters of Sant Francesc

Modernista influences at Casa Rey

and immaculately restored merchants' *palacios*, which retain the elegance of the 15th and 16th centuries when Palma enjoyed its heyday as a maritime trading centre. The area is best explored on foot or in a *galera*, one of Palma's red, horse-drawn carriages. Most of the sights lie within this area, and apart from a seafront walk and trips to the Poble Espanyol and Castell de Bellver, there is little need to stray outside the ancient boundaries of the Old Town.

VIBRANT CITY Palma has 320,000 citizens – almost half the population of the Balearic Islands – and with the summer influx of visitors its population swells to well over 600,000. For many of those visitors, the city's main appeal is its sheer vitality, the flair and *savoir-faire* of its inhabitants, the chic shops and avant-garde art galleries, the chatter in the *tapas* bars and pavement cafés and the scores of excellent restaurants offering the very best in Spanish, Catalan and Mallorcan cuisine. Hardly surprising that a survey conducted by the Spanish national newspaper *El País*, voted Palma as the best place to live in the whole of Spain.

THE CITY
Most Mallorcans refer to Palma simply as "Ciutat" ("City") – a reference to its first name, "Civitas" (Latin for city), given by the Romans, who also called the city "Palmaria". Under Moorish rule "Civitas" became "Medin" (Arab for city), and when the Christians replaced the Moors, the town was renamed "Ciutat de Mallorca". The Roman name of Palmaria came back into official use in the 16th century, but in today's shortened form – Palma.

47

Opposite: Palma's historic Old Town

Relaxing over a refreshing drink in Plaça Major

FROM FIGUREHEADS TO FINILS

As you stroll past the Ajuntament, be sure to look up at the unusual wood carvings of caryatids and atlantes overhanging the façade, for they are the work of a naval carpenter, who was more accustomed to carving the figureheads of ships than adorning state buildings.

▶ **Ajuntament (Town Hall)** *53B2*

Plaça Cort

Palma's 17th-century town hall is grand, yet at the same time charming and characterful, surrounded by stone benches where the locals sit. If you are passing when the great doors are open, enter the grand foyer to catch a glimpse of the *gigantones*, folkloric "giants" that are paraded in the streets during Palma's flamboyant fiestas.

▶ **Banys Arabs**
(Arab Baths) *53B1*

Carrer Serra 7 (tel: 971 721549)
Open: daily 9:30–7:30.
Admission: inexpensive

Hidden away in the tiny streets east of the cathedral, Palma's Arab Baths are an atmospheric souvenir of Medina Mayurqa, the Moorish city that stood here from the 8th to 13th centuries, and represent the last important trace of Islam's presence on the island.

The baths date from the 10th century and were originally part of a noble-man's house. Bathers would move between two chambers, the hot, steamy caldarium and the cooler tepidarium. The domed, colander-like roof of the caldarium, pierced with 25 small skylights, is supported by 12 columns, each slightly different and probably salvaged from the ruins of other buildings. The baths also served as meeting-places, and the court-yard with its cactus, palm and orange trees would have made a pleasant place to cool off.

▶▶ **Basílica de Sant Francesc** *53C2*

Plaça Sant Francesc 7 (tel: 971 712695)
Open: daily 9:30–12, 3:30–6:30.
Admission: inexpensive

Visitors to this imposing church are greeted by a statue of Junípero Serra, California's found-ing friar (see page 50). Behind him rises a sober, sun-baked façade with an ornate portal added in 1700. The original foundations for the church and monastery were laid in 1281, but were remodelled in 1580 after being struck by lightning. To enter, ring the doorbell of the building to the right, which leads straight into the cloisters, whose slender Gothic pillars, lemon trees and a central well all help create a serene atmosphere.

Intricate carving at the entrance to the Basílica de Sant Francesc

The interior of the church, in contrast, appears over-ornate, with its extravagant side chapels, vaulted ceiling and high altarpiece, typical of the baroque exuberance which took Spain by storm in the 17th century. Behind the altar, in the first chapel on the left, lies the spotlit tomb of Ramón Llull, the Mallorcan mystic stoned to death for

attempting to convert the Muslims of Tunisia (see page 50). His effigy rests high up in the wall, adorned by an inverted crescent symbolising his missionary work in North Africa.

▶▶▶ Castell de Bellver

42A3

Tel: 971 730657
Open: Apr–Sep, 8 AM–8:30 PM; Oct–Mar, 8–7:30.
Admission: inexpensive

The castle is one of Palma's great landmarks. The name in Catalan means "castle with a fine view", and to stand on its roof and survey Palma and its bay spread out below is an experience not to be missed. This great castle can be seen from Palma's seafront, picturesquely framed by thick pine woods.

Begun by Jaume II in 1309, and built by Pere Salvà (who also remodelled the Almudaina palace), it is the only castle in Spain that is entirely circular in design. It is arranged around a central courtyard on two levels. Four round towers mark the compass points, with the largest, the Tower of Homage, connected by an arch to the centre. Note the ingenious sweeping stone roof, carefully designed to feed every drop of rain into a central cistern. A deep moat completes the defences.

The castle was originally used as a summer residence by Mallorcan kings, then became a political prison – you can still see the graffiti carved into the stone by French prisoners-of-war. The Palma Historical Museum in the castle contains Talaiotic, Roman, Arab and Spanish artefacts. The castle is also a popular venue for concerts.

Looking west towards Castell de Bellver

REWARDING CLIMB
If you do not have a car, consider taking a taxi up to the castle, then walking back to the city centre through the pine woods. The shady path starts opposite the entrance to the castle, and leads down via a chapel to Carrer de Bellver and the Avinguda de Joan Miró about 1km below. Alternatively catch bus no 3 to Plaça Gomila and from there climb up through the woods to the castle.

Mallorca's two best-known sons gained fame and beatification through their work as missionaries – Ramón Llull was a 13th-century scholar, philosopher and scientist, and Junípero Serra, an 18th-century friar, played an important role in the settlement of North America.

REMEMBERING THE RIGHTEOUS

Llull's flowing-bearded statue enjoys a commanding position on Palma's busy seafront, poised with scroll and quill, apparently making notes of traffic violations. The pedestal dedication, in Catalan, Arabic and Latin, recalls his literary contributions on the island. A striking statue of Junípero Serra, together with a Native American to celebrate his founding of California, can be seen in front of the Basílica de Sant Francesc.

50

Below: statue of Ramón Llull in Palma
Right: Junípero Serra's statue in front of Sant Francesc

Noble missionary Ramón Llull was born in 1235 of noble parentage. An irrepressible rake when young, his sudden conversion is alleged to have occurred when, during a hot-blooded courtship of a married lady, Ambrosia de Castillo, he rode his horse into Palma's Santa Eulalia Church where she was praying, then pursued her down the street. Unable to deter his ardour, she lifted up her blouse to reveal her diseased breasts.

Duly chastened, the 40-year-old Llull devoted his life to the Catholic faith. He founded a monastery and missionary school on top of Puig de Randa (see page 173), where he spent ten years in seclusion. A dedicated scholar, he produced over 250 books and treatises in Latin, Catalan and Arabic on subjects ranging from metaphysics to gastronomy.

He is said to have been stoned to death by an infidel mob while spreading the word in Tunisia at the age of 80, and is now buried in the Basílica de Sant Francesc in Palma (see page 48).

Founder of California Junípero Serra (1713–1784) was born of humble family in the town of Petra (see page 142). Joining the Franciscan order aged 17, he later sailed to Mexico to convert its natives to Catholicism. In 1768, Serra led a crusade to convert the Native Americans of California. The first missionary station was established at San Diego in 1769 and, by the time of Serra's death, a line of nine missions stretched to San Francisco. He was beatified by Pope John-Paul II in 1988.

▶▶ Fundació La Caixa   53B2

Plaça Weyler 3 (tel: 971 178500)
Open: Tue–Sun 10–9. Admission free

Palma's first quality hotel – the Gran Hotel – opened in 1902, the first of several Modernista buildings to grace the city (see page 36). It was restored by the Fundació La Caixa and is now a cultural centre, staging temporary art exhibitions and musical events. The ground floor contains a chic café-bar.

▶ La Llotja (The Exchange)   53A2

Plaça Llotja (tel: 971 711705)
Open: Tue–Sat 11–2, 5–9, Sun 11–2.
Admission free

The majestic, old Maritime Exchange – half-castle, half-church – with twin octagonal turrets, massive windows and an angel over the doorway, bears witness to the maritime might that underpins Palma's prosperity.

Built between 1426 and 1456, it is one of many masterpieces designed by Guillem Sagrera. In its heyday, shipping merchants and commercial traders would meet here to do business in the elegant interior with its twisted columns and rib-vaulted ceiling, suggestive of a palm grove.

When the city's seafaring fortunes declined, La Llotja became a granary but today it is one of Palma's most prominent forums for cultural exhibitions.

▶▶ Museu d'Art Espanyol Contemporani (Fundación Juan March)   53C3

Carrer de Sant Miquel 11 (tel: 971 713515)
Open: Mon–Fri 10–6:30, Sat 10–1:30.
Admission: moderate.

This display of 20th-century Spanish art belongs to the collection started in 1973 by Fundacíon J March, founded by Mallorcan banker Juan March in 1955. There are 59 works of art, each by a different artist – Picasso, Miró, Dali and the Mallorcan-born Miquel Barceló (see panel, page 168) among them.

Dazzling display of Fundación J March

CITY GALLERIES
Mallorca has long attracted painters, and besides the Fundación J March, Fundació La Caixa and La Llotja, there are several other notable galleries in Palma. Can Solleric, in a former palace on the Passeig des Born, holds regular free exhibitions of contemporary art, and Ses Voltes, in the vaults of the ancient city walls below the cathedral, hosts a permanent exhibition of 19th- and 20th-century paintings.

EVENING MAGIC
It is a magical experience to approach Palma and its bay by sea, especially at dusk when the boat lights in the harbour are sparkling and the cathedral and Bellver Castle are illuminated. Boat tours of the Badia de Palma leave regularly in summer from jetties opposite La Llotja. For further information, phone 971 242006 or pick up the tourist leaflet *Excursiones en Barca* from the tourist office.

An early Mallorcan ceramic from the Museu de Mallorca

►► Museu de Mallorca 53B1

Carrer de Portella 5 (tel: 971 717540)
Open: May–Sep, Tue–Sat 10–1, 5–8; Oct–Apr, Tue–Sat 10–1, 4–6. Admission: inexpensive

Mallorca's leading museum is housed in the former 17th-century Palau de Desbruill, built on the foundations of one of the island's earliest Arab houses, and set in one of the most atmospheric corners of Old Palma (see page 54). Inside is a treasure trove of sculptures and paintings, with Arabic ceramics and other artefacts produced by Muslim and Christian cultures, providing a useful overview of Mallorcan history.

On the ground floor are Talaiotic and Roman tools, weapons and jewellery, which are followed by bowls, jars and pottery oil lamps. The latter date from the Moorish occupation of Mallorca. It has to be said that these would be more interesting if they were better displayed and clearly labelled. The Christian art upstairs is more tourist friendly, notably the rooms devoted to Mallorcan Primitive painters and a superb assortment of Gothic paintings rescued from the island's churches and monasteries. Changing exhibitions on themes such as Mallorcan cartography and local writers add to the museum's appeal.

PALAU MARCH
The beautiful Palau March near the cathedral was built in the 1940s at the height of Joan March's power and contains the most important private library on the island.

The Museu Diocesà has a wide variety of exhibits

► Museu Diocesà 53B1

Carrer de Mirador 5 (tel: 971 712827)
Open: Apr-Oct, 10–1, 3–8, Sat and holidays 10–1:30; Nov–Mar, daily 10–1, 3–6.
Admission: inexpensive

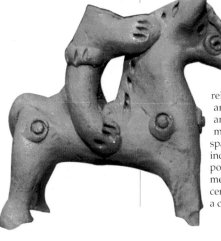

This museum, hidden round the back of the cathedral in the Episcopal Palace, is one of the most appealing in Palma. Its charm is that it resembles an antiques shop more than a museum. On offer is a wide-ranging and interesting mixture of religious and historical *objets trouvés* from around the island, including Roman amphorae, Moorish tapestries, Bibles, missals and paintings as well as ceramics spanning five centuries. The many surprises include a 13th-century Mudéjar pulpit, a portrait of Sant Jordi (St George) with medieval Palma in the background, a 17th-century painting of the infant Jesus carrying a cross, and Jaume II's jasper sepulchre.

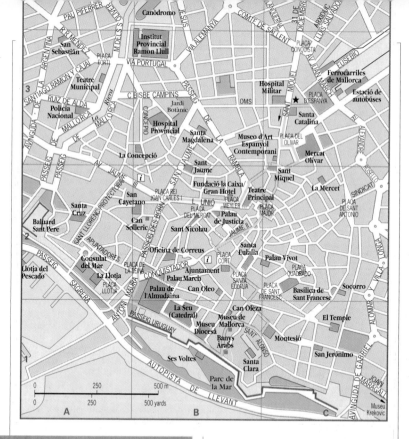

Walk

Historic Palma

This introductory walk is best done in the morning when the markets and churches are open. Allow 2 hours.

Start at Plaça d'Espanya, dominated by an equestrian statue of Jaume I, Conquistador of Mallorca. Walk west via Plaça de la Porta Pintada to Carrer de Sant Miquel. Turn south, past the church of Santa Catalina, and veer left to reach Palma's main market, the Mercat Olivar. Don't miss the spectacular fish displays in the *pescadería* before a mid-morning *sol y sombra* (coffee and brandy).

From the market, take Carrer de Josep Tous I Ferrer back to pedestrianised Carrer de Sant Miquel, and continue past the **Church of Sant Miquel** (see page 58) and the **Fundación Juan March** (see page 51), through an arch into **Plaça Major** (see page 54). Leave by the opposite arch and proceed along Carrer de Jaume II. Turn left into Plaça Cort, dominated by the **Ajuntament** (see page 48). Continue past the 13th-century Church of Santa Eulalia, until you reach the **Basílica de Sant Francesc** (see page 48).

Wind through the narrow lanes of the old town towards the **cathedral** (see page 58). Walk along the sunny south front of the cathedral, descend the steps at the end, and stroll through the Moorish-style **S'Hort del Rei** gardens (see panel page 54), up the historic **Passeig des Born** (see page 57). At the top, turn right, up to leafy **Plaça del Mercat** and the adjoining **Plaça Weyler** with their striking Modernista grandeur (see page 37). Just around the corner, past the Teatre Principal, is **La Rambla** (see page 58).

PALMA'S *PALACIOS*

Some of Palma's *palacios* (palaces) are still owned by the descendants of the wealthy merchants who originally built them, while others have been converted into apartments. Unfortunately, few are open to the public. However Can Oleo and Can Oleza in Calle Morey do occasionally open their doors to the public (check with the Tourist Office for details).

THE KING'S GARDENS

A statue in S'Hort del Rei (the King's Gardens) beneath the Palau de l'Almudaina commemorates Mallorca's famous *honderos* (slingers, see page 30). The garden contains several other modern sculptures and makes a pleasant place to sit among fountains and rose bushes watching the world go by.

▶ **Museu Krekovic**   *43E2*

Carrer de Ciutat de Querétaro (tel: 971 249409)
Open: 10–1, 3–6, Sat 10–1. Closed: August and holidays.
Admission: inexpensive

Hidden in the Queretano Quarter, in the east of Palma, is a functional, purpose-built building devoted to the romantic paintings of the Croatian artist Kristian Krekovic, who died in 1985. The main themes of the collection cover Spanish life and the early civilisations of South America. Though Krekovic's garish style is currently unfashionable, his depictions of suffering in Bosnia in the 1940s are depressingly relevant to more recent conflicts.

▶▶▶ **Old Town**   *53B2*

The best way to capture the ancient charm of Palma's *centre històric* is on foot – exploring the maze of tiny lanes and alleyways behind the cathedral, sitting in the shaded squares, and admiring the magnificent Renaissance mansions and imposing baroque and Gothic churches. It is also a good district for people-watching from one of the bars or cafés in and around Plaça Major, an arcaded square, popular for its street entertainment and artisans' stalls.

One of Palma's main shopping areas is squeezed into the bustling streets around the square – Carrer de Sant Miquel, Via Sindicato, Carrer de Colón and Carrer de Jaume II, a broad mixture of exclusive boutiques, traditional stores and shops selling everyday items. As people still live in the old town, the area is always vibrant.

Further south, behind the cathedral, is where the real architectural gems of the city are to be found – palatial Renaissance mansions (palacios) built by powerful merchants and modelled on the fashionable Italian designs of the 15th and 16th centuries (most of medieval Palma was destroyed by fire). The narrow streets, with their high-walled buildings, are filled with the introspective spirit of old Palma. Yet behind every doorway, you can glimpse a sunny, cobbled patio, magnificent arches, staircases and galleries reminiscent of Palma's heyday as a trading centre (see panel).

▶▶ **Palau de l'Almudaina**   *53B2*

Carrer de Palau Reial (tel: 971 727145)
Open: Apr–Sep, 10–7, Sat and holidays 10–2; Oct–Mar, 10–2, 5–6. Admission: inexpensive

Palma's Royal Palace rises out of the city's defensive walls on the seafront. A palace has stood here since the Muslim *walis* (governors) built their *alcázar* soon after the Arab conquest. The only remaining part of the original building is an archway, the Arc de la Drassana Reial, marking the entrance to the royal shipyards beside the palace. The rest of the edifice was rebuilt in Gothic style during the reign of Jaume II (1276–1311), though elements of Moorish architecture remain – such as the delicate arcades of the loggia.

Tours start in the central courtyard (Patio del Rey) which, flanked by palm trees, is best seen in late afternoon when the sun lights up the cathedral towers overhead. Just off the courtyard is the Chapel of Santa Ana with an important 15th-century altarpiece. The palace museum contains a fine collection of Flemish tapestries and the state apartments offer kingly views of Palma.

Today the palace houses the island's legislature, and it is also used as the official residence of King Juan Carlos of Spain whenever he visits Mallorca.

▶ Parc de la Mar   53B1

A steep flight of steps leads down between the Palau de l'Almudaina and the cathedral to the mighty city walls which once edged the Mediterranean. Today these handsomely restored fortifications overlook a lush area of trees, terraces and the ornamental lake of the Parc de la Mar, which offers shade from the midday sun and views of the bay, the old centre and La Seu. The lake was specifically created to reflect the cathedral. Several cafés provide a welcome break from the city bustle.

Above: Almudaina – eclectic architecture
Opposite: Carrer de Sant Domingo - steps to Plaça Major

SCANDAL AT THE PALACE
At the end of the 14th century, a great scandal broke out at the Palau de l'Almudaina, when it was discovered that the eccentric Aragonese king, Juan I, had installed an alchemist in the royal apartments, in the hope that he would replenish the treasury by turning base metal into gold!

Walk

Maritime Palma

An easy stroll along the waterfront shows how Mallorca's long-standing love affair with the sea is far from over. The walk takes roughly 1.5 hours and is particularly enjoyable in the early evening.

Start on the pedestrian Passeig Sagrera, lined with tall palms, and flanked to the north by historic buildings recalling Palma's maritime past, including **La Llotja** (see page 51) and the galleried **Consulat del Mar**, decorated with flags and cannons.

Cross Avinguda Gabriel Roca and continue to walk westwards along the seafront. A monumental pair of sundials and lines of vivid blue nets strung along the quayside mark the **Port de Pesca▶**, Palma's traditional fishing port, where you can still see fishermen painting their boats and mending their nets.

Continue through a small garden, and onto the **Passeig Marítim**, a waterside promenade round the side of the harbour. On the left you will see Palma's Reial Club Nautic (Royal Yacht Club) frequented by the Spanish royal family, and on the right, the surprising sight of the remains of five **windmills**. On the horizon ahead you can see the imposing silhouette of **Castell de Bellver** (see page 49).

Further along, you reach a tree-lined jetty where excursion boats offer tours of the harbour, and a monument commemorating Palma's 15th-century cartographers.

Look back across the bay at Palma Cathedral before continuing past rows of Mediterranean cruisers and massive "gin palaces" moored at the Club de Mar. Then follow the pavement east, passing under a bridge into the **Estació Marítimo**, Palma's ship terminal, where naval ships, cruise liners, and ferries from mainland Spain and the other Balearic Islands call throughout the year. Continue as far as a large anchor set on a lawn, and you will see two more signs of Palma's maritime prowess – the 15th-century **Torre Paraires**, looking like a chess-piece castle, and beyond it the medieval **lighthouse** at Porto Pi.

To return to the city centre, take a taxi or a no 1 bus back from Estació Marítimo 2.

►► Passeig des Born

53B2

You have not experienced Palma until you have walked "The Born", watched the world go by from one of its old stone benches or argued with its newspaper-sellers, who are famous for getting upset if you try to read a paper before deciding to buy it.

Palma's Passeig des Born has been the city's main promenade since the early 15th century, when the inlet that ran here was filled in, following a disastrous flash flood. It then became the venue of popular festivals, including jousting. Nowadays, despite being very traffic congested, the Born still lies at the very heart of the city, surrounded by some of Palma's smartest shops, bars and restaurants. Its old walkways, bordered by ancient lime trees and furnished with stone benches and flower-filled urns, still retain the elegance of bygone days.

► Plaça del Mercat

53B2

This tiny, leafy yet always busy square presents a scene typical of traditional Palma. A statue of Mallorca's most famous politician, Antoni Maura, a conservative prime minister of Spain several times at the start of the 20th century, stands beneath an ancient rubber tree in front of the church of St Nicolau. To the left are two striking Modernista buildings, commissioned in 1908 by a wealthy resident, Josep Casasayas. Further along stands the Palau de Justicia, once a private palace but today Palma's courthouse.

► Poble Espanyol

42B3

Carrer de Poble Espanyol 39 (tel: 971 737075)
Open: daily 9–7
Admission: moderate

This purpose-built, touristic "Spanish Village" on the outskirts of Palma is a celebration of everything Spanish, including faithful reproductions of around 20 important buildings, among them Granada's Alhambra palace and El Greco's house in Toledo. These are surrounded with typical houses from the Spanish regions, which provide a whistle-stop tour of Spanish architecture, showing its development through Muslim and Christian influences. In the buildings are numerous workshops which demonstrate local craft-making skills, and offer a comprehensive range of Spanish and Mallorcan souvenirs.

Shaded stroll along "The Born"

EL BORN
In Franco's day, the Passeig des Born was inevitably renamed Paseo de Generalísimo Franco. However, everyone refused to use its new name, always referring to it as El Born, a name derived from its days as a jousting ground.

Opposite: Boat repairs in the Port de Pesca
Below: Poble Espanyol

PALMA'S GREATEST TREASURE
"The Cathedral of Palma has one of the finest situations of any cathedral in the world. Its foundations are almost washed by the waves...and the city around and behind it becomes nebulous, a thing of insignificance, a splash of white out of which towers this vast rose-tinted creation of gothic grace and beauty. Like a mother she stands there by the ocean's edge, and like children the buildings of the city gather behind her at her sides: a perfect symbol of the Church she represents."
(*Jogging round Majorca* by Gordon West, 1929)

▶ La Rambla   53B3

Although La Rambla is a mere shadow of its Barcelona namesake, it still makes an enjoyable place to stroll among the colourful, sweetly scented stalls of Palma's flower market. This impressive tree-lined avenue was once the main watercourse through the city. Today, three-generation families show off their best clothes in the evening *passeig*. The two statues at the southern end of the promenade, representing Roman emperors, date from the time of Franco.

▶▶ Sant Miquel   53C2

Carrer Sant Miquel (tel: 971 715455)
Open: Mon–Sat 8–1, 5–8, Sun and holidays 10:30–1:30, 5–7:30.
Admission free

It was in this church that Jaume I celebrated Mass after capturing the city from the Moors in the name of Christianity, and ever since, Sant Miquel has remained one of Palma's most popular churches. Its richly gilded high altar celebrating St Michael, by Spanish artist Francesc Herrara, is considered a baroque classic.

▶▶▶ La Seu   53B1

Palau Reial 29 (tel: 971 723130)
Open: Apr–Oct, Mon–Fri 10–6, Sat 10–2; Nov–Mar, Mon–Fri 10–3, Sat 10–2. Closed: Sun, except for Mass. Admission: inexpensive

Tradition has it that, as Jaume I was setting sail to conquer Mallorca, he vowed to build a cathedral to reach the sky in honour of the Virgin if his venture succeeded. La Seu (the Catalan word for a bishop's see) was also an expression of political power, built on the water's edge for all to see, on the site of the Great Mosque, inside the old Moorish citadel. Rising high above the roofs of the Old Town and the harbour, the "Cathedral of Light" is one of the largest and most beautiful Gothic cathedrals in the world.

Jaume laid the foundation stone on New Year's Day in 1230, after the capitulation of the Arabs, but construction was not completed until 1601. As a result, the exterior demonstrates a variety of architectural styles, but is essentially Gothic. Its best-known (and most photogenic) view is the south front with massive flying buttresses of mellow, golden Santanyí sandstone, surmounted by turrets and pinnacles. The magnificent doorway here, Portal del Mirador (1389), was the work of island sculptor Guillem Sagrera. Seen from the sea, the cathedral seems to glow in the hazy Mediterranean light – for centuries a welcome sight to home-bound sailors.

Detailed carving on the Portal de Mirador at La Seu

The cathedral is entered through the northern door, the Portal del Almoina, where alms were dispensed to the poor. This leads into the Diocesan Museum, full of religious artefacts and holy relics, including a solid silver tabernacle, used for ceremonial processions, and a piece of Christ's tunic.

Inside, the most immediately striking feature is the building's sheer size and proportions, best appreciated from the western end, by the Portal Major. The massive central nave (121m long and 44m high) is supported by 14 pencil-thin pillars which soar to a height of 20m before branching out like palm fronds to form the rib-vaulted ceiling. The high aisles are flanked by a series of chapels containing massive baroque altars, and the entire edifice glows with kaleidoscopic light from its stained-glass windows. There are seven rose windows, including the huge 15th-century one above the presbytery, made up of 1,236 pieces of glass, and with a diameter of 13.3m.

Much of the interior was remodelled at the start of the 20th century by the celebrated Catalan architect Antonio Gaudí (see page 37), who worked here intermittently from 1904 to 1914. He removed the high baroque altar and shifted the beautifully carved choir stalls from the centre of the cathedral to the sides of the presbytery. He introduced electric lighting, placing lamps and candelabra throughout the church, and created the gigantic wrought-iron canopy over the High Altar, symbolising the Crown of Thorns. To appreciate the full effect of Gaudí's work, it is best to see the cathedral illuminated, so join the large congregation for Mass at 10:30 on Sunday mornings.

The lofty splendour of La Seu

A ROMANTIC RIDE
As you leave the cathedral, you will find ranks of smart, red, horse-drawn *galeras* lining the Costa de la Seu, waiting to take you on a leisurely, romantic tour of the old city. The tariffs are displayed on a sign near by, the carriages seat four passengers, the tour takes about one hour and a tip is expected at the end of the trip.

The large sign "Benvinguts a Mallorca" at Son Sant Joan airport welcomes visitors with an immediate reminder of the complexities and politics of Mallorca's language issue. Banned during the Franco dictatorship, the local language – Mallorquín – is back with a vengeance.

Caixa Cash Caja

Local language Mallorquín is a closely related dialect of Català (Catalan), a Romance language spoken in the autonomous community of Catalonia, in north-eastern Spain, around Barcelona, and in the extreme south-west of Mediterranean France. Most Mallorcans are bilingual, and Catalan shares dual official status with Castilian throughout the Balearic Islands.

History Català has been the islanders' everyday language since the conquest of the Balearics by Jaume I in 1229, when it replaced Arabic as the official language. Arabic, nevertheless, has left its mark on the island in a few expressions and in some place names, including Binissalem, Banyalbufar and Alcúdia.

As a literary language, Catalan enjoyed an early flowering in the 13th century through the work of Mallorca's famous son, Ramón Llull (see page 50). However, following the unification of Spain, the Castilian spoken at court gained in importance and by 1715, it was declared the official language of the whole kingdom, including the Balearics. Mallorquín became the colloquial language of the peasants, and rarely achieved written form again, until the Romantic movement of the early 19th century. Special societies were formed and Catalan became the subject of detailed linguistic studies, but still most Spanish literature remained in Castilian.

Castilian was once again rigorously reinforced in Mallorca by Franco. Then, during Spain's political controversies of the late 1970s, Catalan received a boost, reinforced by the granting of autonomy to the Balearics.

Catalan revival Today, the preservation and celebration of the Catalan language is seen by most islanders as the cornerstone of regional identity. The most obvious sign of this has been the change of all the old Castilian town and street names into Catalan versions. For several years Catalan has predominated in the Church, schools and university.

LANGUAGE OF THE LOCALS

It is not too difficult to get the gist of written Catalan if you know a little Spanish and French, but the harsh sound of the spoken word is extremely difficult to understand. Problems can usually be sorted out, however, because everyone in the towns and coastal resorts speaks Castilian Spanish, and usually some English and German too.

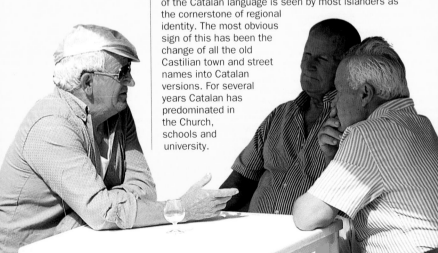

SOME USEFUL EXPRESSIONS

Numbers

	CATALAN	CASTILIAN
1	un(a)	un
2	dos (dues)	dos
3	tres	tres
4	quatre	cuatro
5	cinc	cinco
6	sis	seis
7	set	siete
8	vuit	ocho
9	nou	nueve
10	deu	diez
11	onze	once
12	dotze	doce
13	tretze	trece
14	catorze	catorce
15	quinze	quince
16	setze	dieciseis
17	disset	diecisiete
18	divuit	dieciocho
19	dínou	diecinueve
20	vint	veinte
21	vint-i-un	veintiuno
30	trenta	treinta
40	quaranta	cuarenta
50	cinquanta	cincuenta
100	cent	cien(to)
101	cent un	ciento uno
102	cent dos (dues)	ciento dos
200	dos(dues)-cents	doscientos
500	cinc-cents	quinientos
1,000	mil	mil
2,000	dos (dues) mil	dos mil

Days of the week

	CATALAN	CASTILIAN
Monday	dilluns	lunes
Tuesday	dimarts	martes
Wednesday	dimecres	miércoles
Thursday	dijous	jueves
Friday	divendres	viernes
Saturday	dissabte	sábado
Sunday	diumenge	domingo

61

Basics

	CATALAN	CASTILIAN
Hello/Goodbye	Hola/Adéu	Hola/Adiós
Good morning	Bon dia	Buenos días
Good afternoon/night	Bona tarda/nit	Buenas tardes/noches
Yes/No/OK	Si/No/Val	Sí/No/Vale
Please	Per favor	Por favor/
Thank you	Gràcies	Gracias
Sorry	Ho sento	Lo siento
Excuse me	Perdoni	Con permiso
I don't understand	(No) ho entenc	(No) entiendo
Do you speak English?	Parla anglès?	¿Habla (usted) inglés?
I (don't) speak Catalan/ Spanish	(No) parlo Català	(No) hablo Español
cheap	barat(a)	barato
expensive	car(a)	caro
open	obert	abierto/a
closed	tancat	cerrado/a
hot	calent(a)	caliente
cold	fred(a)	frío
good	bo(na)	buen(o)/a
bad	dolent(a)	mal(o)/a
big	gran	gran(de)
small	petit(a)	pequeño/a
with	amb	con
without	sense	sin
today	avui	hoy
tomorrow	demà	mañana
yesterday	ahir	ayer
left	a l'esquerra	izquierda
right	a la dreta	derecha
straight on	tot recte	todo recto

Palma

62

*A traditional olive-wood
carving*

Shopping

Palma is the place to shop in Mallorca. The main shopping area falls within the boundary of the city's old walls, and can easily be explored on foot.

Most shops close in the afternoon for a siesta (see panel) but, for the truly indefatigable shopper, Palma's branch of Spain's leading department store, **El Corte Inglés**, at Avinguda Jaume III 15, is open Monday to Saturday from 10 AM until 10 PM.

MAIN STREETS Avinguda Jaume III has long been considered Palma's main shopping street, lined with famous names such as Cartier, Benetton and Charles Jourdan, and interspersed with plenty of Mallorcan shops. Try **Majorica** for pearls and jewellery, **Persepolis** for antiques, and **Tutto Chicco** for children's clothes. Carrer de Jaume II and pedestrianised Carrer de Sant Miquel, linking Plaça Major with the market, are good for reasonably priced boutiques whereas the ancient mansions of exclusive Ca'n Veri house the likes of Versace, Escada and Armani. Head to Carrer de l'Argentería for jewellery; **Orquidea** in Plaça de Rei Joan Carles I sells artificial pearls; **Artesanías** at Carrer de l'Unio 13 is good for ceramics; and **Estil Gotic**, at Carrer Palan Reial 10, has beautiful pottery and leatherware. **Vidrierías Gordiola**, Carrer de la Victoria 2, is the best place for glass, while **Artesanjes Pol**, at Carrer de l'Unio 13, is a treasure trove of Mallorcan ceramics and glass. For shoes, try the shops in Carrer de Sindicat.

FASHION For clothes, look out for the sales (*rebajas*) where you can sometimes find top-quality merchandise at reductions of up to 50 per cent. Some shops appear to be in a permanent state of sale, but beware – their quality is not always guaranteed. Clothes will be in metric and European sizes (see panel on page 190 for conversion tables). You will find all the latest fashions in the popular Spanish chain stores, **Cortefiel** and **Mango** in Avinguda Jaume III or **Zara** along the Passeig des Born or, for a bit of fun, head to **Eurocarnavales**, Carrer de Porta de Jesus 16, which sells costumes for fiestas.

HIDDEN TREASURES Some of the most fascinating shops in Palma are hidden away in the narrow streets and alleyways of the old town. Here you can find genuine Mallorcan articles that have largely disappeared from the mainstream shops and department stores – glass, olive-wood, authentic lace and crochet work, decorated with the traditional Mallorcan *llengua* (tongue) pattern. Look out for **La Casa del Olivo**, an olive-carver's workshop in Carrer dels Paners, and **Alpargateria Llinas**, Carrer de Sant Miquel 43, with its countless straw-woven goods.

GASTRONOMIC DELIGHTS For gourmet shoppers the choice is similarly enticing. Start at the tiny **Colmado Santo Domingo**, Carrer de Sant Domingo 5, where you have to fight your way through hundreds of hanging sausages. Near by, at Carrer de Jaume II 29 you will find one of Palma's top delicatessens, **La Montana**. Chocolate-lovers will be unable to resist **Frasquet**, Carrer de Brossa 19 or **Forn Fondo** round the corner in Carrer de l'Unio, the

Palma has an excellent choice of well-stocked supermarkets both in and out of town. If you are staying in self-catering accommodation, it may help to load up your car at one of the hypermarkets, such as **Continente** or **Pryca** on the outskirts of Palma. For easy one-stop shopping, visit the new **Porto Pi** hypermarket-cum-shopping centre on the waterfront – a cluster of over 100 shops including delicatessens, fashion boutiques, gift, chocolate and handcraft shops and a safe, lively play area for the children.

63

Palma's most photogenic bakery

place for *ensaimadas* (see panel, page 91). Everyone goes at least once to the **Forn des Teatre** bakery at Plaça Weyler 11, if only to photograph its Modernista shopfront. For Spanish wines, **El Centro del Vino**, Carrer Bartomeu Rossello-Porcel 19, offers the best choice.

MARKETS Mercat Olivar, near Plaça d'Espanya, is held every morning except Sunday and is the best place for fresh produce. The **Rastrillo** (flea market) takes place on Saturday mornings in Avinguda Villalonga. Palma's flower sellers can be seen daily on La Rambla (see page 58).

La Rambla – always a riot of colour

Enjoy a snack al fresco

Food and drink

The impressive range of restaurants in Palma should suit every taste and budget, ranging from international gourmet restaurants to the inevitable fast-food outlets like McDonald's and Wimpy, not to mention the family restaurants, the Mallorquín speciality restaurants, the fish restaurants, the meat restaurants, the Continental restaurants, the quick snack restaurants, vegetarian café-restaurants, even special "tourist" restaurants with the dishes actually laid out in a display cabinet.

For details of establishments mentioned below, see pages 198–199.

INTERNATIONAL CUISINE The rapid growth of tourism over the past few decades has led to more and more international restaurants being opened in Palma. As a consequence, the number of restaurants serving traditional Mallorcan food has decreased. In their place is a profusion of Chinese, French, German, Italian, Japanese, Moroccan, and Lebanese restaurants.

For a little taste of Paris, head to **Le Bistrot**, for the most delicious sushi, try **Shogun**. Alternatively, **Basiakhi** offers a good-value Indian buffet. If you would prefer to sample different Spanish regional dishes, try the Basque cuisine at **Bilbaína** or the Galician seafood buffet at **Casa Gallega**.

MEALTIME BEHAVIOUR
If you want to dine like the locals, follow this simple guideline: eat hugely, talk a great deal and drink in moderation (you never see a drunk islander!). Mallorcans love to spend time over their dinner, with good lively conversation, and never rush their food. Mealtimes are important social occasions, when friends and family gather together around the table.

LA CUINA MALLORQUINA There are, however, still a few good Mallorcan speciality restaurants to be found, such as **Ca'n Carlos** and **Asador Tierra Asanda**, offering wholesome, unpretentious local dishes without frills but surprisingly subtle in flavour.

Many restaurants have similar menus offering adequate but unmemorable international fare with the occasional Mallorcan dish thrown in for good measure: perhaps a soup or stew to start after the inevitable bread, olives and a bowl of garlicky *allioli* (served prior to most meals), next a paella or some other rice dish, local fish or roast suckling pig, followed by fruit, cheese, ice-cream or crème caramel (*flan*). Note however, paella is not a Balearic dish (it actually comes from the Valencia region). Nor is the cold tomato soup called *gazpacho* (which is an Andalucian dish from Southern Spain), although both are on just about every restaurant menu in Palma. At the **Arrosseria Sa Cranca** there is a choice of seven different paellas, including Valenciana, vegetarian and lobster.

Generally along the seafront and up Avinguda Antonio Maura you will find restaurants mainly geared to the tourist trade, although exceptions include **Caballito del Mar** and the **Taverna de la Boveda**, both of which serve delicious food and are popular with Mallorcans. Other local haunts offering fine cuisine include **Es Parlament**, **Ca'n Eduardo** and **Los Gauchos**.

Although the Mallorcan diet is heavily meat based, vegetarians need not despair. **Na Bauçana** serves a daily-changing lunch menu, and **Bon Lloc** is good for an evening meal.

A LIGHT BITE If you only want a light meal, head for a cafeteria, a bar serving food or a *celler* restaurant, with its characteristically rustic atmosphere. Several can be found in Carrer dels Apuntadors, Palma's principal wining and dining street. Try **Sa Volta** or, further afield, **Celler Sa Premsa**.

One of the best ways to snack while shopping and sightseeing is in one of the many inexpensive cafés and *tapas* bars in the city centre, especially in the side streets around the Passeig des Born (see page 57) and the Carrer de l'Unio. Many restaurants, such as the ever-crowded **La Boveda**, also serve light snacks as well as full meals.

THE WINE LIST
Most of the wines you will encounter are brought over from mainland Spain. They tend to be lighter and fresher than the rather heavy Mallorcan wines (see panel, page 99). Recently, Mallorcans have developed a taste for beer (*cerveza*), now almost as popular as wine. Wine is rarely drunk outside mealtimes, but it is common in Palma to meet friends or colleagues for a *copa*, a quick sherry, liqueur or cognac. The average bar has an astounding array of Spanish cognac. Look in and try one!

65

Paella is not a traditional Balearic dish, but is hugely popular

IN WITH THE "IN" CROWD
It is currently fashionable for Palma's jet set to head to the chic waterfront cafés of Porto Portals, to Bar del Titanic with its impressive cocktail list, or the romantic Havana Moon. For late-night dining, there is yachty Flanigans or trendy pizzeria Diabolito.

FLAMENCO
For a truly Spanish experience, go to El Porton at Passeig Marítim 32 or La Luna, Carrer dels Apuntadors after midnight. Or, if you prefer *sevillanas* and *rocieros*, try El Patio de Triana, Carrer Joan Miró 15.

Nightlife

According to local artist Santiago Rusinyol, "The people of Palma take the moon as others take the sun". In other words, Palma has as much to offer by night as it has during the day. With dinner eaten late, theatre performances rarely begin before 10 PM, cinemas frequently have late-night showings which always attract large crowds, and the terraces of cafés, bars and ice-cream parlours buzz with activity way past midnight on summer evenings. While for those who fail to make it home before dawn, **Café Cappuccino** opens at 7 AM and serves a wicked breakfast of *churros*, traditional Spanish dough-sticks, dipped in coffee or chocolate.

ON STAGE There are three main theatre venues in Palma. The waterfront **Auditòrium** (Passeig Marítim 18) stages theatre, opera and classical concerts, and its main hall is also a popular venue for visiting Spanish and international ballet companies. Chamber music is frequently performed in the more intimate Sala Mozart. Check at the ticket office (tel: 971 234735) for details.

The bill at Palma's second theatre, the grand 19th-century **Teatre Principal** (Carrer de la Riera 2) is predominantly theatre (mainly comedies) and classical music and, from March until May, a variety of Spanish *zarzuela* (light opera) companies present a spring opera season. Further details are available from the box office at the theatre (tel: 971 725548).

The **Teatre Municipal** (Passeig Mallorca 9B tel: 971 739148) offers a more varied programme of contemporary drama, classic films, dance and ballet.

CINEMAS Palma's main cinemas are **Chaplin Multicines**, (Carrer Bartolome Torres 56, tel: 971 277662), **Hispania** (Carrer de Benito Pons 41, tel: 971 270475) and **Rialto** (Carrer de Sant Feliu, tel: 971 721245). Programmes and times are advertised in the local papers and most films are dubbed in Castilian Spanish.

CAFÉS AND BARS The most popular nighttime activity in Palma is without doubt sitting on a terrace, enjoying a *tertulia* (chat with friends) while sipping a beer or a *café con hielo* (coffee with ice). The suburb of El Terreno, around Plaça Gomila, once accommodated Palma's best late-night bars, but now it is quite a seedy district, catering for teenagers, disorientated tourists and sailors. The hub of nightlife is now in the city centre, mostly in the lively, ancient side streets backing Plaça Llotja, with traditional cafés such as **Café La Llotja** (Plaça Llotja), **Café Lírico** (Plaça de la Reina) and **Bar Bosch** (Plaça Joan Carles I) filling up around 10 and staying busy until their doors close at 2 or 3 AM. Other popular late-night haunts include **Gothic** jazz bar in Plaça Llotja and **Made in Brazil**, on

Passeig Marítim, with its Latin music and cocktails. The quieter, candlelit terrace tables of the *tapas* bars on Plaça Llotja will add a touch of romance to your evening.

LIVE MUSIC If it's live music you're after, **Ses Voltes** in the Parc de la Mar is a swinging open-air spot with live pop, jazz and rock bands most weekends. **Hogans**, Palma's first Irish pub, has occasional Irish music. For something more intimate, head to **Bar Barcelona**, Carrer dels Apuntadors, for mellow jazz every night from midnight.

NIGHTCLUBS The disco crowd makes for **Tito's Palace**, a top-rate nightclub which once played host to Marlene Dietrich and Charles Aznavour, but now offers a mega-disco with six bars, laser show and room for 2,000. Their exotic theme fiestas are especially lively. The wealthy "in" crowd can be found bopping at **IB's Club**, Passeig Marítim. There is a tight selection policy at the door but, once inside, you may find yourself dancing with the Crown Prince of Spain. Michael Douglas, on the other hand, frequents neighbouring **Pacha**, Passeig Marítim 42, while the local yachting fraternity and visiting boaties head to the smart **Club Mosquito** beside the Club de Mar, in the marina on Avenida Gabriel Roca.

Tito's – a favourite Palma hotspot

A SPECIAL TREAT
Don't miss the entrance to Abaco, Palma's most unusual and extravagant bar, tucked inside a 17th-century mansion on Carrer Sant Joan. Enter the massive wooden door and step into another world. Sip expensive but exotic cocktails here late into the night, on an elegant patio surrounded by antiques and caged birds, hidden amid luxuriant foliage. Candles and gentle classical music provide the finishing touch.

Accommodation

There are around 50 hotels and *hostales* dotted around Palma providing ample choice for all pockets. If you are planning to arrive in high season (July–September or around Easter) it is vital to book in advance. If you have not made a reservation, pick up the official list from the tourist office. They will not arrange the accommodation for you, leaving that to the telephone booking facility of the Central de Reservas de la Federación Empressarial Hotelera de Mallorca (FEHM, or Mallorcan Hotel Federation), open daily 9–2 and 4:30–7:30 (tel: 971 706007).

For a room with a view, choose from one of the hotels overlooking the harbour around the Passeig Marítim or to the west of the centre along Avinguda Gabriel Roca, overlooking the waterfront. If you are without transport, stay in the heart of the city, where the bulk of Palma's budget accommodation can be found, around the Passeig des Born and the Plaça d'Espanya. Avoid the suburbs – it is better to take a short bus ride westwards out of the city to the leafy resorts of Illetas or Bendinat.

LUXURY HOTELS Three of Palma's four 5-star hotels are just outside the city: **Son Vida**, a 13th-century castle with its own golf course is 5km north-west of Palma. The **Arabella Golf Hotel**, in the same area, offers sporting facilities and a health farm, while **Valparaiso Palace**, in lush gardens in Bonanova, is the least expensive of the three and has views over the Badia de Palma.

THE OLD CITY If you are looking for something more affordable but nonetheless special, why not stay in a converted palace in one of the narrow streets of Palma's historic centre? Book early for the elegant **San Lorenzo**, Carrer de Sant Llorenç as it only has six rooms, or make **Hotel Born** in Carrer de Sant Jaume your base, a lovingly

Prime position on the waterfront at Paseo Marítimo

renovated *palacio* which is the best value 2-star hotel in town. The ultimate luxury must be to stay in the ancient, 5-star **Palacio Ca Sa Galesa**, on Carrer Miramar with magnificent views of the cathedral and the bay beyond.

ON THE WATERFRONT For the most romantic setting choose from the hotels overlooking the harbour, with their magnificent views towards the cathedral. The area around the Passeig Marítim is good for nightlife and restaurants too, but some way out from the *centre històric*. The rather dated, 4-star **Meliá Victoria** dominates the harbour area, with entrances onto both Plaça Gomila and the seafront. Also on the Passeig Marítim, the **Bellver Sol** and **Palas Atenea Sol** are both owned by the Sol group, Spain's premier hotel chain. For a cheaper alternative, the **Costa Azul** and the **Mirador** are 3-star hotels which cost about half the price of their fancier neighbours.

PASSEIG DE MALLORCA This promenade on the site of the old western walls, makes a better-value alternative close to the heart of the city. The 3-star **Palladium** is reasonably priced (ask for a top-floor room for a view of Castell de Bellver), whereas the Jaime III Sol and the Saratoga are more expensive.

BUDGET ACCOMMODATION To see Palma on the cheap, you should consider booking a package deal to one of the Badia de Palma resorts, such as Can Pastilla or Magaluf. Nevertheless, there are several modest *hostales* such as the **Ritzi**, in the lively centre.

HIDDEN EXTRAS Watch out! 6 per cent IVA (VAT) is added to some hotel bills, 15 per cent in 5-star hotels. Breakfast is not usually included in the price of a room, unless you are on a package holiday.

YOUTH HOSTEL
Palma's nearest youth hostel is the Playa de Palma, Carrer Costa Brava 13, in the resort of Sometimes, 20 minutes out of town. To get there, take bus 15 from Plaça d'Espanya, get off at Hotel Royal Cristina, then it's a couple of minutes' walk away between Balneario no 4 and no 5. There are only 65 rooms so it is advisable to book well in advance (tel: 971 260892).

BARGAIN BUS FARES

The Bono-Bus scheme offers books of ten bus tickets, either for the city centre or the outer zone, available from most tobacconists (look out for brown and yellow "tabac" signs). This will be a definite saving if you're planning to stay a while.

AN ESCORTED WALK

Possibly the best way to discover the old city in a short time is to take a guided walking tour. These start at Joan Miró's Egg sculpture in the S'Hort del Rei gardens at 10 and 12:15 Monday to Saturday. The tour takes two hours and only leaves if at least eight people turn up.

70

Travel in style in one of Palma's famous galeras

Practical information

ORIENTATION Palma is compact enough to explore easily on foot. It has three distinct areas: the city centre, including the Casco Viejo (Old Town) around the cathedral; the harbour and promenade area, called the Passeig Marítim; and the new modern city, which stretches along the bay.

Most sights are conveniently located in the city centre, a roughly circular area, originally marked out by the city walls, about 2km in diameter (approximately 40 minutes' stroll from one side to the other). It is crossed by four interconnected avenues, the Passeig des Born, Avinguda Jaume III, Carrer de l'Unio and Passeig de la Rambla. The capital's maze of ancient side streets can be confusing at times, and these major thoroughfares act as useful reference points.

TOURIST OFFICES Palma's main tourist offices can be found at Sant Domingo 11 (tel: 971 724090), Plaça de la Reina 2 (tel: 971 712216), Palma Airport (tel: 971 260803) and Plaça d'Espanya (tel: 971 711527). They all provide city and island-wide information, and seem to have pamphlets covering most topics, including bus schedules, ferry and boat-trip timetables, accommodation lists, and lists of top city shops and restaurants. For furthur information check the Web site: www.a-palma.es.

OPENING TIMES Most shops, banks, post offices and museums in the capital follow the same opening hours as the rest of the island (see page 189). The cathedral is open all day.

DRESS CODE The people of Palma are chic dressers, so make sure you are clothed appropriately. Don't wander about in scanty beachwear, or you will be made the subject of derision by the locals (men without shirts are referred to scathingly as *descamisados* or "shirtless ones"). If you go into a bar or restaurant in your swimwear, you are unlikely to be served. For places of worship, to show respect, make sure your shoulders and knees are covered.

PARKING In Palma, parking can be a nightmare. If you want to park in the city centre, you will need an ORA (Ordenación Regulación Aparcamiento) ticket on weekdays 9:30–1:30 and 5–8, and on Saturdays 9:30–1:30. Although tickets are readily available from parking meters, and the charge minimal, it is virtually impossible to find a vacant place and you can only stay for a maximum of 90 minutes. Thereafter fines are immediate and steep. Multi-storey car parks are expensive. Travelling by public transport is a better bet.

PUBLIC TRANSPORT Palma has an efficient bus network that connects the capital to most places on the island, and is also the best way to reach the city suburbs. All buses pass through the central bus station (Plaça d'Espanya), and route maps and timetable details can be found at every *parada* (bus stop). Pay the driver as you enter and keep hold of your ticket for inspection.

Useful routes include:
1 Along the Passeig Marítim
4 Plaça de la Reina – Fundació Joan Miró
15, 23, 26 Plaça d'Espanya – Plaça de la Reina – Can Pastilla – S'Arenal
17 Plaça d'Espanya – Aeroport
21 Plaça d'Espanya – Plaça de la Reina – Palma Nova
22 Plaça d'Espanya – Portals Nous

Black and white taxis can be hailed in the street, picked up at ranks, or ordered by phone on 971 401414. A green light saying Lliure/Libre indicates they are available for hire. In town, prices are reasonable, but they increase at night and weekends. If you stray outside the city, tariffs rise steeply so it is best to check the cost in advance.

Ranks of horse-drawn carriages can be found along Carrer de Palau Reial alongside the Almudaina Palace, on the Avinguda d'Antoni Maura, and the Passeig Sagrera, or beside the cathedral in Costa de la Seu (see panel on page 59).

PERSONAL SAFETY Take the normal precautions you would in any bustling city. Don't leave anything visible in a parked car. Don't carry excess cash. Use the hotel safe to store valuables. At night, keep to well-lit, populated areas.

Visitors in the Born plan their next excursion

WHAT'S ON WHERE?
Find out what's showing at the cinema or theatre by visiting the venues or your nearest tourist office, or by looking at the listings in the *Majorca Daily Bulletin*. A monthly guide to cultural and sporting events in Palma, published in Spanish and Catalan by the city council, is available at most hotels.

ON YOUR BIKE!
One of the most pleasurable ways of exploring Palma is by pedal-power. There is even a special lane for bikes and joggers running for 4.5km along the seafront. You can rent a bike from Ciclos Bimont, Plaça de Progrés 19 (tel: 971 450505) or a moped from RTR Rental, Avinguda Joan Miró 340 (tel: 971 402585).

West of Palma

▶▶▶ REGION HIGHLIGHTS

La Granja *pages 80–81*
Port d'Andratx *page 86*
Portals Nous *page 86*
Portals Vells *page 86*
Sa Dragonera *page 86*

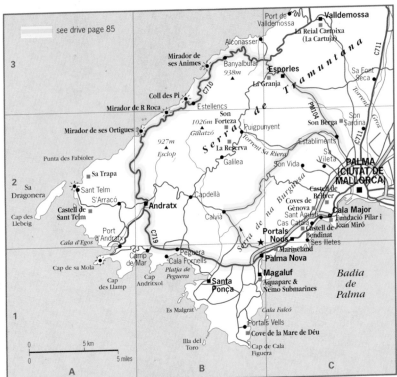

see drive page 85

3

Port de Valldemossa
Valldemossa
La Reial Cartoixa (La Cartuja)
Alconasser
Mirador de ses Animes
Banyalbufar
938m
Esporles
La Granja
Sa Font Seca
C711
Coll des Pi
C710
Estellencs
Mirador de R Roca
Son Forteza
1026m
Puigpunyent
Son Berga
Son Sardina
PM104
Mirador de ses Ortigues
Galatzó
Serra de Tramuntana
Establiments
927m
Esclop
La Reserva
Torrent Sa Riera
Sa Vileta
Punta des Fabioler
Galilea
Son Vida
PALMA (CIUTAT DE MALLORCA)

2

Sa Dragonera
Sa Trapa
Sant Telm
S'Arracó
Capdellà
Serra de na Burguesa
Coves de Gènova
Sant Agustí
Castell de Bellver
Castell de Sant Telm
Andratx
Calvià
Cas Català
Cala Major
Fundació Pilar i Joan Miró
Cap des Llebeig
Port d'Andratx
Cala d'Egos
C719
Portals Nous
Castell de Bendinat
Ses Illetes
Peguera
Marineland
Cap de sa Mola
Camp de Mar
Cala Fornells
Palma Nova
Platja de Peguera
Cala Falcó
Cap des Llamp
Cap Andritxol
Santa Ponça
Magaluf
Aquaparc & Nemo Submarines
Badia de Palma

1

Es Malgrat
Portals Vells
Cove de la Mare de Déu
Illa del Toro
Cap de Cala Figuera

0   5 km
0   5 miles

A   **B**   **C**

74

WEST OF PALMA The western corner of Mallorca was one of the first areas to be settled by the Spanish in the 13th century – a cross at Santa Ponça commemorates the spot where Jaume I and his troops landed on 12 September 1229. Now a ribbon of resorts decorates the south coast all the way to Sant Telm, the port closest to the dramatic, lizard-shaped island of Sa Dragonera, whereas inland and along the precipitous north coast, you can tour some of the most enjoyable mountain scenery on the island. It is in this region west of Palma, with its stark contrasts, that you can appreciate how, despite the tourist boom, there still remain places that are more or less untouched by outside influence.

EPICENTRE OF TOURISM The stretch of coast to the west of Palma, once an area of hills, rocky headlands and pristine beaches, has since been smothered by ugly tourist-industry urbanisation. This is where mass tourism has most completely taken hold – the Badia de Palma alone has more tourist beds than Greece – where developers of the 1960s and 1970s bulldozed their way in to create the hideous resorts that have made Mallorca synonymous with the cheap and tacky: loud, throbbing discos, blazing neon lights, topless music bars, all-night gift shops and chips-with-everything cafés.

Even so, most resorts have evolved their own identities, either in terms of the nationalities they attract, the age range they cater for or the income group they appeal to.

Cala Major, once the playground of the jet set, has gone downmarket in recent years; neighbouring Bendinat is less developed, giving a fleeting glimpse of how appealing this region must once have been; Portals Nous has a sophisticated atmosphere born of its ritzy marina; British-dominated family resort Palma Nova fuses with frenetic Magaluf (Mallorca's nightlife capital), as two major package-holiday destinations.

The German-dominated "villa-land" resorts of Santa Ponça, Peguera and Camp de Mar were counted among the most desirable destinations on the island not so long ago but, although still very picturesque, they are now over-developed. By contrast, Port d'Andratx

Above: sophisticated Portals Nous
Opposite: Magaluf
Pages 72–73:
Portals Vells – an idyllic cove

THE CALVIÀ COAST
The Calvià coast covers a 50km stretch from Cas Català beach on the Bay of Palma to Cala Fornells, and includes some of Mallorca's best beauty spots (deserted coves) and indisputably some of its worst eyesores (Palma Nova and Magaluf). Yet, when you stand in the tranquil, totally untouristic town of Calvià, a few kilometres inland, it seems hard to believe that this is the administrative centre for all those concrete jungles on the coast, and the richest municipality in Spain.

offers a beautiful harbour, popular with the yachting fraternity, with a touch of St Tropez glamour.

Public transport is speedy, efficient and inexpensive between Palma and the resorts. Unlike in many parts of the island, most of the hotels here are open during winter months, providing visitors with the full tourist treatment all year round.

"LA OLTRA MALLORCA" Somewhat surprisingly, this over-developed area encapsulates most vividly the contrasts that the island has to offer. The concentration of visitors is so centralised, that it is easy to escape the madding crowd and to find *la oltra Mallorca* ("the other Mallorca") – peaceful villages, market towns and even quiet hidden coves, just a few kilometres away from the monster resorts.

The rugged, fjord-like coastline of the Andratx peninsula in the extreme west around Sant Telm offers walkers stunning scenery, and the pine-studded peninsula that lies south of Magaluf is one of the most undeveloped and picturesque parts of the island, with its horseshoe-shaped sandy beaches and rocky coves,

Former sentinel,
Mirador de Ses Animes

76

Below: Banyalbufar

including Cala Felcó, Cala El Mago (nudist beach) and charming Cala Portals Vells.

HEADING INLAND Rich agricultural land starts immediately beyond the coastal resorts, with tiny, tranquil villages encased in almond groves, orchards, woods of holm oak and pine, and whitewashed farmsteads that are smothered in prickly pears. This region contains two excellent attractions for those who want to sample the Mallorcan countryside but only have time for a day trip: the country house at La Granja, with its antiques, gardens and displays of Mallorcan traditions, and the nature reserve at La Reserva, high in the wooded Galatzó mountain range near Puigpunyent, which offers a gentle introduction to Mallorca's wildlife and mountain scenery.

SENSATIONAL SCENERY The road between Banyalbufar and Andratx is one of the best scenic drives in Mallorca. Clinging high above the coast, the road looks down over a succession of sheer cliffs, hanging woods and tumbling terraces of vines, lemons, olives and scarlet poppies, before twisting through a chain of mountain hamlets. Lookout points dotting the coastal road as it descends towards Andratx include a 16th-century watchtower, built as a sentinel against pirate attack, providing awesome views over the surf-buffeted coves below.

DAY TOUR
To get a taste of both sides of this western region, take a day trip from Palma by car. In the morning, follow the busy coast road through the packed resorts of Palma Nova and Peguera to Port d'Andratx. After a fish lunch by the harbour, return inland to Andratx and take the mountain road to the sparsely populated north coast, skirting the great peaks of Esclop (927m) and Galatzó (1,026m) on your way up to the terraces of tiny Banyalbufar, before winding back to the southern coastal road via Puigpunyent, Es Capdella and Calvià.

▶▶ Andratx 74B2

This charming country town lies gently draped over a rich hillside of almond, orange and olive groves. Known to the Romans as Andrachium, Andratx is typical of those towns built slightly inland as a precaution against pirate attack. During the 13th century, it was the home of both the Bishop of Barcelona and King Jaume I.

The best time to visit is on a Wednesday morning when the streets are packed with stalls selling fruit, vegetables, fish and local cheeses. Find time to explore the old houses and cobbled streets of the upper town, culminating in the 13th-century fortress-like church of Santa Maria. From here, the views across sun-drenched rooftops to the sparkling blue harbour of Port d'Andratx (see page 86) near by are magnificent.

View across Andratx to the port

▶ Cala Major 74C2

Of the string of tourist developments which fringe the Badia de Palma, Cala Major is the closest to Palma, located on a hilly stretch of coastline just beyond Palma's ferry port. The resort combines elegant high-class residences with ugly mass-market complexes and offers visitors plenty of restaurants, shops and bars and a fine sandy beach, with Palma only a short bus-ride away.

Cala Major's most prestigious address is Palau Marivent, owned by the King of Spain and visited three times a year (see panel). This "Palace of Sea and Wind" sits on a rocky outcrop, overlooking Palma's yacht harbour where the King's 40m yacht *Fortuna* is moored.

Further west are two more resorts, Sant Agusti and Ses Illetas. The three resorts are fast becoming one, although which is devouring which is uncertain.

▶ Calvià 74B2
Tourist office: Ca'n Vich 29 (tel: 971 139109)
Calvià initially appears to be just another attractive country town, surrounded by highly fertile farming land, with green-shuttered houses, a handful of shops and bars, and chickens scratching beneath the olive trees. But look closer and you will find signs of prosperity that include the ostentatious new sports stadium and the over-sized town hall, paid for by the profits from tourism. When tourists discovered the nearby beaches, Calvià hit the jackpot as the administrative centre for the district of Calvià (covering all the resorts from Portals Nous to Peguera).

Of historic interest, the huge parish church of **Sant Joan▶** (Plaça Sant Joan. *Open* Mon–Sat 9:30–1:30) was built in the late 19th century around the 13th-century original. Look out from the church square across the lush countryside flecked with almond, olive and carob trees, and it is difficult to believe you are just a stone's throw from the pulsating resorts of "Maganova" (see page 84).

Calvià's historic mural was created by local students

▶ Camp de Mar 74B1
This popular, low-key holiday resort offers an extensive beach and fine bathing off the rocks, but it has been spoilt by a couple of new large hotels and a supermarket which back onto the beach. The bay's most notable feature is a tiny islet just offshore, accessible by a frail wooden bridge, where there is a pleasant restaurant. From Camp de Mar, an enjoyable 5km walk, along a rugged coast with fine views and fragrant pines, leads to Port d'Andratx (see page 86).

SUCCESS STORY
In Calvià, be sure to see the large ceramic mural made of *majolica* tiles by local art students in the neatly laid out square beside the church, showing a map of the district and telling the story of the town's historic development.

▶ Coves de Gènova 74C2
Carrer de Barranc 45 (tel: 971 402387)
Open: 10–1, 4–7. Closed: Mon afternoon. Admission: inexpensive
Nature appears to have created the Coves de Gènova for the convenience of visitors staying in the Palma area. For those who do not fancy travelling to see the great multi-coloured caverns at Artà (see pages 140–141), Drac (see page 167) and Hams (see page 167), these caves offer a brief insight into the colourful wonderland of stalactites and stalagmites that lies just below the surface of Mallorca. The village of Gènova sits high on the slopes of the Serra de na Burguesa above Palma, and contains a surprising number of good bars and restaurants.

Typically Miró – modern and abstract

NAIVE STYLE
Miró's paintings are almost childish – vivid splashes of bright primary colours, influenced by his love of peasant traditions. Indeed, his expressive freedom and wild calligraphy prompted André Breton, leading theorist of the Surrealist movement, to describe Miró as "the most Surrealist of us all". However, anyone tempted to say that their child could do better should look at the heavily realistic pictures that Miró was producing aged eight – the fantasy came later.

▶▶ **Fundació Pilar i Joan Miró**　　74C2
*Carrer Joan de Saridakis 29, Cala Major
(tel: 971 701420)
Open: 15 May–14 Sep, Tue–Sat 10–7, Sun 10–3;
15 Sep–14 May, Tue–Sat 10–6, Sun 10–3.
Admission: moderate*

In Mallorcan eyes, the artist Joan Miró is nothing less than a saint. Apart from a brief spell in Paris when Miró became involved with the Surrealist movement there, he spent most of his life in Barcelona. But both his wife and mother were Mallorcan and he always longed to return to the scene of his childhood holidays to draw inspiration from what he called "the light of Mallorca". In 1956, aged 63, he bought a house and studio overlooking the bay in Cala Major on the outskirts of Palma, where he lived and worked until his death in 1983.

Today, Miró's studio remains almost untouched since his death, with incomplete canvases and open tins of paints. Opposite, a small, rotating sample of his work is on display in an appropriately modern, angular gallery. The Miró Foundation owns most of the work he completed on Mallorca – around 6,000 works, including 134 paintings, 300 engravings and 3,000 studio pieces. The garden contains statues, murals and other examples of Mironian work.

▶ **Galilea**　　74B2
This charming village of whitewashed farmsteads, arranged in tiers 480m above sea level in the shadow of the mighty peak of Puig de Galatzó, has recently become an artists' colony, and half of its 400 inhabitants are foreigners. The stolid 19th-century church that tops the village has two distinguishing features: two sundials (one over the principal doorway, the other on the south wall) and only one window. On a fine day, you can see far out to sea, while eating *tapas* (see pages 174–175) in the local bar and listening to the sound of sheep-bells on the hillsides.

▶ **Hort de Palma**　　74C2
The "Garden of Palma" is a fertile area of countryside to the north-west of the city, dotted with small villages, estates and country houses, including Son Berga (6km north of Palma), an 18th-century mansion with magnificent gardens, and Son Vida (5km north-west of Palma), once the seat of the Marqués de la Torre, now a luxury hotel (see page 69).

▶▶▶ **La Granja**　　74C3
*Carretera d'Esporles, Esporles (tel: 971 610032)
Open: daily 10–7. Admission: expensive*
Time seems to have stood still at the handsome old hacienda of La Granja, tucked in a tranquil wooded

valley, 10km south-west of Valldemossa. There has been a house here since Moorish times, which was later occupied by Cistercian monks, before passing in the 15th century into the hands of the Fortuny family, who still own it today. It presents a fine blend of Moorish architecture and Mallorcan rural tradition with unspoilt authenticity.

A vast collection of antiques, furniture, ceramics and art adorns the house. Highlights include an elegant drawing-room with its own theatre, the nursery, the family chapel and the torture chamber in the dungeons. However, the real reason for visiting La Granja is to learn about rural Mallorcan traditions, and in the various workshops and outbuildings, you can watch costumed artisans demonstrating lacemaking, embroidery and spinning, pottery and candle-making before tasting samples of fig cake, wine, herbal liqueurs, deep-fried *bunyols* (doughnuts) and other delicacies in the shaded courtyard.

►► La Reserva 74B2

Puigpunyent (tel: 971 616622)
Open: daily 10–4, (until 5 in summer).
Admission: expensive

If you do not have time for a full excursion into the mountains, a visit to this privately owned nature reserve will give you a taste of the countryside of Mallorca's Serra Tramuntana. La Reserva describes itself as "Mallorca's paradise" – a 3km-long, clearly defined footpath exploring the lower slopes of Puig de Galatzó. Wooden plaques provide polyglot information on subjects such as plants and birdlife. Additional points of interest include waterfalls, the Cave of the Moor, a fig orchard and a charcoal burner's hut.

AN IDYLLIC GARDEN
Escape the tour groups at La Granja by taking a walk in the magnificent fountain-filled grounds. These contain ornamental and botanical gardens, as well as waterfalls and a thousand-year-old yew. There is a 1,200m signposted walk in the company of roaming deer, pigs and goats, as well as a natural spring which spouts water some 9m into the air.

A potter at La Granja demonstrates his craft

Mallorca has everything you need for a family holiday by the sea. As in most of Mediterranean Europe, society here is very child-friendly and, besides the usual beach holiday fun and games, the resorts all have purpose-built activities and amusements to bankrupt Mum and Dad.

AN UNUSUAL TREAT
Fancy a day trip with a difference, without the need to hire a car or pile into a crammed coach with screaming children? Then consider catching the vintage train from Palma to Sóller (see pages 108–109). The dramatic journey through the Serra de Tramuntana takes about an hour, then from Sóller you can take an ancient tram down to the Port de Sóller (see pages 106–107) for a swim and an ice-cream.

Resorts Mallorcans love children and constantly make a fuss of them. Most hotels and *hostals* welcome them and many offer rooms with three or four beds. Restaurants and cafés encourage families and many package holidays offer child-minding facilities and a children's entertainment programme. Children's facilities lean towards physical activities, but besides the beach, swimming pools and indoor games, large hotels often put on special children's shows, a magician or clowns. Funfairs and circuses also visit Mallorca. A novel summer attraction in Palma Nova is **Flik Flac**, a circus with a difference – no animals, but a dazzling two-hour show of comedy, dance and acrobatics.

Beaches Scattered around the island are lots of good sandy beaches with safe, shallow water and first-aid stations, ideal for children. Try Santa Ponça or Magaluf, to the west of Palma, both with broad family beaches, ideal for youngsters, and plenty of watersports for older children. To the north-east, children love the clear, shallow water at Port d'Alcúdia and Port de Pollença, or playing in the dunes behind the Platja de Muro. Cala Millor and Sa Coma are also classic family holiday beaches. In the south, choose between the tiny, sheltered coves of Cala Pi, Cala Llombards and Cala Santanyí or the unbridled fun of popular beach resorts, Can Pastilla and S'Arenal. Beach games, sports and fishing equipment can be bought in the abundant seaside shops.

Funparks and animals

There are four aquaparks on the island: **Aquaparc** (tel: 971 130811) at Magaluf, **Aqualandia** (tel: 971 511228) on the Palma–Inca road, at km 25 (also with a wax museum), **Hidroparc** (tel: 971 891672) at Port d'Alcúdia, and **Aquacity** (tel: 971 440000) at S'Arenal, one of the largest water funfairs in the world (see page 176). Still on a watery theme, it's hard to beat **Nemo Submarines** (tel: 971 130227) at Magaluf, which offers a rare chance to experience the myriad fish and wrecks of the underwater world, or **Marineland** (tel: 971 675125) at Cala d'en Blanes (see page 84), where visitors see performing dolphins, sea lions and a parrot circus.

Animal lovers should visit the **Reserva Africana** (tel: 971 810909) near Sa Coma (see page 148), with its lions, crocodiles and wildebeest or, for monster fun, visit the giant plastic dinosaurs at **Son Gual Parc Prehistòric** (tel: 971 742960) 16km east of Palma on the Manacor road.

Sport There is a whole host of sporting activities geared specially to youngsters. Most riding clubs have small ponies suitable for young riders, and a mini-golf course is rarely far away, the most exotic being **Golf Fantasia** (tel: 971 682349) at Palma Nova. Most resorts have go-karting facilities and offer exciting boat trips, often in glass-bottomed boats. For tiny children, it is possible to rent bicycles with child-seats, or to ride along the seafront in many resorts on a tourist train.

Evening fun Older children are thrilled by the flamenco and jousting at the **Castillo Comte Mal's** "Medieval evenings" (tel: 971 617766) in Palma Nova, or the rip-roaring, swashbuckling, **Pirate Adventure** (tel: 971 130411), an evening show with audience participation in Magaluf.

For something more educational, visit a glass-blowing factory (see page 104), one of the island's **caves** (the Coves del Drac are the most impressive, see page 167), or learn about traditional crafts at **La Granja** (see page 81).

CHILDCARE
- Remember that small children are particularly vulnerable to the sun and need to be well protected.
- If you need a child seat in a hire car, a cot or a high-chair in your hotel or apartment, these should be booked in advance and checked for safety on arrival.
- Nappies and formula milk are sold in shops and supermarkets.
- Outside main resorts, baby-changing facilities are not widely available.

The beach at Magaluf

▶ Magaluf 74B1

Tourist Office: Avinguda Magaluf 22 (tel: 971 131126)

Magaluf was among Mallorca's earliest tourist developments and is synonymous with cheap 'n'cheerful sun, sand, sea and *sangría* package holidays. Today, however, the authorities have smartened up the resort. By knocking down some of the monstrous concrete hotels built during the tourist boom, widening the golden, sandy beach and building an attractive beach promenade, they are trying to promote more of a family image.

Nevertheless, summer visitors are still assaulted by fast food, neon lights, noisy bars such as the Britannia Pub, Benny Hill's and Fred's Fish 'n' Chips, and scantily clad youths intent on having a riotous holiday. Out of season, the whole scene changes. Discos are closed, bars shut early and the resort is popular with older visitors who are looking for a quiet, yet reasonably priced, winter holiday.

▶ Marineland 74C1

Costa d'en Blanes (tel: 971 675125)
Open: daily 9:30–5:30. Closed: 18 Nov–25 Dec.
Admission: expensive

Stars of the daily shows here are the performing dolphins and sea lions, whose zealous aquabatics attract appreciative crowds. In the Parrot Circus, trained macaws ride a comic cavalcade of bicycles, jeeps and roller skates. Other attractions include an aquarium and a reptile zoo.

▶ Palma Nova 74B1

Tourist Office: Passeig de la Mar 13 (tel: 971 682365)

Once a beauty spot, with its wide, shallow bay and golden beaches set against a backdrop of pine-covered hills, "New Palma" is another prime destination for cut-price, package tour holidays. Its waterfront clutter of hotels and tourist facilities now merges into Magaluf, creating a continuous resort, sometimes referred to as "Maganova". However, it has more character than Magaluf, smarter hotels, and makes a better base for family holidays.

▶ Peguera 74B1

Tourist Office: Carrer Sebelli (tel: 971 687083)

Peguera, with its two generous sandy beaches, Platja de Palmire and the smaller Platja de Tora, is a favourite resort with families and older visitors. To the west, it is a 1km stroll to the tiny beach and clear waters of Cala Fornells, with its chic, modern pueblo-style villas, that cling to the steep slopes above the bay.

MEGA-DISCO

Not only does Magaluf have Mallorca's only casino, but also the largest and probably the loudest disco in Europe. BCM mega-disco is open daily from 10 PM until 5 AM (tel: 971 132715) and takes place on two levels: the upper level, with spectacular laser shows and a swimming pool, is for the soon-to-be-deaf trendy young crowd, whereas the lower level is for what the upstairs group calls *carozas* (carts) – in other words, anyone over 30!

Drive

West of Palma

See map on page 74.

You need not drive far from Palma to enjoy the peace of Mallorca's interior. This 86km circuit guides you through the mountains up to the spectacular cliffs and sea views of the north coast. Allow 5 hours.

From Palma Nova, take the PM1015 northwards to **Calvià** (see page 79). Before long, the concrete high-rise resorts of the coast are replaced by woods, farms and fields flecked with olive and carob trees. In Calvià town centre, turn right at a T-junction and climb steadily past several grand country houses guarded by decorative wrought-iron gates to the small village of **Establiments▶**. It was here that George Sand and Chopin first stayed during their visit of 1838–1839, amid a landscape Sand considered worthy of Poussin's paintbrush. From here, take a left turn to **Esporles▶**.

This pretty town of tree-lined streets, sheltered by mountain ridges, makes a pleasant stop for a drink or lunch, or to buy apples, pears, oranges and figs, grown on the local terraces and sold in its shops.

Continue north following signs to Banyalbufar and **La Granja** (see pages 80–81), typical of the beautiful *fincas* (country houses) that adorn the island's interior. A sinuous drive along the northern coast leads to the small farming community of **Banyalbufar▶▶**, clinging perilously to a narrow ridge – some of the buildings lining its narrow main street are supported by stilts. Its steep terraces, which were originally constructed by the Moors, support thriving crops of tomatoes, grapes and flowers, and are still worked mostly by hand.

Heading west along the coast, several *miradores* (viewpoints) provide a chance to stop for refreshment and to take in the magnificent views of mountains, high cliffs and the sea far below. After the tiny village of **Estellencs▶▶**, a harmonious ensemble of ochre houses offset by a backdrop of similarly coloured cliffs, the road winds gently down to the stately old town of Andratx (see page 78). From here it is a simple 13km drive along the fast C719 to Palma Nova.

Precarious farming on Banyalbufar's coastal terraces

85

COVE DE LA MARE DE DÉU

According to local legend this remarkable church, hewn from the soft rock, was the work of shipwrecked Genoese seamen who took shelter from a storm in the bay. In thanksgiving for their survival, they placed a small figure of the Virgin from their ship inside the cave. In 1866, it was removed for safe-keeping and can now be seen in the seafront church at Portals Nous.

86

Opposite: Cove de la Mare de Déu, Portals Vells

CASTELL DE BENDINAT

Just inland from Portals Nous lies a medieval 13th-century castle complete with battlements and fortified towers. Enlarged in the 18th century and today used as a conference hall, it makes a majestic sight surrounded by dark pine woods on the Palma–Andratx road. It is said that its name derives from a remark uttered by a contented Jaume I in 1229 after he had dined here – "*Havem ben dinat.*" ("We have eaten well"!)

▶▶▶ Port d'Andratx   74A2

Port d'Andratx is a good example of a picturesque fishing port turned upmarket holiday resort, while still keeping a turn-of-the-century fishing village charm. The setting is idyllic, with the deep natural harbour flanked by wooded hills, rich with peach trees and vines, that lead up to Andratx town 5km inland (see page 78). The old harbour on the east side of the bay is particularly agreeable, with a string of waterfront cafés and *tapas* bars lining the promenade. In summer months, pleasure boats run to Sant Telm (see page 88) and the nearby island of Sa Dragonera (see below).

▶▶▶ Portals Nous   74C2

Do not be put off by the rather disappointing main street of Portals Nous until you have explored the exclusive pine-shaded side streets lined with gracious, high-walled mansions. For this is one of Mallorca's most stylish resorts, and its glitzy marina, **Porto Portals** – considered by many to be the best yachting marina in the Balearics – is where the rich and famous "hide away" to be noticed. This is the St Tropez of Mallorca, and one of the most rewarding venues for people-watching and celebrity-spotting.

▶▶▶ Portals Vells   74B1

The discreetly scattered villas and tiny bay of glistening turquoise water that comprise Portals Vells are located down a pretty, pot-holed country lane, a mere stone's throw from the urban jungle of Maganova (see page 84), at the end of a pine-scented peninsula barely touched by development. There are several delightful beaches, including Cala Portals Vells and the tiny nudist beach of Platja Mago. Walk along the south side of the cliffs to reach the Cove de la Mare de Déu (see panel). The view across the bay towards Palma cathedral from here is surely one of the most splendid on the island.

▶▶ Puigpunyent   74B2

You will inevitably pass through this quaint little town of cream-coloured, sun-bleached houses surrounded by mountains, if you are touring the Serra del Nord. Stop to visit the 17th-century parish church with its mighty rectangular tower, and to buy some apples, melons and plums grown in the lush wide valley, before continuing 2km to the north to see the source of the Torrente Sa Riera (which flows through Palma), spanned by a picturesque old aqueduct. Near by is the 17th-century *finca* (country house) of **Son Forteza▶**, a typical Mallorcan country residence which occasionally opens its beautiful gardens.

▶▶▶ Sa Dragonera   74A2

In the 15th century one of the Balearics' most notorious pirates, Redbeard, had his base camp on the rocky islet of Sa Dragonera just 1km off the western tip of Mallorca. Today this dragon-shaped bare wedge of rock, 7km long, 400m wide and rising steeply to 310m, is a protected nature park. Although you are not allowed ashore, many visitors like to tour round the island in the hope of spotting ospreys or Eleonora's falcons. Sa Dragonera also offers good scuba diving. Boat trips run regularly out of Port d'Andratx (see above) and Sant Telm (see page 88).

Right: Inspiring views from Sa Trapa

SA TRAPA

It is still possible to wander round the ruined chapel, kitchen and living quarters of this isolated mountain community. Almond trees continue to blossom on its perfectly built terraces, the mill still has its ancient machinery and it is easy to make out the wide sweep of the threshing floor, now punctured by pines that have grown up since the monastery's closure in the late 18th century.

►► Sant Telm

74A2

The tiny former fishing village of Sant Telm lies on the western tip of Mallorca, overlooking the island of Sa Dragonera. It is a quiet, little-known holiday resort that, at the moment, consists of little more than one main street draped along a small rocky bay with a small sandy beach at one end, a harbour at the other, and several excellent seafood restaurants in between.

In the surrounding countryside there are excellent cliff-top and forest walks that follow well set out paths, up to the ruined 14th-century Castillo de Sant Telm to the south-east of the village or to the ruined Trappist monastery of Sa Trapa (see panel, this page, and walk opposite), which now belongs to the island's ornithological society.

► Santa Ponça

74B1

Tourist Office: Carrer Puig de Galatzó (tel: 971 691712)
This busy, cosmopolitan resort enjoys an attractive site just west of the Badia de Palma, with pine woods and a large sandy beach washed by clear, shallow water. Popular with British tour operators, it gets packed out in summer although it never attains the brash atmosphere of nearby Magaluf (see page 84). Nevertheless, if you are looking for a fast tan by day and fast fun by night, the numerous discos and bars are as busy as the broad sandy beaches.

Historically, Santa Ponça is more than just another coastal holiday resort. It was here in 1229 that Jaume I first came ashore to conquer the island. He came well armed, with 150 ships carrying 16,000 troops and 1,500 horses, and eventually landed on the rocky promontory of Sa Caleta, 2km west of Santa Ponça, on 12 September 1229. In the ensuing battle, some 1,500 Moors were killed. Others fled to the mountains, enabling Jaume and his *conquistadores* to press eastwards to besiege Palma for three months before it finally surrendered on 31 December. Look out for the tall white Victory Cross erected here in 1929 to commemorate the 700th anniversary of this historic landing, with its sculpted scenes depicting the bravery of the Christian troops.

Santa Ponça – a popular mooring

Walk

Sa Trapa

Hidden away in the cliffs north of Sant Telm is the abandoned Trappist monastery of Sa Trapa. Take a light picnic and plenty to drink. Allow 3 hours return, excluding time at Sa Trapa.

Start at the northern end of Sant Telm (see opposite) in Plaça de Mosser Sebastià Grau by the blue and white windmill. From here, take Avinguda de la Trapa inland, which becomes a country track through pine woods leading to a farmhouse named C'an Tomevi. Turn right behind the house following a sign for Sa Trapa. At the next sign, either turn left for a steep ascent of the cliffs, or continue straight on up an easier but longer inland track.

If you turn left, walk through the woods until you reach a pair of small concrete gateposts. Turn right here – the first of many black paint arrows show the way. The path narrows, crosses several walls and passes the stone ruins of a lime-kiln. Eventually you ascend above the pines. After a short scramble up, a well-established path leads up to a clifftop viewpoint and over the promontory to the romantic buildings of **Sa Trapa** (see panel opposite) in the valley beyond.

Sa Trapa is currently being restored by the Grupo Ornithologia Balear (GOB) and the track they use leads inland from behind the monastery, over a pass then gently down the mountain. The track then crosses a bridge, curves through a farm and, forking right, leads back to C'an Tomevi.

In common with other areas of Spain, Mallorca has, after many years of neglect, experienced something of a renaissance in its cuisine. For the more discerning tourist, Mallorcan food has become an essential part of the holiday experience.

Mallorcan cuisine *La cuina mallorquína* is hearty peasant fare, based on nourishing pork, fish and vegetable dishes, steeped in tradition and rooted in local ingredients. Its simple, generous portions are served without frills but are nonetheless delicious and surprisingly subtle in flavour.

The main ingredients of traditional Mallorcan dishes are typical of the Mediterranean kitchen: tomatoes, garlic, olive oil, aubergines and courgettes, peppers and herbs. Fried together, these form a *salsa mallorquína* (Mallorcan sauce) served with many meat dishes, and used as the basis for a variety of *caldereta* (stews), which include a bouillabaisse-style *caldereta de peix* (fish stew).

Above: Sobrasada *and* botifarró – *sausage specialities*

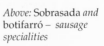

Staple diet For centuries pork has been the cornerstone of the islanders' diet, and no visit to Mallorca is complete without trying *lechona asada* (roast suckling pig) at least once. Not long ago every village celebrated the *matança*, the winter slaughter of pigs, with singing and dancing and the making of hams and sausages for the coming year. In some villages such as Sant Joan, it remains an important cultural event.

The different varieties of sausage can often be seen hanging from the rafters of restaurants and deli-catessens – *sobrasada*, or minced pork with hot red peppers, and *botifarró*, cured pork with blood, as well as spicy *chorizo* from Spain. And every bar or restaurant has its *jamón serrano* or *jamón iberico*, a whole cured ham on display on an attractive slicing-board.

A side effect of the *matança* was *frit mallorquí*, a tasty fry-up of the most perishable pork offal with potatoes, onions and tomatoes. Nowadays you find it on menus as a starter alongside *tumbet*, a Mallorcan-style ratatouille of aubergines, potatoes and peppers in olive oil, and *sopes mallorquínes*, a thick broth of thinly sliced brown bread with vegetables. Classic meat dishes include *llom amb col* (pork wrapped in cabbage with pine nuts and raisins) and its winter cousin, *tords amb col*, with thrush instead of pork, and *escaldums* (chicken casserole with potato and almonds). Look out also for roast lamb (*cordero*) and *conill all i oli*, char-grilled rabbit smothered with a heavily garlicked mayonnaise. Mallorcans love hunting and so pheasant (*faisán*), partridge (*perdius*) and quail (*codorniz*) are frequently on menus. Veal is often used for stews (*estofat de vedella*) while poultry is often combined with fruit or seafood. *Pollastre amb gambas*, chicken stuffed with prawns, is especially delicious.

Coastal delights Near the coast, fish dishes reign supreme, varying from simple grilled sardines (*sardinas*) to *caldereta de langosta* (lobster casserole). Try the local speciality, *anfós al forn* (sea bass baked in a case of rock salt), *musclos al vapor* (steamed mussels), *calamares farcits* (stuffed squid), *salmonetes* (red mullet) and *greixonera de peix*, a hearty fish stew, cooked in an earthenware bowl. Prawns come *a la parilla* (grilled), *al ajilla* (fried in garlic) or *a la Romana* (in batter).

A number of traditional dishes use eels, a favourite island delicacy. They include *greixonera d'anguiles* (eel casserole) and *espinagada* (spicy eel and vegetable pie). Perhaps the strangest dish of all (which tastes better than it looks!) is *calamares en su tinta*, jet black rings of squid stewed in its own ink, served with white rice.

Even though paella is not a Mallorcan dish (coming from Valencia), it is widely available and makes a memorable meal; *paella ciega* (blind man's paella) comes without bones. The local equivalent is *arròs brut* ("dirty rice"), saffron rice cooked with chunks of chicken, rabbit and vegetables. *Arròs negre* is blackened with squid ink and *arròs marinera* contains seafood.

Above: jamón serrano

ENSAIMADAS

Life without *ensaimadas* to the Mallorquín would be as unthinkable as breakfast without croissants to the French. These fluffy, spiral-shaped sweet pastries dusted with icing sugar are sold in bakeries and range from bite-sized ones to great cartwheels up to half a metre in diameter. Eaten plain for breakfast and tea, stuffed with spicy sausage as a snack or filled with cream, almonds and fruit as a delicious dessert, they are without doubt Mallorca's gastronomic pride and joy.

The North-west

93

▶▶▶ REGION HIGHLIGHTS

Deià *page 101*

Fornalutx *page 102*

Serra de Tramuntana
pages 120–121

Sóller *pages 110–111*

Valldemossa
pages 116–117

94

The North-West map (page 94 of 208)

0 ——— 5 km
0 ——— 5 miles

see drive pages 120–121

Punta Beca

838m

Pollença

C710

Torrent de Pareis 1003m
Sa Calobra
Puig Roig
Cala Tuent
1102m
Puig Tomir

Morro de Cala Roja
Escorca
Monestir de Lluc

Sa Illeta
Gorg Blau 1348m
Lluc
Punta Grossa
Mirador de ses Barques
1445m
Puig Major
Puig de Massanella

Port de Sóller
C710
Torrent de Sant Miquel

Coves de Campanet

Fornalutx
Campanet

Cala de Deià
Sóller
Biniaraix
Caimari
Büger

Punta de Deià
Lluc-Alcari
Serra d'Alfàbia
Moscari

Sa Foradada
Selva

Son Marroig
Deià
Mancor

S'Estaca
Serra des Teix
1068m

Port de Valldemossa
1064m
Es Teix
Coll de Sóller
Orient
Castell d'Alaró
Lloseta
Inca
Ermita de Santa Magdalena

Camí de s'Arxiduc
Alfàbia

Valldemossa
Alaró

La Reïal Cartoixa (La Cartuja)
Bunyola
Binissalem
C713
Torrent des Rafal Ences
Agualandia

Esporles
Consell
Biniagual
Costitx

Sa Font Seca
Santa Maria del Camí
Sencelles

Torrent ses Mates
Biniali
Lloret de Vista Alegre

Son Berga
Son Sardina
Sa Cabaneta
Santa Eugènia
Pina

Establiments
PM27
C713
Pòrtol

Son Vida
Sa Vileta
Sa Indioteria

Son Gros

PALMA (CIUTAT DE MALLORCA)
Son Ferriol
Casa Gordiola
C715
Montuïri

Castell de Bellver
Gènova
C715
Sant Jordi
Son Guai Parc Prehistòric
Algaida

Cas Català
Cala Major
Coll d'en Rabassa
Es Molinar
S'Aranjassa

Portals Nous
Sant Agustí
Ses Illetes
Can Pastilla
PM19
C717
Sant Francesc
C717
Randa
Santuari de Cura

A

Serra de Tramuntana

THE NORTH-WEST One of the big advantages of the mass-tourism resorts being concentrated in the south, is that about 80 per cent of the island is left uncrowded. Drive a short distance northwards from these big resorts and you would be forgiven for thinking you were on another island, one filled with citrus groves, almond orchards, pine and palm trees, mountain ranges, and isolated coves and inlets.

"MOUNTAINS OF THE NORTH WIND" The entire length of the north-west coast is protected by the Serra de Tramuntana (Mountains of the North Wind), which stretch from Andratx to Pollença, at times almost plunging into the sea. This, the most scenically attractive region of Mallorca, is also one of the hardest to reach, even though it is served by the island's only two railway lines. Besides offering spectacular scenery, the Serra de Tramuntana holds many secrets. Take the slow train up to Sóller, the wiggly descent to Sa Calobra, pay a visit to the monasteries at Valldemossa and Lluc and, by the end of your tour, you will have a completely different image of Mallorca.

In the southern foothills lies a mosaic of fields of dark red soil, covered with gnarled olive trees, orange groves, fig orchards and wild fennel. Driving through the tiny honey-coloured hamlets snoozing in the sun – where the only sounds come from sheep-bells, the chatter of the locals in the sunlit squares and the clatter of horses and carts – is rather like entering a time-warp; it is as if the villagers are unaware that the rest of the island is a leading holiday destination.

Of all the mountain villages, Fornalutx is the most photogenic, while Sóller is one of the most atmospheric with its Modernista architecture, its café tables spilling out into the main square and its old-fashioned railway carriages trundling through the streets to the region's only beach of note, a few kilometres away at Port de Sóller.

MOUNTAIN SAFETY
When walking in the mountains, remember the following precautionary measures: never go alone, never overestimate your capabilities, dress properly, take a good supply of food and water, and get a weather report. The "Island of Calm" can be very deceptive and the weather can change within minutes.

Pages 92–93: Orient – a typical mountain village

95

Stunning north-western scenery – olive and orange groves

PILGRIMAGE CENTRES The two best-known mountain villages in Mallorca, however, are Deià, where the poet Robert Graves is buried, and Valldemossa, in whose Carthusian monastery Chopin and George Sand lived together for several months. The monastery and scenery have changed little since that ill-fated winter of 1838 (see pages 118–119), and remains today well worth visiting for a Chopin concert or purely for the monastic peace.

Deià is dramatically cupped in a giant natural amphitheatre between the mountains and the sea. Graves spent most of his working life in the village and helped to give it the image of an artists' colony. Nowadays, it still has a few resident painters and writers but it is really more of an exclusive and expensive retreat for expatriates from Germany, Britain and the Spanish mainland. An 1878 guidebook noted that Deià had "a collection of strange and eccentric foreigners" and it appears to have changed little since.

Near by, nestling at the heart of the Serra, is the famous pilgrimage centre of Lluc, a 13th-century monastery containing Mallorca's most sacred relic, a black Virgin known as La Moreneta.

Deià village square (top), the monastery church in Valldemossa (above) and La Moreneta (opposite)

WALKERS' PARADISE Undoubtedly the best way to discover the north-west of Mallorca is on foot, to fully appreciate the dizzy gorges and the stony pastures, the rock-roses and dazzling yellow sprays of broom, the scent of the pines and the spray of the sea, the sound of the cicadas and the swirling of birds overhead. The mountains offer some of the most breathtaking views of the island, from the highest peaks across the orchards and olive groves of the central lowlands. On a clear day, you can just make out the urban edges of Palma simmering in the haze, a world away from the Mallorca of the mountains.

Entrance to the house at Alfàbia surrounded by delightful gardens

►► Alfàbia 94A2

Sóller–Palma road (at entrance to the Sóller tunnel)
(tel: 971 613123)
Open: May–Oct, Mon–Fri 9:30–6:30, Sat 9:30–1; Nov–Apr, Mon–Fri 9:30–5:30, Sat 9:30–1. Admission: moderate

The gardens of Alfàbia are a delightful memento of when Mallorca was under Moorish rule and a legacy of the Arab talent for landscaping and irrigation. Their name derives from *"al fabi"* – "jar of olives" in Arabic. The lush gardens were designed around a grand hacienda with veranda by Benihabet, the Muslim governor of Inca who, following the Spanish invasion of 1229, converted to Christianity and was therefore able to retain possession of the estate. Today, its ownership remains in the direct line of his descendants.

The cool, fragrant garden makes a special spot for an afternoon siesta – take a book or some postcards, find a shady seat and drift off to sleep to the soothing sound of gently splashing pools and fountains. Or stroll along creeper-covered walkways, past cascading trellises of

ROYAL SHOW
In mid-August, Bunyola's equestrian centre is the venue for the famous HRH Princess Elena Horse Jumping Trophy, attended by members of the Spanish royal family.

jasmine, wistaria and honeysuckle, through twining subtropical plants and citrus groves to the small outdoor bar, which serves delicious freshly squeezed orange or lemon juice.

The house, though somewhat rundown, is a fascinating relic of halcyon days, with its faded wall panels and antique furniture. Note the library of old books, the fine 14th-century *mudéjar* (post-Reconquest Moorish style) ceiling inside the porch, and an oak chair, considered one of the most beautiful and most valuable antiques on Mallorca. It was commissioned as a throne by the uncrowned Jaume IV and adorned with carvings depicting the story of the children of Jaume III, who died while imprisoned in Bellver Castle. Sadly, Jaume IV never had a chance to sit on it. After the Battle of Llucmajor in 1349, in which his father was killed by the Aragonese, he was captured and spent the rest of his days in exile.

▶ Binissalem 94B2

This small country town is the centre of Mallorca's wine-making industry. Viticulture was introduced to the islands by the Romans and survived the Moorish occupation (Binissalem means "House of Salem" in Arabic, and the town originally grew up round a Moorish country house). Production reached a peak in the late 19th century until phylloxera devastated the vineyards. It has taken a long time to re-establish wine production on the island, but the quality and reputation of Mallorcan wines is growing.

Binissalem's **Festa d'es Verema** (Grape Harvest Festival) with folk-dancing and freely flowing wine takes place in the spacious main square every September.

▶ Búger 94C3

Four windmills and a small 17th-century church pierce the skyline of Búger, one of dozens of sleepy hilltop villages in Mallorca's interior which have been totally overlooked by the tourist industry. Soak up the atmosphere in one of the bars of the main square – Plaça de la Constitutitó – where local men sit at pavement tables, while the women go about their daily chores, stopping to chat to their neighbours in the cool shade of the narrow, flower-filled streets and stepped alleyways. In the surrounding area, there are several prehistoric burial sites (see pages 28–29).

▶ Bunyola 94A2

The wooded southern foothills of the Serra de Tramuntana are probably the least known region of Mallorca. In the midst of them is this delightful mountainside town of plane trees and sun-baked cottages, known locally for its Saturday morning market. The tiled, yellow spire of Villa Francisca, one of Mallorca's few intact examples of Modernista architecture (see page 36), on the outskirts, is surrounded by orchards and is a striking landmark.

Bunyola's Modernista masterpiece

It's a steep climb to the Castell d'Alaró

"FISH-FACE"
The Castell d'Alaró was the scene of a tragic episode during the Aragonese invasion of 1285. Alfonso III of Aragon was so irritated by the struggle to capture the castle, and so riled by the garrison's two commanders Guilermo Cabrit and Guillermo Bassa, who had punningly (and foolishly) called him "fish-face" ("*anfos*" means "perch" in Catalan!) that, when the castle eventually fell, he had the pair arrested, impaled and roasted alive. Cabrit and Bassa now rank among the great figures of Mallorcan history, venerated almost as if they were saints.

CALA DE DEIÀ
A 20-minute stroll north of the village, down a wooded ravine (turn left off the road to Sóller at the sign marked Depuradora), leads to the beautiful Cala de Deià. This tiny shingle cove of jagged cliffs and deep, clear water is bounded on the west by the promontory of Punta de Deià. It is a wonderful place for a swim, and there is even a ramshackle beach bar and restaurant for refreshments.

▶▶ Castell d'Alaró   94B2

A castle has stood on this lofty, impregnable rock since Moorish times. Indeed it was so invincible that the Arab commander was able to hold out here for two years after the Christian conquest. Later, in 1285, it was the last stronghold captured during the conquest of Mallorca by Alfonso III of Aragón (see panel).

To reach the castle, drive north-east on the PM210 towards Orient. At km18, a turning left leads to a narrow road bordered by stone walls and fields of olives and almond trees. This degenerates into a rough dirt track full of potholes, best suited to four-wheel-drive vehicles or hikers with sturdy footwear. About 4km up through terraced olive groves is a small, rustic bar-restaurant, **Es Pouet**. From here, it is just under an hour's trek up steep and winding stone steps to the fragmentary ruins of the 15th-century castle. A tiny pilgrims' church, Mare de Déu del Rufugi, has stood here since 1622, and there is also a snug inn at the top, the Hostal Castillo de Alar, with log fires, delicious home-cooking and basic dormitory accommodation (bring a sleeping bag if possible).

The climb up to Castell d'Alaró is one of Mallorca's most popular walks – especially on Sundays – and the views from the terrace, 871m above sea level, extend across the entire island.

▶▶ Coves de Campanet   94C3

3km north of Campanet (tel: 971 516130)
Open: daily 10–6 (7 in summer).
Admission: expensive

It is worth stopping in the peaceful town of Campanet, if only to visit the **church of Sant Miquel▶** (Plaça Sant Miquel. *Open* Mon–Sat 9:30–1:30) built in 1220 and recognised as a Christian place of worship even during the Arab occupation, and to enjoy a drink in the friendly bar opposite.

The main sources of income in Campanet are farming, basketwork, glass manufacture (see page 104) and the Coves de Campanet, a veritable tourist honeypot. Discovered in 1945,

the limestone caves are the smallest of the five Mallorcan cave systems open to the public, and considered by many to be the finest. Stout footwear is recommended for the fascinating 40-minute conducted tour through the subterranean maze.

►►► Deià 94A2

This picturesque village has long attracted foreign artists. The painter Santiago Rusinyol and the writer Anaïs Nin both lived here, and Pablo Picasso worked here briefly, but Deià's most famous resident was the English poet and novelist Robert Graves (see page 35). Graves wrote some of the 20th century's greatest love poems in Deià.

Graves strove hard to stop Deià being ruined by the encroaching tourist developments, and even in high season the village is rarely crowded as buses are not allowed to stop. The sleepy, green-shuttered houses and steep, cobbled streets form a harmonious ensemble, crowned by a pretty country church. Nearly a quarter of its 400 inhabitants are "expats" and artists, drawn by Deià's beauty and relaxed atmosphere and history. The village has a large number of galleries, top restaurants (see page 200) and luxury hotels (see page 196), – notably La Residencia, an idyllic mansion turned hotel. As author Robert Elms put it, "Everything in Deià is taken slowly, except your money".

"WILD OLIVES"
Robert Graves' family continues to live in his house in Deià and, since the writer's death, his son and biographer, William Graves, has described Deià in his book, *Wild Olives – Life in Majorca with Robert Graves*.

Deià has long attracted foreign artists and celebrities

101

▶ ▶ ▶ Fornalutx 94B3

Not only does Fornalutx claim to be Mallorca's most picturesque village but also the most beautiful village in all Spain, and it is hard to disagree – unless you accept the claims of its neighbour Biniaraix. Indeed, Fornalutx is graced with an idyllic setting in a valley scented by orange and lemon groves, with Puig Major, the highest mountain on the island, as its dramatic backdrop.

The village itself is a quaint huddle of ancient, honey-coloured stone houses (many still retain remnants of Moorish paintings under the eaves) and steep, cobbled streets, frequently stepped to facilitate the passage of mules. There are several terrace restaurants and bars, where you can sit and soak in the views of olive and orange groves climbing until they reach the pines on the foothills of the mountains.

▶ Inca 94C2

This busy industrial town at the end of the railway line from Palma is heavily promoted as a place all tourists should visit. Excursions usually coincide with the vast Thursday market, and many include a visit to one of the town's countless leather factories or their retail outlets along Avinguda General Luque and Gran Vía de Colon. Prices do not warrant a special trip, but you will find there is plenty of choice.

Pursuers of Mallorcan cuisine will enjoy a meal in one of the town centre's *cellers* – rustic restaurants, where the wine is drawn from the giant vats lining the walls. Celler C'an Amer is the most famous (see page 200). You could try their local specialities of *caracoles* (snails) or roast suckling pig. In the bakeries you may see *concos d'Inca* ("Inca bachelors"), a type of cake made by the nuns who inhabit the

Fornalutx – narrow streets give way to olive and orange groves

Monasterio de las Jerónimas.

Outside town, a turning right off the Inca-Alcúdia road, signposted to the **Ermita de Santa Magdalena▶**, leads up to the summit of Puig d'Inca (304m) and a small sanctuary offering far-reaching views over the countryside and mountains. There is a small chapel and a café for visitors. Every year, a pilgrimage, said to have been followed for 800 years, is made to the hermitage on the first Sunday after Easter.

▶▶ Lluc

94C3

Tel: 971 517025
Open: Museum 10–5:30.
Admission: inexpensive. Information and accommodation
office 8 AM–10 PM. Basilica and chapel 9 AM–8:30 PM;
Masses at 11:30 and dusk

The Monestir de Lluc (Lluc Monastery) has been a centre of pilgrimage since the 13th century when an Arab shepherd boy, recently converted to Christianity, discovered a dark wooden statue of the Virgin in the forest. The image was placed in the church at Escorca, but three times it returned miraculously to the same spot in the forest. Local people recognised this as a message from God and a chapel was built to house it.

This chapel forms part of a colossal ensemble of pink-tinged stone buildings along with a church, a choir school, the old Augustinian monastery, a small museum and gallery, Els Porxerets (the former pilgrims' quarters with stables), 100 monks' cells now used to accommodate visitors (see page 194), a restaurant (see page 201), a souvenir shop and the Way of the Rosary, with added touches by Gaudí (see page 37).

The best time to visit Lluc is at 11:15 AM to hear the famous choristers, **Els Blavets**, during the service. The black Virgin, La Moreneta ("the Little Dark One"), Mallorca's patron saint, stands in the chapel, encrusted with jewels donated by the people of Mallorca. Pilgrims and tourists still flock to see her in their thousands.

"Ave Maria" –
magnificent artwork

PILGRIMAGE TO LLUC
In 1973, Todo Güell, owner of the Bar Güell in Palma, revived an ancient pilgrimage from the capital to Lluc monastery on foot. The 48km walk takes place in the last week of July and attracts up to 50,000 participants, who set out from the Bar Güell crying : "Let's go to Lluc, on foot and as brothers!"

Do not be put off by the glut of tasteless holiday merchandise on sale in all the resorts, with virtually every item bearing the word "Mallorca" or a touristic image of the island. It is well worth searching out some of the traditional crafts of the local artesania (craftsmen).

Special souvenirs – glass and siurells...

Glassware and pottery It is ironic that the best souvenirs Mallorca produces are also the most breakable. Glass, for instance, has been made on the island since Roman times, and glassmaking techniques have changed little since then. In the 16th century Mallorcan glassware rivalled that of Venice, and today's bestselling products often reproduce historic designs. Since the 1960s the island has had three glassmaking centres – the best known is Casa Gordiola at Algaida. Here visitors can see craftsmen at work in their sauna-like workshop, hand-blowing the glass, made in dark green cobalt and amber hues. In the nearby shop, jugs, drinking glasses, vases and candle-holders are popular buys.

Another local handicraft found throughout the island is pottery. Most of Mallorca's potters (*ollers*) live and work in Pórtol, where you can visit some of their workshops. Felanitx is famed for its robust semi-glazed terracotta pottery and its Sunday morning market provides a good opportunity to pick up rustic cooking bowls, plates or jugs at bargain prices (see panel opposite). With the decline of the island's olive oil industry, olive wood is now a popular resource, with souvenirs ranging from salad bowls and servers to earrings and eggcups. A hard-wearing, mellow-grained wood, it makes an unusual gift.

The one craft product that feels truly Mallorcan has to be the brittle, curiosity-provoking *siurell*. These clay whistles have been made in Mallorca and given as tokens of friendship since Arab times. They come in all shapes and sizes – the most common form of *siurell* is a behatted man playing a guitar or sitting on a donkey – and are painted white with flashes of red and green. They are cheap, children love them, and Joan Miró, the artist, was much influenced by their brightness and simplicity.

BORDADOS
One of the finest traditional Mallorcan craft specialities is *bordados* (crochet). Sadly, nowadays most pieces are manufactured by machine, although it is still possible to search out some fine handmade samples. Try **Bordados Orduna**, Plaça Rei Joan Carles I in Palma (tel: 971 712253) or **Casa Maria**, Colóm 10, Pollença (tel: 971 530341).

Leather and "roba de llengües"

Mallorca has a world-wide reputation for its leather, so shoes, belts, wallets and handbags are generally a good buy. Inca is the centre of Mallorca's leather industry, a bustling city full of leather factories and retail outlets, offering an exceptional range of shoes, belts, wallets and clothing. Catch the "Leather Express" train from Palma for a shopping spree. Or stay in the capital where every second shop seems to sell shoes.

...and olivewood

Mallorcan cloth also has a good reputation and the traditional *roba de llengües* (literally "cloth of tongues") is one of the most striking features of any Mallorcan home – a durable and reversible cotton material, taking its name from the colourful zigzagging red, green or blue patterns stamped onto the woven cloth. Until the turn of the 20th century weaving was a thriving industry, with dozens of cotton mills around Palma, Sóller, Esporles, Santa Maria and Pollença. Today it continues to be made mainly in Santa Maria and Pollença; it is used for curtains, bedspreads, wall furnishings and upholstery.

SHOPPING LIST

(Ask in any tourist office for a complete list of handicrafts and recommended shops.)

Ceramics: Art de Mallorca, Carrer de Convent 4, Manacor (tel: 971 550790); Artesanías, Carrer de l'Unio 13, Palma (tel: 971 724299).

Fabrics: Tejidos Flaquer, Carrer Segadors Gabellins 2, Capdepera (tel: 971 563057), Galeries Vincenç, Rotonda Ca'n Berenguer, Pollença (tel: 971 530450), Herederos de Vincente Juan, Carrer de Sant Nicolau 10, Palma (tel: 971 721773).

Glass: Vidrios Gordiola, Carretera Palma–Manacor, Algaida (tel: 971 665046); Lafiore, Carretera Vieja de Valldemossa 1, S'Esgleieta (tel: 971 610140).

Leather goods: Munper, Carretera Palma–Alcúdia km30, Inca (tel: 971 500500); Mar-Piel, Avinguda Lluc, Inca (tel: 971 503779).

Olive wood: Art Olivo Sansó, Carretera Palma– Manacor, Manacor (tel: 971 552800); La Casa del Olivo, Pescateria Vella 4, Palma (no phone).

Siurells: Roca Llisa, Carrer Roca Llisa 26, Portol (tel: 971 602497); Ca'n Bernardí Nou, Carrer Jaume I,6, Sa Cabaneta (tel: 971 603171).

COOKING POTS

Pottery is an ancient craft on the island and some of the original workshops (*alfarerías*) date back to the Moorish period. Look out for *plats morenos*, glazed bowls decorated with traditional symbols of cockerels, flowers and fish, the *olla*, a typical clay storage jar, and the *greixonera*, a heavy earthenware casserole which has given its name to a number of local dishes. These include *greixonera de peix* (fish soup), *greixonera de frare* (a sausage and vegetable stew) and *greixonera de peus de porc* (pigs' trotters with cheese and breadcrumbs).

Typical mountain scenery around Orient

The pebble beach at Sa Calobra

▶▶ Orient

94B2

Nervous drivers should not even think about tackling the road to Orient from Bunyola, with bends at alarming angles and no barriers to stop you tumbling down the mountainside. (There is a much easier approach from Alaró and Inca.) Those who make it to this picture-book village are rewarded with a marvellous sight – one of Mallorca's smallest hamlets, with a population of 26, nestling among olive and apple trees at the foot of Puig d'Alfábia. Its inaccessibility keeps Orient free of tourist coaches, but it is popular with walkers (numerous walks start from here, including an ascent to the Castell d'Alaró (see page 100), and day-trippers from Palma, who visit its four restaurants for an away-from-it-all lunch in the countryside (see page 201).

▶▶ Port de Sóller

94A3

Tourist Office: Plaça Constitució 1, Sóller (tel: 971 630332)
A sheltered and quiet resort popular with French visitors, Port de Sóller's natural harbour was once the main outlet for produce grown in the valleys and terraces around

Sóller. A long, curving seafront bordered by shops and restaurants caters to the daily influx of visitors arriving by the historic orange trams that connect the port to Sóller (see page 109). Their vintage carriages are still in use, stopping at a choice of hop-offs along the waterfront, before reaching the terminus at the end of the bay.

You can swim from two small sandy beaches on the bay, one near the tiny marina and the other to the south. Other attractions include the boat trips along the north coast, particularly to Sa Calobra, and the hour-long walk to the lighthouse (see page 112), for panoramic views of the bay. A longer path, through rock gardens and olive groves, connects with an old mule track from Deià to Sóller.

►► Sa Calobra   94B3

Do not believe anyone who tells you they have discovered an idyllic, unspoilt cove on the north-west coast called Sa Calobra. It is indeed a beautiful spot, which is why busloads of tourists crowd in every day, even in winter, to see one of the most visited sights on Mallorca.

The journey to Sa Calobra is more memorable than the cove itself. A snaking road known as the **Nus de la Corbeta** (Knotted Tie) plunges 800m in 12km, with terrifying hairpins, hair-raising loops and dramatic views. The easier approach is by boat from Port de Sóller, which takes you past isolated coves, and gives an excellent view of Puig Major.

Everybody visits Sa Calobra to see the impressive box canyon at the mouth of the **Torrent de Pareis►** (Twin Streams), reached by a 10-minute walk through a set of dimly lit tunnels. Up to 400m high and only 30m wide, with some sections never seeing daylight, this dramatic gorge culminates in a small pebble beach, hidden beneath a sea of sun-worshippers. In summer, when the gorge is dry, you can hike between the cliffs to see its two splendid waterfalls (see panel).

► Santa Maria del Camí   94B2

Santa Maria is a historic market town, celebrated for its craft products and vineyards. It also contains some notable old buildings. In Plaça Caidos stands the 18th-century church of **Santa Maria►** (*Open* Mon–Fri 9:30–1:30) with its belltower clad in deep blue tiles. The interior is in Churrigueresque style (a Spanish development of Baroque) and contains an unusual painting of the Madonna and Child with a goldfinch.

To the north-west, signposts direct visitors to a former Minorite friary, the 17th-century **Convent dels Mínims►**, on the C713. On the first floor is a museum, containing an eccentric mix of curios, and the ground floors are now a *bodega* (wine bar), where you can taste and buy local wines and spirits.

MALLORCA'S "GRAND CANYON"
To walk Mallorca's awesome "Grand Canyon" is a famous, testing expedition for which rock-climbing skills, ropes and even diving equipment are recommended. It takes about five hours to navigate the 7km-long and, at times, treacherous route from Sa Calobra to Escorca. Be warned, flash floods can render the rocks dangerously slippery and the river waist high. Don't even attempt to walk in the canyon except at the height of summer.

Santa Maria's striking blue tower

Train ride

Palma to Port de Sóller

A ride on the vintage train, all mahogany panels and brass fittings, which hisses, hoots, whistles and rattles through the Mallorcan countryside to Sóller, combined with a tram ride down to Sóller's scenic port, makes a great day out for all the family.

The railway line from Palma to Sóller, audaciously cut through the mountains of the Serra de Tramuntana, first opened in 1912 and was quickly followed by a connecting tram service to Port de Sóller. By 1917 Mallorca's railway system was at its most extensive, and you could have travelled by train from Palma to Inca, Manacor, Artà, Felanitx and Santanyí. By 1927 the entire line was electrified. Today, the train from Palma to Port de Sóller is used by commuters, but it is, first and foremost, an evocative survivor from a bygone age, a popular part of the island's appeal.

The following itinerary is based on weekday timetables only. While the timetables allow for a shorter trip, it is worth making this a whole day out. If you intend to return to Palma by the last bus, tram or train of the day, check they are running.

The train leaves Palma from the Sóller station in Carrer Eusebio Estada (just north of Plaça d'Espanya). There are five departures a day, but only the 10:40 train makes a special photo-opportunity stop during the hour-long, 27km journey. The train passes through Palma's

poorer suburbs, then rattles across a pancake-flat plain, passing small country stations with pigs rooting beneath olive trees, then uphill to the market town of **Bunyola** (see page 99). Get off here to visit the **Tunel factory▶** where Mallorca's herb-based liqueurs are made or continue on the roller-coaster ride across the spectacular Serra de Tramuntana, through a series of 13 tunnels. The longest, Tunel Major, runs for 3km.

The train eventually chugs to a halt at the **Mirador del Pujol d'en Banya**, a purpose-built viewing stop overlooking the houses of Sóller. The 10:40 train arrives at Sóller at about 11:40. The station building is almost as full of character as the train, cool and lofty, with a fountain. The "Orange Express" tram to the port leaves from just below the station, but do not join the rush to board it straight away. Walk down the hill instead to enjoy the sedate delights of **Sóller** (see pages 110–111). There is time to visit its two museums before they close, and have a drink or lunch in one of the cafés in the main square.

Return to the railway station to catch one of the half-hourly trams to **Port de Sóller** (see pages 106–107).

The journey takes 30 minutes in the original wooden carriages that have been running since 1913 (although in summer you may find more modern open-sided carriages are also used). As it clatters through orchards and back gardens you can imagine you are living half a century ago.

Port de Sóller is a delightful place for a dip in the sea and a lazy lunch, a stroll along the seafront or, if you fancy something more energetic, a walk up to the lighthouse at Punta Grossa (see page 113) before heading for home.

The most scenic way to return to Palma is by bus from Port de Sóller. Buses depart at 4 or 5:30 from the quayside stand near the tram terminus and take an epic 90-minute route around the coast via Deià (see page 101) and Valldemossa (see page 116), terminating in Palma by Bar La Granja in Carrer de Arxiduc Luis Salvador, just north of Plaça d'Espanya.

If you prefer to return by train, get the 6 PM tram from Port de Sóller and the 7 PM train from Sóller.

Take the tram (opposite) to Port de Sóller and explore the town (below)

*The Modernista church
of Sant Bartomeu*

▶▶▶ Sóller   94A3

Tourist Office: Plaça Constitució (tel: 971 630332)

However you approach Sóller – whether by road, crossing the mountain pass at Coll de Sóller or speeding
through the newly opened tunnel, or on the old-world
train from Palma (see page 108) – this affable town of
sleepy green-shuttered houses and shady fountain-filled
squares makes a memorable impression. Spread across
the broad fertile Valle de los Naranjos (Valley of the
Oranges), Sóller is still redolent of the late 19th- and early
20th-century days when its citizens grew prosperous
from the fruit trade.

Today's abundant harvests are largely due to the excellent irrigation system introduced by the Arabs when they

settled here around AD 950, and still in use. Their merchant ships, which brought such wealth to the region, once anchored in the nearby port.

Take a seat in Sóller's central square, Plaça Constitució, with its venerable plane trees and fountains, and look up at the ostentatious Modernista façades of the Banco de Sóller and the church of Sant Bartomeu next door to see the strange results of the vagaries of the fruit business. In the 1860s the orange groves were struck by blight, and many of Sóller's residents were forced to seek their fortunes elsewhere. Those that succeeded returned with new, fanciful ideas from abroad. Examples are the buildings by Joan Rubió, a pupil of Gaudí, who also created a fluid, Modernista mansion, called **Can Prunera** (see page 37).

Can Prunera – fancy wrought-ironwork

Many visitors seem to do little but sit outside the cafés in Plaça Constitució, soaking up the sun and the atmosphere. With several good cafés and *tapas* bars (see page 175) and a fine selection of pastry shops, there is little temptation to move on. Try the tangy orange and lemon ice-cream from **Heladería Can Pau, Pastelería Ses Delicies'** mouth-watering fruit tarts – *tartaleta manzana* – and don't leave without savouring a freshly squeezed orange juice at **Es Planet**.

On the edge of town, the **Museu Balear de Ciencias Naturales (Natural Science Museum)▶** is in an elegant manor house dating from the early 20th century. Its enthusiastic staff look after a cherished collection of fossils, animal skulls, bones, rocks and natural curiosities as well as a section devoted to past botanists, including Archduke Luis Salvador (see page 35). Another part of the collection identifies and illustrates many species of local flora – a helpful introduction to the **Jardí Botànic (Botanical Gardens)▶▶**, in the grounds around the museum, with its terraces specifically devoted to shrubs and herbal, aromatic and culinary plants of the Balearic Islands. (Camp d'en Prohom, tel: 971 634064. Museum and gardens *Open* Tue–Sun 10–5:30. *Admission*: moderate.)

Stroll past the elegant railway station, flanked by cypress trees and filled with potted plants, reminiscent of Sóller's glorious heyday then on to the interesting town **cemetery▶▶▶**, with its Modernista tombs adorned with metal wreaths and ceramic flowers. Several of the epitaphs are in French, revealing the significant French community of the town.

Also worth visiting is the **Museu de Sóller▶▶▶**, the ethnological museum. It is located on three floors of the Casa de Cultura (Carrer de Sa Mar 9. tel: 971 634663. *Open* Mon 11–5, Wed 10–6, Sat 10–2. *Admission:* inexpensive). A homely 18th-century manor house, it is crammed with antiques and relics of old Sóller.

TRAIN TIMES
The old-fashioned Palma–Sóller railway line means the north-west coast is within easy reach of the capital and ideal for day trips. Five trains a day leave from Palma's Plaça d'Espanya, at 8, 10:40 (the "turístico" train), 1, 3:15 and 8:05 (7:45 in winter). In the opposite direction trains leave Sóller at 6:45am (the commuter train), 9:15, 11:50, 2:10, 7 (6:30 in winter) and 8:05 PM (7:35 in Jul, Aug, Sep). Antique trams trundle down to Port de Sóller approximately half-hourly from 6 AM until 9 PM. Check local time-tables for changes.

Walk

Badia de Sóller

This walk follows a narrow road along the curve of the bay up to the lighthouse which overlooks the charming fishing village of Port de Sóller. Keen walkers can then continue across the cliffs to enjoy the fine views from Punta de Sóller.

The starting point is at the tram terminus on the seafront of Port de Sóller, next to the Restaurant Marisol. Allow 90 minutes to the lighthouse and back, 3 hours (with sturdy footwear) if you include Punta de Sóller.

Walk south along the seafront road, passing the Hotel Miramar. In the

distance, you will see the white salt-cellar-shaped lighthouse you are aiming for, the **Faro de Punta Grossa**, high up on the cliffs opposite, overlooking the bay. Turn right by Bar Pepe, crossing the tramlines and a blue-railed bridge to follow the curve of the shore. This easy stroll on the level provides ever-changing vistas of the wide, virtually enclosed bay.

The road now makes a steady climb, twisting up the side of the cliffs, passing through pine woods and a variety of well-placed villas, which are mostly owned by foreign residents. From the euphorbia-covered hills, which sparkle with small yellow flowers in early spring, you can look down to the turquoise waters of the bay below.

Around one hairpin bend, you can see in the valley below the stony ruins of what was either a watchtower or a *forn de calça* (limestone kiln), built to make the whitewash with which the islanders once painted their houses. A little further on is a memorial to a local soldier killed here in the opening days of the Spanish Civil War.

When you reach the lighthouse (closed to the public), there are fine views back across the port and the mountains behind, including the island's highest peak, Puig Major, easily identifiable by its crown of communications antennae.

For those planning to continue on to Punta de Sóller and who haven't brought a picnic, this is a good spot to take a break. A first class meal can be had on the terrace of the **Es Faro** fish restaurant beside the lighthouse.

To continue to **Punta de Sóller**, take the track to the left of the lighthouse, ducking under two chains. When the wall on your left ends, continue downhill as the path curls around the lonely cliffs. The route is well trodden but overgrown in places – look for the small piles of stones that mark the path at key points. Fragrant pines and wild rosemary enhance the hike, and

The lighthouse, Faro de Punta Grossa, set high on the cliffs overlooking Port Sóller

you will pass more ruined limekilns before the path descends still further to a river valley.

Crossing a stone wall, you scramble up the bare rocks, keeping well away from the cliff-edge and passing a red "67" painted on the rocks. From the summit there are rewarding views northwards to Cap Gros, and south along the coast towards the **Punta de Deià** (see page 101) and **Lluc-Alcari**, the smallest village on the island with only 11 inhabitants, on the winding coast road between Deià and Sóller. Once an Arab country estate, today it consists of three Moorish watchtowers, a couple of artist's villas, the **Costa d'Or** hotel (see page 196), a bar and a tiny, rocky beach.

To return, retrace your steps to the lighthouse and walk back down to Port de Sóller.

ISLAND GOSSIP

Stories of the Archduke's scholastic endeavours are frequently spiced with gossip about his affair with a local girl stricken by leprosy. Every islander has an Archduke story to tell. One recalls how a farmer, unaware with whom he was dealing, gave the nobleman a few coins in reward for helping him shift some barrels. "That is the first money I have earned in my life," quipped the Archduke.

▶▶ Son Marroig 94A2

Deià–Valldemossa road C710 (no telephone)
Open: Mon–Sat 9:30–2, 3–5:30 (7:30 in summer).
Admission: inexpensive

This stately, L-shaped mansion, perched high above the coast, was once the favourite residence of the wealthy Austrian aristocrat, Archduke Luis Salvador, known to the islanders simply as S'Arxiduc. Today the mansion is open to the public as a museum and shrine to Mallorca's greatest admirer.

The Archduke was born in 1847 in the Pitti Palace, Florence, the son of Leopold III of Tuscany and Marie Antoinette de Bourbon. He first came to Mallorca 20 years later, to escape Viennese court life, and immediately fell in love with the island. An ecologist before his time, and an early hippy who wore Mallorcan peasant clothes, he bought up estates on the north-west coast to save them from development and devoted himself to studying and recording Mallorcan wildlife and traditions. His seven-volume *Las Baleares* (see page 35) took 20 years to produce and is still considered *the* authority on its subjects. He died in 1915 in a Bohemian castle.

Even without these associations, Son Marroig would be worth visiting in its own right, simply for its setting overlooking the coastline of north-west Mallorca. Only part of the ground floor and one room of the first are open to the public, but you can see the Archduke's large library and a wealth of memorabilia, which include photographs, furniture and paintings owned by S'Arxiduc.

In the romantic garden, a short walk leads to a graceful, neo-classical, white-marble rotunda, where the Archduke would sit and contemplate the mountains and sea. From here you have a spectacular view of **Sa Foradada** ("pierced rock")▶▶, which is a rocky headland jutting out to sea with a massive 18m hole at its centre. Get a ticket from the custodian in the house before you walk down to the peninsula, where you will find a tiny landing stage built to enable the Archduke and his guests to moor their yachts and swim off the rocks.

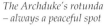

The Archduke's rotunda – always a peaceful spot

Walk

Camí de S'Arxiduc

This full-day walk, originally mapped out by Archduke Luis Salvador during tours of his estates with an umbrella and a mule, is highly recommended for keen hikers.

The Archduke's Bridlepath not only affords spectacular views of the entire north coast but also an introduction to traditional mountain industries. En route, you pass *sitjas* (round charcoal ovens), *cases de neu* (snow pits where winter snows were stored beneath a layer of ash), *forns de calç* (limekilns) and *caças a coll* (thrush nets, slung between the trees).

Begin by walking through the car park opposite Bar Sa Mata on the main road through Valldemossa. Turn right into Carrer de Joan Fuster, then first left and on to a rough track at the top of the hill. You climb gently at first, towards a group of pines, then gradually more steeply, following red waymarks until you reach a clearing.

From here it is a short, tough climb to a *mirador* and the start of the Camí de S'Arxiduc, marked by a romantically ruined stone refuge. For the best views of all, a one-hour diversion takes you to the summit of Puig Teix, from where most of Mallorca is visible on a clear day.

The path drops back down to Valldemossa through the wooded Cairats valley, passing a shelter where you can camp in summer, then a *sitja* and a kiln.

For a shorter walk to the foot of the Teix, you can simply do this last section in reverse. Leave Valldemossa by walking past Son Gual, the large old house with a tower, and turn left after ten minutes onto a wide track signposted "refugi". To the shelter and back will take a brisk couple of hours.

The full walk takes at least six hours and should only be attempted by experienced hillwalkers with proper boots. Take plenty of food and water, a compass, map (available from good bookshops) and whistle, a sunhat, sweater and waterproofs – the weather on the mountains can change very quickly.

Views of Valldemossa and the wooded Cairats valley

115

Painted tiles dedicated to the island's saint

▶ ▶ ▶ **Valldemossa**
94A2

Tourist office: Plaça de la Cartuja (tel: 971 612106)
This hillside town is associated with two very different women. Dominating the pretty houses and cobbled streets is La Reial Cartoixa (La Cartuja in Castilian), the Carthusian monastery where George Sand and her lover Frédéric Chopin spent the winter of 1838–1839 (see pages 118–119).

Walk down the hill to the parish church, and you will discover that Valldemossa is more concerned with remembering Mallorca's saint, Santa Catalina Thomás, than that one cold, damp winter long ago. There is scarcely a house without a painted tile beside the front door asking for the saint's support. Take Carrer de Rectoría to the left of the church to see the tiny dwelling where she was born, now restored as a shrine.

The **Reial Cartoixa**▶ ▶ ▶ (Plaça de la Caruja, tel: 971 612106. *Open* Mon–Sat 9:30–4:30 (6 in summer), Sun 10–1) developed from a royal palace given to the Carthusian order in 1399. Most of the buildings date from the 18th century. Visitors enter through the gloomy neo-classical church, with frescoes by Bayeu, Goya's brother-in-law. You walk into huge whitewashed cloisters, where signs point out a circuit of the rooms and cells where the monks lived.

The monks prepared and dispensed medicine in the pharmacy, where you can almost smell the herbs in the ancient jars; after their expulsion in 1835, one remained to continue treating the villagers. The head of the monastery

SANTA CATALINA THOMAS
Mallorca's very own saint was born in Valldemossa in 1531. A humble peasant girl, Catalina spent most of her 43 years as a nun in Palma's Santa Magdalena convent, where she is buried. Her life was truly exemplary – she even mixed sand with her soup as a precaution against gluttony. Canonised in 1627, Santa Catalina is now a revered presence in many island churches and houses.

Valldemossa – a village not to be missed

resided in the prior's cell, where you can see memorabilia associated with Santa Catalina Thomás and the library where monks used to meet for half an hour each Thursday, their only human contact. Solitude led to introspection and in one of the cells you can see instruments of flagellation used in penitential moments.

Cells 2 and 4 re-create the rooms where Sand and Chopin spent their notorious winter. The rooms contain manuscripts, letters, portraits, original scores, the manuscript of *A Winter in Majorca* (see page 119) and the two pianos used by the composer. Cells 6–9 contain a 16th-century printing press, books and paintings belonging to the Archduke Luis Salvador (see page 112). Upstairs is a small display of modern art containing works by Picasso, Francis Bacon, Henry Moore and the Mallorcan painter Juli Ramis, as well as Joan Miró.

Next door to the monastery, the **Palau del Rei Sanç (King Sancho's Palace)**▶ was originally built in 1311 as a hunting lodge. It was donated in 1399 to the Carthusians, who lived here until 1767 when the new monastery was occupied. Today the palace is stuffed with a miscellany of antiques, furniture, books, utensils and religious treasures. During the summer, short concerts and folk dancing take place several times a day. (Tel: 971 612106. *Open* Mon–Sat 9:30–1:30, 3–6. *Closed* Sun. *Admission:* expensive.)

Before you leave Valldemossa, take time to explore the streets and shops. Do try the local sweet delicacy, *coca de patatas* (fluffy, light potato buns) washed down with a chilled almond milkshake at Bar Meriendas. Then drive six twisting kilometres along a hair-raisingly narrow but beautiful, cliff-hugging lane, which leads down to an isolated handful of stone cottages and fishing boats on a stony beach at Port de Valldemossa – pleasant for a swim and a paella on the waterfront (see page 201).

CHOPIN
Chopin composed several pieces during his short stay including the "Raindrop Prelude" and a "Funeral March", reflecting his depressed state of mind. These and other Chopin "classics" can be heard in a series of 15-minute concerts which take place several times daily in the Palau del Rei Sanç. Serious Chopin fans should visit in July and August for the acclaimed Chopin Festival (contact the tourist office in advance for tickets and programme details).

Mallorca still remembers the visit paid to the island in 1838 by the French literary celebrity George Sand and her lover, the Polish composer Frédéric Chopin, even though they only stayed for three months.

Monastery home of Chopin and Sand

Hopeful arrival "Sand", the *nom de plume* of Baroness Amandine Aurore Lucie Dupin (1804–1876), and Chopin were accompanied by Sand's 14-year-old son Maurice and eight-year-old daughter Solange. They arrived in December, hoping to carry on their love affair away from the gossipmongers of Paris, and hoping too that the warm climate would benefit the health of Chopin and that of Sand's son.

At this time there was little accommodation available on the island. The party stayed first in a villa in Establiments (see page 85), but they were soon forced to move out because rumours spread among the villagers that Chopin had tuberculosis, the disease from which he eventually died in 1849.

Move to Valldemossa A new home was found in three cells in the former Carthusian monastery at Valldemossa (see page 116), just three years after its monks had been expelled. At first Chopin described Valldemossa as "one of the most beautiful places on earth", but disillusionment soon set in and their short stay of three months proved far from idyllic, characterised by poor food and "lugubrious rain". Chopin's declining health and ostracism by the locals, who disapproved of the couple's adulterous relationship, did not help either. The fact that Sand, a free-thinking, pioneer feminist, smoked cigars and wore trousers was found quite shocking. Sand later commented how different things might have been had they conformed to the extremely religious community's ways and bothered to attend Mass.

Sad finale It was a venture doomed to failure – moving with an invalid and children to the remote mountains of a foreign land, only recently declared to be in a state of war, during the worst months of winter, and hoping that the comforts of modern France would not be missed. As Chopin's illness became more acute, Sand grew increasingly disillusioned and antagonistic towards the islanders among whom they were living.

Mallorca has never forgiven the writer for the outspoken, opinionated account of her stay in her book *Un Hiver à Majorque* (*A Winter in Majorca*), published in 1842, in which she took her revenge for her hardships and frustrations by distastefully labelling the islanders liars, monkeys and Polynesian savages and describing them as "crafty and thieving...heartless, selfish and impertinent". (Strangely enough, it is said that the people of Valldemossa are still considered cold and suspicious of outsiders, compared with their neighbours in Deià who continue to welcome eccentric foreigners.)

As a result, the book makes sad reading. It is, however, appreciative of the Mallorcan countryside, Sand's vivid descriptions providing a memorable glimpse into 19th-century life here. Many of the descriptions of scenery show that the landscape has barely changed over the past 150 years including that of her arrival in Valldemossa: "The torrent was still a delightful stream which glided along among tufts of grass and clusters of flowers; the mountain was in a smiling mood, and the valley in which Valldemossa nestled opened before us like a garden in spring. To reach the Cartuja you have to leave the coast for it is impossible for any vehicle to clamber up the stony track that leads to it. It is a fascinating approach with its sudden twists and bends among magnificent trees, and with wonderful views that are unfolded at every step, and increase in beauty the higher one rises."

Somewhat ironically, Sand's and Chopin's visit has contributed to the image of Mallorca as an island of romance and cultural pedigree, and her book can be bought in several languages in Valldemossa itself. The English translation is by Robert Graves with his own idiosyncratic annotations. As Graves observed, the whole sad episode was a fascinating clash of the classical and romantic worlds.

Above: George Sand
Below: Chopin's cell in the Reial Cartoixa

119

Serra de Tramuntana

See map on page 94.

Escape the busy resorts and sun-scorched beaches by spending a cool, refreshing day touring the Serra de Tramuntana, the magnificent mountain range which runs parallel to the north-west coast and offers breathtaking scenery. Allow 5 hours.

The drive takes you from Palma up to the peaks of the Serra de Tramuntana, passing the highest point of the island, Puig Major, and returning across the central plain via Inca.
The round trip of 110km incorporates some steep roads and hairpin bends, and is likely to appeal most to

Sweeping views from the Mirador de Ses Barques

confident drivers with a good head for heights.

Leave Palma by the Via Cintura ring road, taking the exit marked Sóller (C711). The city's industrial estates are soon left behind as the road makes a beeline north towards the mountains.

A sharp bend heralds the start of the dizzying climb to the Col de Sóller – on the right you pass the Moorish gardens at **Alfàbia** (see page 98), at the entrance to the tunnel through the mountains to Sóller.

Col de Sóller offers panoramic views of the island and its peaks, along its 65 sharp bends rising to a height of 496m, before dropping down into the Sóller Valley.

If you intend to stop in **Sóller** (see page 110), drive through the congested inner streets to the northern outskirts, where there is a car park.

Leave Sóller, following signs to Lluc, and join the C710 as it climbs east through the fragrant pine woods. A turning to the right offers a worthwhile detour to Mallorca's prettiest village, **Fornalutx** (see page 102).

A little way on, the **Mirador de Ses Barques▶▶** is a stunning viewpoint overlooking the Badia de Sóller: a convenient place to pause for refreshments and photographs. The bar-restaurant serves freshly pressed orange juice, made with fruit from the valleys below. From the terrace you can look down to Port de Sóller. To the west is the Cap Gros lighthouse, and to the east the headland of Punta Grossa with the old watchtower of Torre Picada.

Continue east, climbing to a far starker landscape overshadowed by craggy peaks, and Puig Major (1,445m) in the northern distance. Even though Mallorca's highest peak is capped with a spiky crown of radar installations, and military use prevents close

Gorg Blau – a tranquil mountain reservoir

access by members of the public, Puig Major makes a formidable sight. The road skirts the mountain, burrowing through two tunnels and passing two reservoirs, **Embalse de Cúber** and **Embalse del Gorg Blau▶**, surrounded by a nature reserve. The first is enlivened by a group of photo-friendly black donkeys, while Gorg Blau is good for a walk or picnic.

When leaving Gorg Blau, look out for a sharp bend to the left (sometimes obscured by parked cars), which leads into a short tunnel. This is the turning down to **Sa Calobra** (a 2-hour detour, see page 107). Continue along the C710 through Escorca, until you reach a junction where you turn right on to a minor road signposted to Caimari.

This gentle road descends slowly through the fields of the foothills of the Serra de Tramuntana, through the villages of **Caimari** and **Selva▶** with their interesting churches, to reach Mallorca's leather capital and third largest town, **Inca** (see page 102). From here drive south-west to vinicultural **Binissalem** (see page 99) then on to Palma taking either the motorway or the old highway (C713) via **Santa Maria del Camí** (see page 107).

The North-East

▶▶▶ REGION HIGHLIGHTS

Alcúdia *pages 130–131*

Cap de Formentor
pages 136–137

Pollença
pages 144–145

Port de Pollença
page 147

S'Albufera *page 148*

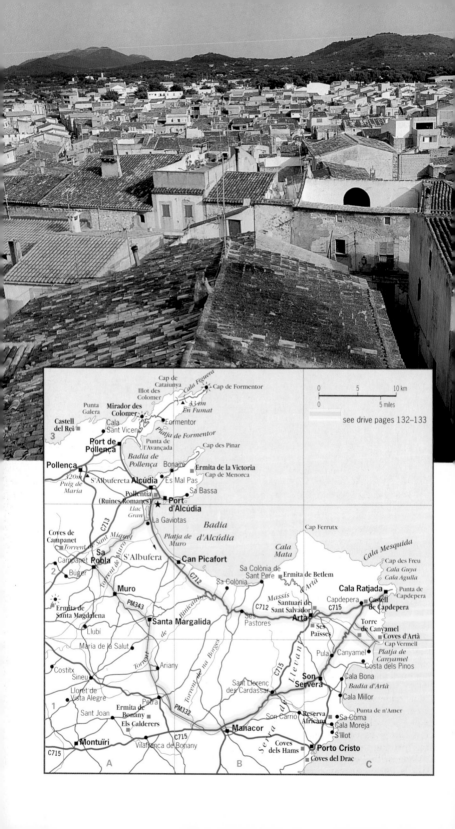

see drive pages 132–133

Map labels:

Cap de Catalunya
Cala Figuera
Cap de Formentor
Illot des Colomer
Punta Galera
Mirador des Colomer
33 m En Fumat
Castell del Rei
Cala Sant Vicenç
Formentor
Platja de Formentor
Port de Pollença
Punta de l'Avançada
Cap des Pinar
Pollença
Badia de Pollença
Bonaire
320 m Puig de Maria
Ermita de la Victoria
Cap de Menorca
S'Albufereta
Alcúdia
Es Mal Pas
Pollentia (Ruïnes Romanes)
Sa Bassa
Port d'Alcúdia
Llac Gran
La Gaviotas
Badia d'Alcúdia
Cap Ferrutx
Coves de Campanet
Torrent de Sant Miquel
Platja de Muro
Cala Mata
Cala Mesquida
Sa Robla
Campanet
Can Picafort
Cap des Freu
Cala Guya
Cala Agulla
Búger
Torrent de Muro
S'Albufera
Sa Colònia de Sant Pere
Ermita de Betlem
Punta de Capdepera
Muro
PM343
Sa Colònia
Cala Ratjada
Ermita de Santa Magdalena
Binicaubell
Massís d'Artà
Capdepera
Castell de Capdepera
C712
Santuari de Sant Salvador
C715
Llubí
Santa Margalida
Ses Pastores
Artà
Torre de Canyamel
Maria de la Salut
Ses Païsses
Coves d'Artà
Cap Vermell
Costitx
Ariany
Pula
Canyamel
Platja de Canyamel
Sineu
Son Servera
Costa dels Pins
Lloret de Vista Alegre
Cala Bona
Badia d'Artà
Sant Joan
Ermita de Bonany
Sant Llorenç des Cardassar
Cala Millor
Petra
PM332
Punta de n'Amer
Montuïri
Els Calderers
Reserva Africana
Sa Coma
Cala Moreja
C715
Vilafranca de Bonany
C715
Son Carrió
S'Illot
Manacor
Coves dels Hams
Porto Cristo
Coves del Drac

Serra de Llevant
Torrent de na Borges

Scale: 0 — 5 — 10 km / 0 — 5 miles

Grid labels: A B C / 1 2 3

THE NORTH-EAST

Two great bays fringed with fine sand and shallow water bite deep into Mallorca's north-eastern corner. The resorts here are among the most relaxed on the island, and there is plenty to discover near by – the illuminated caves of Artà, the wetlands of S'Albufera, the windmill-studded hinterland of the Plá, sea views from the Cap de Formentor peninsula, and the historic towns of Pollença, Alcúdia and Artà.

RUGGED LANDSCAPES

The amazing scenery of the Cap de Formentor peninsula represents Mallorca at its unspoilt , breathtaking best. The mountains of the Serra de Tramuntana continue to inspire right up to the north-eastern extremity of the island. Massive cliffs jut into the sea, producing weird rock formations, attracting nesting seabirds, and hiding small but plentiful *calas* (coves), most only reachable by sea. Indeed, having tunnelled by car through the En Fumat mountain near the end of this rocky finger of land, you will get a bird's eye view over the beautiful inlet of Cala Figuera and Mallorca's most inaccessible beach. Eventually you will reach the lighthouse with the inevitable bar and shop and yet more amazing views, all the way to Menorca on a good day.

CONTRASTING RESORTS

The Cap de Formentor forms a perfect northern protection for the bays of Pollença and Alcúdia, with their busy resorts and beautiful clean, white sandy beaches. Be careful not to confuse the picture-postcard inland town of Pollença with Port de Pollença, an ideal seaside resort for all the family, located on the Badia de Pollença. Likewise the town of Alcúdia is one of Mallorca's historic gems, whereas Port d'Alcúdia is a modern industrial port and package-holiday resort on the bay of the same name. Beyond the purpose-built resort of Can Picafort, the coastline becomes rocky again, dotted with cliffs and coves, with the mountains of Artà forming an impressive backdrop.

Along with Pollença and Alcúdia, Artà is the other major town in the

BLOSSOM TIME

One of the most popular times to visit the Plá is in January and February, when the pink and white almond-blossom attracts large numbers of visitors and displays in a most spectacular way the extent of the orchards on the plain. The land between the rows of trees is frequently used for grazing or, around Llubí, for the growing of capers.

Pages 122–123: Pollença's Calvary Hill *leads to a tiny pilgrimage chapel*

Left: Artà
Below: Countless calas *indent the coastline*

north-east, a medieval hilltop town famous for its crowning glory, the Sanctuary of Sant Salvador, and its Bronze Age settlement at Ses Païsses on the outskirts of the town. Further east, many of the ancient fishing villages have been transformed into mega-resorts, such as Cala Millor. The lively resort of Cala Ratjada, with its pine-shrouded coastline, choice of excellent sandy beaches and atmospheric marina, has remarkably managed to retain some Mallorquín character. Also along this stretch of coast, the Coves d'Artà (Caves of Artà) are one of the great natural wonders of the island.

Sunset in the "Land of a Thousand Windmills"

MIRACULOUS MARSHLANDS The 17,000-hectare Parc Natural de S'Albufera is the largest area of marshland in the Mediterranean and a magnet for wetland birds. The reserve lies just to the south of Alcúdia, and close to the main coastal road. Its bogs, sand dunes and narrow canals are a breeding ground for all types of fish and amphibians and there are over 200 species of birds.

LAND OF A THOUSAND WINDMILLS Talaiotic remains found on Mallorca's pancake-flat hinterland with its myriad windmills confirm that Es Plá (the Plain) has been

Almonds and onions of Es Plá

settled since the 4th century BC, although it did not become the agricultural centre of the island until Roman and Moorish occupation. Today, it is one of the least populated regions with many of the young migrating to the coastal resorts for work. It is also one of the most unspoilt parts of the island, offering a gentle rural landscape for those who want a break from the jam-packed beaches and the smell of suntan oil.

Main crops here include grains, pulses, garlic, artichokes, and vegetables. The highly fertile area of reclaimed marshland behind S'Albufera, which surrounds Muro and Sa Pobla, today produces oranges, lemons, strawberries and even some rice, and is frequently dubbed "Mallorca's Fruit Basket", "Land of a Thousand Windmills" or "Huertas de la Puebla" (Garden of the People). Whichever name you choose, there's no denying that the interior plain is another unmissable jewel in Mallorca's many-faceted crown.

S'ALBUFERETA
As its name suggests, S'Albufereta is a smaller version of S'Albufera. This wetland area lies on the north-east coast of Mallorca, between Port de Pollença and Alcúdia. Visitors can look for herons, egrets, warblers and the occasional Eleonora's falcon. Orchids, gladioli and other flowers grow in the scrubland and marshes in springtime, while grasshoppers and mole crickets put in an occasional appearance.

Mallorca offers a host of spectator sports from friendly football games between villages to the passion and pride of a bullfight, where the matador may be awarded the highest accolade – the tail of the bull – for his expertise and courage.

Football (above) and horse-trotting (opposite) are popular spectator sports

BASKETBALL

Basketball is one of Mallorca's most closely followed sports, largely because the island boasts a top division *baloncesto* (team), Prohaci Mallorca. You can see them playing regularly at the Palau Municipal d'Esportes stadium at Camí La Vileta, Palma (tel: 971 739941 for match details).

AN ANCIENT SPORT

It is believed that the Balearic archipelago took its name from the Greek word "*ballein*", meaning "to sling" (see page 30), and in recent years, the ancient martial art of *tiro con honda* (slingshot) has seen a revival on the island. If you want to know where to see it, drop into the Bar España, Carrer dels Oms 31, Palma (tel: 971 726250), home of the Club de Honderos.

Football Soccer is a national obsession in Spain and Mallorca is no exception. On Sundays during the winter season (September to March), games take place all over the island, with even the smaller villages having teams. Mallorca's two main teams are both Palma based and, although they are admittedly not in the league of Real Madrid or FC Barcelona, their matches are well supported by an enthusiastic local crowd and good fun to attend.

Real Mallorca plays in the **Estadi Lluis Sitjar**, just north of the city centre in Plaça de Barcelona (tel: 971 452111), while **Atlético Baleares** play in the **Estadi Atletico**, just north-west of the city beside the Via Cintura (easily reachable by bus 7). Matches take place on alternate Sunday afternoons and tickets are available at the turnstiles.

Horse-racing Another popular spectator sport is horse-racing, or rather trotting, which takes place on Sundays at the Son Pardo Hippodrome in Palma (on the road to Sóller at Carretera Palma–Sóller km3, tel: 971 754031), and the hippodrome at Manacor (Carretera Palma–Artá km50, tel: 971 550023). Enthusiasm for trotting on Mallorca goes back at least 200 years when, during fiestas, there were trotting races between neighbouring villages. Although there were already several trotting courses on the islands in 1965 when the **Son Pardo Hippodrome** was built, it was the first course in Europe to be floodlit and, at over 1km in length with 76 stables, it was also considered to be one of the best.

A day at the races is seen very much as a family outing (interestingly, entrance for a woman is cheaper than for a man, while children enter free). Usually around 3,000 spectators turn out for the Sunday racing at Son Pardo, but on the day of the Gran Premio National there will be around 15,000, all trying to catch a glimpse of local hero and former European trotting champion, a Mallorcan, Juan Antonio Riera.

Bullfighting To the Spanish, bullfighting is more of an artistic performance than a spectator sport – a legacy from pagan rites, involving the sacrifice of the mighty bull,

worshipped throughout the ancient Mediterranean, with the matador, the symbol of superior human intelligence, overcoming the prowess of the bull by slaying it.

In Mallorca bullfighting is still held in high esteem by its *aficionados*, who judge the fight by the quality of the bull and the moves of the matador. However, it does not have the status or following associated with the *corridas* held on the mainland, and Spanish bullfighting critics (similar to theatre critics) are generally rather severe when discussing Balearic bullfights.

If you have attended a bullfight at one of the great arenas in Madrid, Barcelona or Pamplona, the Sunday duels in Palma's bullring may disappoint. Nevertheless, if you have never seen a bullfight and want to do so, look out for splashy posters and newspaper advertisements with details of the programme and how to buy tickets. But be warned: many first-time spectators at a *corrida* experience some unexpected emotions. It is definitely not for the squeamish or faint-hearted.

Palma's Plaça de Toros (Avinguda Gaspar B Arquitecte 32, tel: 971 752639) is the third largest ring in Spain, with a seating capacity of 14,000. The bull-fighting season begins in March and it ends in October.

There are also bullrings in Inca, Muro and Alcúdia where fights are often staged to coincide with local celebrations. For those who do not fancy seeing a real bullfight, organised excursions are sometimes arranged to Alcúdia, where mock bullfights with exhibitions of dressage are staged every Thursday at 6 PM in the summer.

RINGSIDE SEATS
Buying tickets for a bullfight can be quite complicated: seats in the sun (*sol*) are cheaper than those in the shade (*sombra*) while *sol y sombra* (sunny but shady later in the day) are priced in between. Choose your seating row and remember to take a cushion!

Galeras *at the Portal
del Moll*

A STROLL THROUGH THE OLD TOWN

From the church of Sant Jaume, walk along Carrer de Sant Jaume, turning left down Carrer dels Albellons. Turn right past Alcúdia's pompous neo-classical town hall to reach the atmospheric, café-fringed Plaça Constitució at the heart of the old town. Leave by the narrow shop-lined Carrer del Moll, which brings you out at the massive Porta del Moll gate. To the right is Passeig de la Mare de Déu de La Victoria, where the town's market takes place.

►►► Alcúdia   124A3

Alcúdia is strategically situated at the neck of a peninsula separating the Badia de Pollença and Badia d'Alcúdia, and through its carefully restored buildings and monuments it neatly illustrates the development of Mallorcan history.

Originally a Phoenician settlement, the town was built inland from its port (today Port d'Alcúdia) as a defence against pirates and invaders. It was taken over by the Greeks and reached its heyday in the 2nd century AD, when the Roman invaders made it their capital, Pollentia (meaning "power"). Destroyed by the Vandals in the 5th century, the town returned to greatness under the Moors, who built Al-Kudia ("the town on the hill") on the site of the Roman remains. With the conquest of Mallorca by Jaume I, Alcúdia finally returned to Christian rule in 1229.

The **Old Town**►►► is compact, boxed inside medieval walls. To visit it, park on the south side in Avinguda dels Princeps d'Espanya, and enter beside the church of Sant Jaume, at its south-western corner. Walk right round the walls and you will come across a small bullfighting arena at least 100 years old (see page 129), and two ancient gateways. The Portal del Moll, with its two square towers and two massive palm trees standing guard, is the symbol of Alcúdia.

Inside the walls, you will find an attractive maze of narrow cobbled streets reminiscent of Palma's Arab quarter, with its peaches-and-cream-coloured mansions and palaces. Look for the Can Torró library, at Carrer d'en Serra 15, opened in 1990 in a former palace.

The **Church of Sant Jaume▶▶** (Carrer de Sant Jaume. *Open* Mon–Sat 9:30–1:30) goes back to the 13th century, but the present building is mostly 19th century. The interior is designed in Spanish Gothic style with two impressive stone pulpits, and is always crowded with worshippers on Sundays. Next to the church, inside a tiny chapel, is a small museum, the **Museu Monogràfic de Pollentia▶**, devoted to the history of Roman Pollentia and exhibiting finds from excavations in the area. (Carrer de Sant Jaume 30, tel: 971 547004. *Open* generally Tue–Fri 10–1:30, 5–7 (3:30–5:30 in winter) Sat–Sun 10:30–1. However, times frequently change. *Admission:* inexpensive.)

A short walk from the church takes you to three interesting sights outside the Old Town, connected by signposted footpaths. Closest are the remains of Roman houses at **Pollentia (Ruines Romanes)▶**. Near by, on Alcúdia's outskirts, set among olive, pine, lemon and fig trees, stands a well-preserved **Roman theatre (Teatre Romà)▶▶▶**, with tiered seats and stubby pillars, the smallest Roman theatre in Spain. (*Open* at all times. *Admission* free.)

Continue a short distance further along the road to Port d'Alcúdia, and you will find a tiny chapel worth a visit purely for its simplicity and peaceful atmosphere. The **Oratori de Sant Anna▶** (*Open* mornings only) was built in the early 13th century and is believed to be Mallorca's oldest surviving church. Above the entrance is a carved statue of the Virgin Bona Nova.

The peninsula north-east of Alcúdia is worth visiting to see the **Ermita de la Victoria▶**. Take the road towards Es Mal Pas. Leave by the northern gate, Port Roja (near the bullring), and drive through the smart villas of Bonaire towards Cap des Pinar. A watchtower, Torre Major, was constructed on its summit (451m) by Philip II in 1599. En route, a turning to the right leads up to the fortress-like hermitage. On 2 July each year there is a pilgrimage from Alcúdia to the hermitage, in honour of the 15th-century wooden statue of Victoria, the town's patroness. The statue was reportedly twice stolen by pirates and both times miraculously restored to its original place.

Although the road to Cap des Pinar leads to a military zone, much of this scenic headland is a nature reserve with magnificent coastal views, making it a rewarding region for walks, picnics or a cycle ride.

Ancient remains at Roman Pollentia

A TASTE OF LOCAL COLOUR
Mallorca's markets are worth visiting as much for their local character as for their produce. Don't miss Palma's colourful food market in Plaça de l'Olivar (Mon–Sat 8–2), Sineu's traditional livestock jamboree (see page 150) every Wednesday or Inca's sprawling general market on Thursdays. For handicrafts, try Alcúdia's Sunday market where you will find everything from olive wood and pottery cooking utensils to fine leather belts and bags.

Drive

Badia d'Alcúdia

See map on page 124.

Sandy seaside resorts, sleepy market towns, a marshy nature reserve, and the dusty agricultural plains – all seen on this tour – provide a small glimpse into the varied facets of eastern Mallorca. Allow 5 hours.

Following the curve of the Badia d'Alcúdia, this leisurely 120km round trip runs south-east from Port d'Alcúdia to the uplands of the Serra d'Artà, then to Mallorca's eastern-most promontory, Punta de Capdepera. Turning south, the drive continues inland to Manacor, then follows mainly quiet country roads back to the north-east coast.

From Port d'Alcúdia, take the main road south (C712), following signs to Artà. The road follows the pines and dunes of the coast, passing along the edge of the **S'Albufera** inland nature reserve (see page 148). After the resort of **Can Picafort** (see page 136), the road continues through the green hills of the Serra d'Artà to the medieval town of **Artà** (see page 134).

It is worth spending some time in this charming town to visit the Santuari de Sant Salvador with its impressive vistas, and the archaeological museum with finds from the nearby Talaiotic site at **Ses Païsses** (see page 150). Then continue east for 8km to the Capdepera ringroad. From here, follow the signs to Cala Ratjada.

Once a small fishing village, **Cala Ratjada** has since developed into a popular seaside resort with several fine beaches (see page 135), and makes an ideal stop for coffee and a quick dip. Follow the one-way system through the town to the harbour where it is easy to park.

On leaving Cala Ratjada, follow signs to the left in the direction of Canyamel and Son Servera. After about 8km, turn left towards the **Coves d'Artà**

(see pages 140–1), driving past the Canyamel golf course. Turn right at a junction for **Platja de Canyamel►►**.

This resort enjoys a sheltered posi-tion with a beach of fine white sand served by an arcade of shops, bars and restaurants. Stop here for lunch, before heading back to the main road, following signs for Son Servera. En route, you will pass the impressive fortress of **Torre de Canyamel►**, built as a look-out for pirates – now partly converted into a rustic restaurant, which specialises in *la cuina mallorquína* (see page 90).

Pass through the sedate old towns of Son Servera and Sant Llorenç des Cardassar, then take the C715 to **Manacor** (see page 171). Follow the

132

signs for Palma through the town, but after 2km turn right for Petra. The road now crosses the flat, fascinating landscape so characteristic of central Mallorca, the rich agricultural heart of the island, which has been farmed since Roman times. Vines, aubergines, tomatoes and melons grow in the dusty soil, while the silhouettes of windmills and village churches stand out on the horizon.

By-pass Petra (see page 142) and Santa Margalida (see page 150), and head on to **Muro**, a friendly town with an important, albeit oversized church, a bullring and a quirky folk museum (see page 142). Follow the one-way system through Muro's narrow streets and continue to **Sa Pobla**▶▶. Much of

Above: Holidaymakers crowd the busy Platja de Canyamel
Below: Es Plà – Mallorca's fertile and tranquil agricultural plain

the land surrounding this agricultural town was reclaimed from the swamps of the Albufera Gran over a century ago. Now known as the Huertas de la Puebla (Garden of the People), the fertile fields today grow strawberries, artichokes and salad crops. Park in the north-east of the town and walk to the central square, with its fine old houses and 17th-century church.

From here, narrow twisting lanes lead past farms and an electrical power station to the main road (C712). Turn left back to Port d'Alcúdia.

*View over Artà (top);
Sant Salvador's
treasures (inset)*

▶▶ Artà   124C2

The spires and battlements of this medieval hilltop town can be seen from afar. Derived from the Moorish word *"jertan"* (garden), Artà has been occupied for at least 3,000 years, as evidenced by the remains of a Bronze Age site at Ses Païsses outside the town. Nowadays it is a prosperous little town close to the coast, and is particularly lively each Tuesday on market day.

Despite the hurly-burly of daily life, Artà still maintains an atmosphere of great antiquity, thanks to its principal attraction, the **Santuari de Sant Salvador▶▶**, towering high above the town (*Open* Mon–Fri 10–1, 4–7, Sat–Sun 10–1. *Admission* free). It is a stiff, rewarding climb to reach the sanctuary. Start on Carrer de Sant Salvador, behind the Plaça d'Espanya, and follow signs until you reach a long, cypress-lined stone stairway – the Via Crucis (Way of the Cross) – which leads from the town centre past the parish church of the Transfiguració del Senyor, to the top. You can drive up, although the streets are narrow and they are not always one-way!

The sanctuary occupies the site of a Moorish alcázar. The chapel and its castellated walls were built between 1825 and 1832, after the previous hermitage was knocked down as a superstitious countermeasure against the spread of a devastating plague. The church contains some vivid paintings of Mallorcan Christian heroes – Jaume the Conqueror

receiving the surrender of the *walis* (governors), Ramón Llull being stoned to death in Tunisia, and Sant Antoni, patron saint of Artà (see panel). The views from its tranquil, palm-filled courtyard over Artà's yellow, terracotta and grey rooftops with the hazy countryside beyond are absorbing – take a bag of almonds, a cold drink and all your unwritten postcards.

Back down in the town, the **Museu Regional d'Artà▶** (Carrer d'Estrella 4, tel: 971 835017. *Open* Mon–Fri 10–1. *Admission* free) displays archaeological finds such as ceramics, jewellery and bronzes from the nearby site of Ses Països (see page 150) and elsewhere on the island.

▶ Cala Millor   124C1

Tourist Office: Passeig Marítim
(tel: 971 585864) and Parc de la Mar 2
(tel: 971 585409)

Cala Millor is the epicentre of recent tourist-wooing developments along Mallorca's east coast. From Cap des Pinar south to Sa Coma, every little bay and cove appears to have sprouted a holiday complex, with Cala Millor as the largest and most brash. Despite its wide promenade and white sandy beach, the coastline has been ruined by ugly high-rise hotels and apartment blocks. Nevertheless, good sports facilities (including windsurfing, karting, bowling and riding), wild nightlife and flowing beer make this resort in summer one big, crowded party.

To the north, Cap des Pinar, named after the pines that grow on this headland, endeavours to remain an exclusive enclave with luxury hotels and private villas. To the south in the Badia d'Artà is Cala Bona. Its role as a fishing port has been superseded by three man-made beaches and it is now a good spot for watersports. Sa Coma is another large resort with a great beach and a tidy seafront.

▶ Cala Ratjada   124C2

Tourist Office: Plaça dels Pins (tel: 971 563033)

Cala Ratjada is yet another former fishing village turned popular resort. However, unlike many others, it still retains some Mallorcan charm. The beaches close to town are not special but there are magnificent sandy bays further north at Cala Guya, Cala Agulla and Cala Mesquida.

From the port, a short walk uphill (signposted "Faro") leads through woodland to the breezy headland of Punta de Capdepera and its lighthouse. Also above the harbour are the gardens of **Casa March▶▶▶**, owned by the same banking family as the Fundación Juan March in Palma (see page 51). The gardens contain an extensive sculpture park with works by Rodin, Henry Moore, Barbara Hepworth and several Catalan artists. (Visits are by appointment only through the tourist office.)

Traditional street lamp in Artà

THE SAINT WITH A SWINE
In every picture of Sant Antoni – Artà's patron saint – he is always seen with a small pig, because he is also the patron saint of animals. He is honoured each year on 16–17 January with a masked procession, followed by a blessing of all the local pets. Artà's main fiesta, Sant Antoni de Juny, dates back to 1581 and takes place on 13 June when dancers, with papier-mâché horses strapped to their hips, take to the streets for the festivities.

Superb bathing at Sant Vincenç

COASTAL WALK
The bleak, limestone hills surrounding Cala Sant Vicenç provide plenty of spectacular walking opportunities. Perhaps the most scenic is a short hike along a rough lane to Punta de Covas, a headland to the north-west of the resort. The walk takes less than an hour and the views are outstanding.

ZIG-ZAG TO HEAVEN
There's no denying the twisting, narrow 20km drive from Port de Pollença to Cap de Formentor is hair-raising at times. Indeed, a local legend has it that when the parish priest arrived at the Pearly Gates together with the local bus driver, only the driver was admitted, because he had caused far more people to pray.

► Cala Sant Vicenç
124A3

This secluded resort in the north-eastern corner of the island has two main pocket-handkerchief sized beaches, divided by the ugly San Pedro hotel, and a jumble of other hotels, restaurants and souvenir shops along the shoreline. Inland is more attractive, with luxury villas set in profusely flowering gardens.

With its relaxed atmosphere and rugged cliff scenery, Cala Sant Vicenç has always been an artists' haven. A statue on the promenade pays tribute to one local painter, Llorenc Cerda Bisbal.

► Can Picafort
124B2

Tourist Office: Plaça Gabriel Roca 6, Santa Margalida (tel: 971 850310)
This resort, in the centre of the Badia d'Alcúdia, has a good family beach fringed with low pines. A copious supply of restaurants, supermarkets and souvenir shops meets all the needs of its visitors, who are predominantly package holiday-makers staying in the high-rise hotels. For quieter beaches, head north to Platja de Muro.

►►► Cap de Formentor
124B3

The steep and winding road which leads from Port de Pollença to the peninsula of Cap de Formentor offers some of Mallorca's most dramatic scenery. Be sure to stop after 6km at the Mirador d'es Colomer, and scramble up to the awe-inspiring viewpoint high above the sea-pounded cliffs. A small, rocky islet, Illot des Colomer, lies offshore and is a sanctuary for nesting seabirds.

From here the road narrows and twists past two more small viewpoints which conspire to exhaust your film stock, then the road drops down, past a turning right to Platja de Formentor. After a further 11km of pine-scented woods and sun-bleached rocky outcrops punctuated by brilliant blue splashes of sea, you eventually reach the isolated lighthouse at the northernmost point of Mallorca. Like many "Land's Ends" around the world, Cap de Formentor can get extremely crowded, but few will dispute the magnificence of the sea views, which, on a clear day, stretch to Menorca.

On your return, stop at the beautiful Platja de Formentor, a startlingly white, palm-lined beach targeted in summer by boat excursions from Port de Pollença, or visit the grand **Hotel Formentor** (see page 197) for a drink. Tucked into the sheltered south coast of Cap de Formentor, this was Mallorca's first hotel, built in 1926 by the wealthy Argentinian Adan Dielh, and it placed Mallorca firmly on the luxury holiday map.

▶▶ Capdepera   *124C2*

Near the easternmost tip of the island, this hilltop town, capped by a medieval castle, can be seen from afar. It is the centre of Mallorca's basketmaking industry and in the surrounding hills you can see the dwarf fan palms used to make the baskets.

You can reach the **Castell de Capdepera**▶▶ (*Open:* Apr–Oct daily 10–8; Nov–Mar daily 10–5. *Admission:* inexpensive) by climbing the steps from the main square, Plaça de l'Orient, a climb well rewarded by the views from the top. The Romans were the first to build a castle on this strategically important site, to guard the route from the coast to the interior. The Moors later enlarged it, then the Christians destroyed it and built another in its place in the 14th century. King Jaume I is said to have stayed here in 1231 and tricked the Moors into capitulating by lighting dozens of camp fires in order to give the impression that he was accompanied by a sizeable army. In fact all he had with him were 28 men and four horses.

Inside the castle, you can walk round the well-preserved battlements, admire the dazzling cactuses when they're in bloom and visit a small chapel, Nostra Senyora de la Esperança.

"GIVE IT A WHACK!"
It is said that Can Picafort took its name from Jeroni Fuster, a rather heavy-handed labourer who built the first house there. Apparently his nickname at work was "Picafort!" or "Give it a whack!"

137

Visitors to Hotel Formentor enjoy excellent views and one of the island's best beaches

Luxury housing is a feature of the Mallorcan landscape, ranging from the fortified fincas *(country houses) built by Jaume I's conquistadores to the aloof, security-screened villas in the hills owned by the celebrities of today.*

La Granja – one of Mallorca's finest fincas

Former glory In the past, the Spanish aristocracy were exempted from all taxes, and property made a recession-proof investment. Still today, property and land is passed down through the generations in Mallorca, and many families now own second homes.

Getting behind the monumental façades of Mallorca's historic mansions is a haphazard affair. Some have been turned into hotels or offices, others are open by private arrangement only, or have closed their doors because too many visitors were attracted. In the Serra de Tramuntana, **Alfàbia** (see page 98), **Son Marroig** (see page 114) and **La Granja** (see pages 80–1) all give clues to life in the island's stately homes.

The best place to visit, however, is **Els Calderers** (see page 141), open to the public only since 1993. In the heart of the island, this huge 18th-century manor house, framed by level fields and farm buildings, still has an authentic, lived-in feel, as if the owners had just popped out for a while. It is easy to imagine its noble residents receiving their guests, attending Mass in the private chapel, sewing by the log fire or listening to music – and their servants at work in the kitchen, laundry or ironing room. As the publicity puts it, this really is *la oltra* (the other) Mallorca.

Finca features The sun-bleached, white-stone *fincas* of the north differ from their inland counterparts, which are built of honey-coloured sandstone. Look closer and you will notice other contrasts. In the mountainous regions, where olives were the most abundant crop, they usually contained a *tafona* (olive-press), whereas in the central plain, where the economy was based on grain, the building was most likely to have a mill. Around Binissalem, they had wine-presses. Some, such as Son Forteza Vell in Manacor, even built a defence tower.

If the *finca* was of some importance it was divided into three sections; the *casa de los señores* (house of the owners), the *casa de los amos* (house of the farm manager) and other buildings (servants' quarters, stables and workshops). The *casa de los señores* would normally be located on an upper floor (as with their city equivalents), entered by a monumental staircase that led into a grand salon-cum-reception room. Some wealthy *señores* would also have their own *capilla* (chapel), ostentatiously decorated to reflect their social status more than their religious devotion. The *finca* of **Sa Torre►** near

Typical arcaded court-yard in Palma

Llucmajor is a classic example, with its cathedral-like structure, which can be seen for many miles around.

During the 17th and 18th centuries, many aristocrats and country landowners moved to the city, leaving their *amos* to maintain their estate. This created something of a building-boom, with elegant Palmanian mansions such as Can Vivot, Can Oleza and Can Morell (the latter today known as Palau Sollerich) built in the fashionable Renaissance style, complete with spacious patios, finely decorated windows, loggias and arcades.

Modern development At the turn of the 20th century, "traditional" architecture fell from fashion, and many patrician townhouses were converted into small apartments. However, in the wake of the concrete jungles of the tourist boom, visitors are beginning to appreciate these fine *fincas* once more, and rural property is being renovated as authentically as possible to create luxury holiday homes (see panel on page 143, and page 194). Encouragingly, traditional, rustic styling is back in vogue with the package tourist. Leading the way forward today is the resort of **Cala Fornells** (see page 84), designed by Mallorquín Pedro Otzoup, and **"The Anchorage"** at Illetas. This is an imaginative waterfront holiday village designed by François Sperry (who was the architect of Port Grimaud in Provence) to create a more traditional Mallorcan style and ambience.

PATIOS
Peep through the arched doorway of any Mallorcan *finca*, and you will almost certainly find a flower-filled central courtyard or patio, used as a meeting place. Usually they contain a well with an adjacent watering trough, stone benches, wall-mounted rings for the horses and a horse mount.

BEWARE OF THE DOG!
Look out for a most unusual exhibit at La Granja, listed in the guide leaflet simply as "dog". On a chain outside his kennel in the grounds, a large black *ca de bestair* (a smooth-coated guard dog native to the island) greets visitors with a very wary eye.

"GREEN PEARLS"

Mallorcan "green pearls" or *alcaparras* (capers), reputedly the best in the world, make ideal gifts if you are looking for something edible to bring back for friends. The best are found in Llubí, Campos, Sant Joan and Felanitx. There are five varieties: *nompareilles* (7mm), *surfines* (7–8mm), *capucines* (8–9mm), *fines* (11–13mm) and *gruesas* (13mm+). The smaller they are, the greater the flavour – and the price. Capers are, of course, the buds of the plant. Look out also for the *alcaparrones* – the fruit – eaten in the same way as olives.

▶▶ Costitx 124A1

In prehistoric times Costitx was the island's main centre of population, and the surrounding area has proved a rich source of archaeological treasure. Today it is one of the smallest communities on the island with a population of just 800. It is a charming village of crumbling, cream cottages, snoozing in the sunshine of the Plá, its two spacious squares enlivened by the brightly coloured parasols of a cluster of cafés. Most villagers work the land, growing almonds, figs and cereals. The village also has a cottage industry which produces crucifixes, Madonnas and artificial roses.

Costitx's main attraction, however, is a remarkable natural history museum, the **Casa de Sa Fauna Ibero-Balera**▶▶ (Casa Cultura, Carrer Can Font, tel: 971 876070. *Open* Tue–Fri 9:30–12:30, also 2nd and 4th Sat and Sun of month. *Admission:* inexpensive). A child-friendly museum with some 3,500 stuffed and preserved animals, insects and birds, it provides a good introduction to the vast number of species that can be found in the Balearics (see page 15). The building also contains a bar-restaurant with good views of the surrounding agricultural plains, and a swimming-pool.

Coves d'Artà – a dramatic display

▶ Coves d'Artà 124C2

Tel: 971 841293
Open: summer, daily 10–7, winter, daily 10–5.
Admission: expensive.
The Artà Caves are perhaps the grandest of Mallorca's subterranean wonders. Now they have become a popular tourist attraction, it is hard to imagine what French geologist Édouard Martel felt when he first stepped into these

dark, mysterious and terrifying caves in 1876. In fact they had been known about for centuries – Jaume I found 2,000 Arabs hiding here with their cattle during the Christian conquest – but it was Martel who first studied these grottoes, 46m above the sea on Cap Vermell.

A guided tour of the caves comes with special effects and the chambers of vividly illuminated stalactites and stalagmites are given Dantesque names – Hell, Purgatory, Paradise. The descent into Hell is swiftly followed by a *son et lumière* display! The tour emerges from the caves to a view of the sea, beautifully framed by the cavern entrance.

►► Els Calderers 124A1
On the C715 to Manacor, near Sant Joan. (tel: 971 526069)
Open: summer, daily 10–7; winter daily, 10–4.
Admission: moderate
Elegant Els Calderers, built in 1700, offers visitors a rare glimpse inside one of the island's most representative *fincas* (country houses). Sumptuous furnishings, family portraits and photographs, collections of fans, hunting weapons and toys help to bring this noble residence to life (see page 138).

Treasures of the Ermita de Betlem

►► Ermita de Betlem 124B2
This tiny, remote hermitage is hidden away from the tourist track, 10km north of Artà at the end of a long, winding lane. Founded in 1805, its first settlers had to spend their first night in a stall – hence the name Betlem (Bethlehem). Apart from the crudely painted church, its buildings are not particularly noteworthy, but the views over the Badia d'Alcúdia are magnificent. A clearly defined footpath leads down to the seashore from here, to the delightful village of Sa Colònia de Sant Pere (see page 149).

► Llubí 124A2
The economy of this sleepy town of tree-lined avenues and pastel-shaded houses is based on a tiny, almost insignificant plant bud. The caper has become the symbol of the village, and the gently undulating countryside surrounding Llubí is covered in a green carpet of caper bushes (see panel opposite). Llubí is also known for its traditional production of *herbes* and *palo*, both typical Mallorquín liqueurs.

► Montuïri 124A1
The best-known image of this traditional hilltop town are its eight old stone windmills, set against the sky – testimony of a past dependent on agriculture. As you wind your way up the narrow alleyways to the main square – Plaça Major – with its friendly locals' bar and the church, you will catch glimpses of the corn-coloured landscape beyond. Montuïri is also known for its cultural life, maintaining local holidays and traditions, including its famous Cossier dance (see page 19).

A "GOOD YEAR" AT BONANY

In 1609, just five years after the sanctuary was completed, the villagers of Petra climbed up to the chapel to pray for rain. When their prayers to end the severe drought were answered with a *bon any* (good year), they named their sanctuary Bonany. The stone cross beneath the summit is where Junípero Serra bade farewell to the villagers before setting off on his missions, but the real attraction here is the sweeping panoramic views extending over the Serra de Tramuntana, the Badia d'Alcúdia and the central plains.

Portrait of Junípero Serra

▶▶ Muro
124A2

The *pièce de résistance* of this small market town on the edge of the S'Albufera marshes (see page 148) is its **Museu Etnològic de Mallorca▶** (Carrer Major 15, tel: 971 717540. *Open* Tue–Sat 10–1, 4–6, Sun 10–2. *Admission:* inexpensive). Housed in a typical town mansion and devoted to Mallorcan traditions, its displays of furniture, costumes and crafts provide fascinating glimpses into Mallorca's past. A courtyard containing a well, a waterwheel and orange trees leads to more exhibits – blacksmiths' and cobblers' workshops, a collection of carriages, and tools used by silversmiths, sculptors and spoonmakers.

The main square is dominated by the huge Catalan-Gothic **church of Sant Joan Baptista▶** (*Open* Mon–Sat 9:30–1:30) It looks almost Arabic, guarded by palm trees and a square belltower which is linked to the main church by a tiny arch. The cloisters of another church – the **Convent of Santa Ana▶** – were used in the past to stage fights between bulls and bulldogs. Today, bullfights can still be seen in Muro's impressive Plaça de Toros, built in 1910 within the quarry that produced its white stone.

▶▶ Petra
124A1

This remote inland town would be completely off the tourist route were it not for the fact that it is the birthplace of Mallorca's most famous son, Fray Junípero Serra, the founder of the Spanish Missions which grew into the State of California (see page 50).

The town seems hardly to have changed since his day, with its tall, green-shuttered buildings, fountain-filled squares and a maze of narrow little streets. Fortunately there are signs directing you to the house where Serra was born and a small museum in his honour – the **Museu and Casa Junípero Serra▶** (Carrer Barracar Alt 6–8, tel: 971 561149. *Open* generally daily 9–8, but if closed, follow instructions on the door to the keyholder's house in the next street).

Just south-west of Petra, crowning the Puig de Bonany (317m) is the **Ermita de Bonany▶**, a hilltop hermitage built in 1604 (see panel).

> *Until you have driven across Es Plá, the fertile plain at the centre of the island, you have not seen the "real" Mallorca – once described by Santiago Rusinyol as "The Island of Calm".*

Mallorca's fruitbasket The Plá spans the island from the southern flanks of the Serra de Tramuntana in the north-west to the Serra de Levante in the south-east. The plain itself has some small hills, which rise like bubbles from the dusty, flat landscape, and are topped by religious sanctuaries, as at Puig de Randa (see page 173) and Bonany (see panel page 142).

It is a softly hued landscape, patterned with orchards, olive groves and sheep, and scattered with chunky *fincas* and sun-baked towns, which offer few tourist attractions beyond their ancient, outsized churches and weekly markets.

The Plá has been the agricultural heartland of the island since Roman and Moorish times – with a wide variety of crops: almonds and apricots at Llucmajor, melons at Vilafranca, capers at Llubí, garlic at Sant Joan, figs at Sencelles and vines at Binissalem. The area around Muro and Sa Pobla is known as "Mallorca's fruitbasket" or the *Huertas de la Puebla* (Garden of the People), with its extensive strawberry, artichoke, potato and salad crops. There is also flower-growing and a limited amount of stock farming, including a recent revival of the indigenous black pig.

The main roads leading eastwards from Palma to Alcúdia, Artà and Santanyí take you across the plain quickly and efficiently – but if you want to get off the beaten track, take some of the narrow country roads, many of them laid down by the Romans, which criss-cross the plain between small towns like Porreres, Montuïri and Sineu. As you come across horses and carts bringing the produce home from the fields, you might feel that you have finally discovered that elusive but worthwhile destination, the real Mallorca.

Sa Pobla – "Garden of the People"

RURAL HOLIDAY HOMES
For a taste of rural Mallorca, contact the Asociació de Agroturisme Balear (tel: 971 721508), an organisation offering self-catering holidays in over 80 country farms or *fincas*, mostly in the Plá and ranging from basic cottages to luxury manors.

Pollença, characterised by narrow, sun-drenched streets

ROMANTIC SETTING
The massive grey mountain Puig Tomir, which overhangs the west of Pollença, gave English crime-writer, Agatha Christie, the ideal location for one of her romantic short stories. First published in 1936, *Problem at Pollensa Bay* tells of a local boy who broke away from his protective mother to run off with a perfect and well-spoken English girl. The story, together with its characteristic twist at the end, is a reminder of the pre-war world when well-spoken English holiday-makers with "excellent hotel manners" came to Mallorca on the steamer from Barcelona.

▶▶▶ Pollença   124A3

This town is an absolute gem – a haven of sleepy Mallorcan traditions nestling in the foothills at the eastern end of the Serra de Tramuntana; the perfect Mallorcan town, where café life and the siesta roll on as if package holiday-makers had never been invented. The somewhat austere buildings lining the dusty streets, with their ochre roofs, sun-baked walls and faded wooden shutters, could be virtually anywhere in rural Spain. Try to visit on a Sunday morning when the people are gathering at the Café Espanyol or the Club Pollença in Plaça Major after church, and the square is filled with colourful market stalls. Clothes and household goods are sold near the car park, with fruit, flowers and vegetables in the central square, Plaça Major. Local cheeses and roasted almonds are good buys.

The Pont Romà (Roman bridge) on the northern edge of town gives a clue to Pollença's long history. After the Spanish conquest in 1229, Pollença came under the control of the Knights Templar, who initiated work on the parish church, Nostra Senyora dels Angels. The name Pollença dates from the 14th century, when refugees from Alcúdia, fleeing inland to escape continual pirate raids, called the town after their former Roman capital, Pollentia. Since then, the expulsion of the Moors and resistance against pirates has been celebrated every August, with fireworks and a mock battle, Los Moros i Los Cristianos (see page 18), that rages around the town during the local fiesta.

Among many historic buildings is a former Jesuit convent which is now the town hall. From here the 365 steps of the Vía Crucis (Way of the Cross), lined with cypress trees, leads up **El Calvari▶▶** (Calvary Hill) to a tiny pilgrimage chapel, with far-reaching views to the Badia de Pollença and across to Puig de Maria opposite (see below). Inside the church is a much-revered wooden cross dating from the 13th century, placed there by thankful mariners who had survived a shipwreck off Cala de Sant Vicenç. On Good Friday there is a torch-lit procession of penitents, dressed in dark triangular hoods which cover all but their eyes, who solemnly carry the cross down the Calvary steps to the town centre.

South of Plaça Major, the 17th-century Dominican **Monastery of Santo Domingo▶▶** has beautiful cloisters that are the principal venue for Pollença's acclaimed music festival, which attracts a number of internationally renowned musicians every summer. Pollença has also long been popular with artists, and hosts a prestigious annual painting competition. Winning entries can be seen inside the monastery, together with a small **Museu Municipal**, containing the remains of prehistoric sculptures shaped like bulls, as well as a *mandala* (a Tibetan sand painting) given by the Dalai Lama in 1990 (Carrer Santo Domingo, tel: 971 531166. *Open* Jul–Sep, Tue–Sun 11–1, 5:30–8:30; Oct–Jun, Tue–Fri 11–1, 5:30–7:30, Sat 11–1. Check, as times may change. *Admission* free).

Three kilometres south-east of the town, a potholed road of terrifying angles and impossible bends leads up to **Puig de Maria▶** (320m), where nuns settled in 1371 and remained for several hundred years, refusing to leave even when the bishop of Palma ordered them down for their own safety. If you are after an utterly different experience of Mallorca, you can stay here (see page 194) but don't expect luxury... you will have to pay for showers!

Locals in Pollença watch the world go by

Walk

The Bóquer Valley

This easy 6km walk follows the course of the Bóquer Valley – a popular place for bird-watching, particularly in the migration seasons (from April to May and September to October). Allow 2.5 hours return.

Start at the roundabout on the seafront in Port de Pollença, armed with stout shoes, binoculars and a drink or picnic lunch. Follow the road signs that direct you to Formentor and head out of town. Turn left just past the supermarket.

146

Stone pillars mark the entrance to a tree-lined lane, which leads to a ridge and a large farmhouse. As you pass Bóquer Farm, glimpse over the stone wall to the left for a good view across gardens and orchards to the town and bay below.

Go through the gate and uphill along a stony track to the start of the Bóquer Valley. You will soon enter a steep-sided cleft in the rocks. The track across the valley is well worn, weaving through a sparse landscape strewn with wild flowers, small shrubs and windswept pines. Resident birds you may spot include black vultures, ravens, peregrines and, in spring and summer, Eleonora's falcons, ospreys and even a booted eagle soaring overhead. Stonechats and numerous goldfinches can be seen fluttering in the grasses. You may hear red-legged partridges and could even spot a rare rock sparrow.

Soon after a gap in a stone wall, the sea comes into view. Just offshore is the Es Colomer rock and to the left is the high ridge of the Serra del Cavall Bernat. In one place erosion has created a dramatic window in the cliffs; if you have any energy left, climb up for a closer look. The track continues down a sharp incline, passing a lazy freshwater spring, to the small shingle beach of Cala Bóquer.

After a rest, retrace your steps to Port de Pollença.

Looking towards the sea beyond the Bóquer Valley

▶▶ Port d'Alcúdia   *124A3*

Tourist Office: Carretera Artâ 68 (tel: 971 892615)
Port d'Alcúdia plays many different roles: its modern marina is the busiest on the north-east coast, bustling with pleasure craft; its harbour is home to a naval base and it has a busy fishing fleet (if you are interested in fishing trips or sea excursions, this is the place to come). Its commercial port is second only to Palma in importance with daily car ferries to Barcelona and Menorca; and it is the biggest, most crowded resort on the Badia d'Alcúdia – hardly surprising when you see its palm-studded beach, which is a 15km arc of well-groomed golden sand and the longest in Mallorca.

Beyond the beach is disappointing – a seemingly never-ending chain of high-rise hotels and apartment blocks, broken up only by souvenir shops, fast-food outlets, bars and discos. Nevertheless, it remains a popular and suitable choice for families. At peak season, it is virtually impossible to find a room here, but one of Mallorca's very few campsites, Platja Blava (tel: 971 870002), is just a short distance away to the south-east.

▶▶▶ Port de Pollença   *124A3*

Tourist Office: Carretera de Formentor 31 (tel: 971 865467)
Set in a splendid horseshoe bay, Port de Pollença is a genteel, old-fashioned resort which is popular with families and older visitors, particularly in winter. Agatha Christie set a story here (see panel, page 144) and it is easy to imagine her characters staying at the waterfront hotels and sitting in deckchairs on the beach.

The resort has no good nightclubs or discos but offers instead rather a good supply of shops, waterfront cafés and restaurants. Its shallow water and sandy beaches are particularly well suited to young children, and its lively harbour makes it a popular mooring for yachts. During the day the beach becomes the main centre of activity with watersports and boat trips. In the evening, the focus shifts to the long palm-lined promenade, where it is fun to don your finery and join in that admirable Spanish institution, the evening *paseo*.

Port de Pollença – a popular centre for watersports

Don't feed the ostriches!

▶ **Reserva Africana (Auto-Safari)** 124C1

Portocristo–Cala Millor road
(tel: 971 810909)
Open: daily 9–5 (9–7 in summer).
Admission: expensive

This half-day family outing is most enjoyable if you arrive early when the animals are feeding. Tours can be made in your own vehicle or aboard a safari truck, following a one-way route which takes about 45 minutes. The reserve's collection includes lions, zebras, antelope, wildebeest, ostriches and storks, and there is a Baby Zoo with young animals. Take binoculars, and close your windows before the nimble-fingered monkeys spot you!

▶▶▶ **S'Albufera** 124A2

5km south of Port d'Alcúdia
(tel: 971 892250)
Open: Apr–Sep, daily 9–7; Oct–Mar,
daily 9–5. On weekends and holidays in
spring, access to the park is restricted to
pedestrians and cyclists.
Admission free

The name S'Albufera derives from the Arabic "al-buhayra" (small lake or lagoon), although the site has been exploited since Roman times. The marshes became popular hunting grounds until the 17th century, when they were divided into self-irrigating cultivable plots. From the early 20th century to the 1960s (when the northern end was sold off for tourist development), the area was used to grow rice, and paper was produced from the reeds and sedge. Only after 1985, following fears that tourist development was damaging the area's ecology, were 800ha bought by the Balearic Islands government for conservation.

A rare purple heron in the Albufera

Today, the **Parc Natural de S'Albufera** is the largest area of marshland in the Mediterranean, providing visitors with a wholly unexpected aspect of Mallorca – an oasis of welcome peace and a delight for nature lovers. Its comprehensive network of paths (some of which can be cycled) guide you around a hushed world of bridges, hides and observation points that are tucked among the lakes, reed beds and grassy undergrowth. Birds are the main attraction here, but there are also Camargue horses, and eels which migrate here from their birthplace in the North Atlantic. **Es Comu**, an area of sand dunes, includes pine and juniper woods and orchid groves. Frogs, snakes, insects and colourful wild flowers complete the picture.

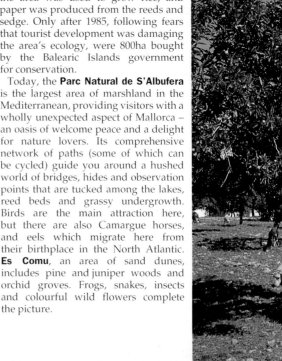

►► Sa Colònia de Sant Pere 124B2

It would be worth visiting this quiet fishing village for the drive alone, with the cliffs of Puig den Ferrutx and the mountains of the Serra d'Artà rising high on the right, and sweeping views of the Badia d'Alcúdia and the distant Formentor peninsula on the left.

But the village itself is also well worth the trip – a remarkably unspoilt hotch-potch of cream, buttermilk, apricot and peach-coloured seaside homes with faded terracotta roofs, one *hostal* (see page 197) and a few simple fish restaurants (see page 202). There is even a tiny beach of golden sand lapped by sheltered, crystalline waters. Unlike on so many of the island's beaches, you cannot hire a sunbed, or a pedalo or even a parasol. How long will it be before this idyllic spot is discovered and spoilt by the tourist hordes?

► Sant Joan 124A1

It is hard to believe that Sant Joan is in the middle of the Plá (see page 143), with all the *capamuntes i capavalles* (uphills and downhills) of the surrounding countryside – a rich farmland of wheat fields, almond groves and orchards. It is like a mountain village, with streets and houses built on terraces on different levels, and steep narrow lanes leading up to a windmill.

The village's main activities are pig-farming and making the traditional sausages. Every October, it hosts the massive **Festa d'es Botifarró o de sa Torrada** (Sausage or Roast Feast) to mark the end of summer and the arrival of the cold weather, the best time to cook *botifarró* (pork sausages). The fiesta's crowds of visitors come to taste the different sausages toasted in the embers of an outdoor fire, and to enjoy the lively dancing.

THE SINGING PRIEST
Sant Joan is often remembered for a former priest, Father Rafel Ginard, who travelled from village to village gathering all the popular songs of the island, which he then published to save them from being forgotten. This monumental *oeuvre*, the *Cançoner Popular de Mallorca*, contains some 20,000 songs and has done much to preserve the culture and traditions of Mallorca and of the Catalan language.

Farming on the outskirts of Sa Colónia

A POET REMEMBERED
Near the main entrance to Ses Païsses, there stands a monolith in memory of the early 20th-century writer, Miquel Costa I Llobera, who set many passages of his famous poem, *The Legacy of Greek Genius* (1900), in the Talaiotic settlement. The poem is an epic work on the subject of Mallorcan prehistory, which in 1947 was made into an opera called *Nuredduna* (*The Virgin Oracle*), with libretto by Miquel Forteza and music by Antoni Massana.

► **Santa Margalida**   *124A2*

This attractive little town in the north-eastern part of the Plà is known mainly for its vine-growing and leather-working and its traditional fiesta, the **Carro de la Beata**, which takes place on the first Sunday in September. Every year a small girl is chosen to represent Mallorca's only saint, Santa Catalina Thomás (see pages 116–117). Dressed in traditional peasant dress, she is carried through the streets accompanied by decorated floats (see page 19).

► **Ses Païsses**   *124C2*

2km south of Artà (tel: 971 835017)
Open: daily 10–6
Admission: inexpensive
The Talaiotic (Mallorcan megalithic) settlement of Ses Païsses is one of the most important archaeological sites in Mallorca. Located on top of a low hill near Artà, in a shady wood of holm oaks, surrounded by fields of almond and carob trees, this Bronze Age settlement is an evocative legacy of the inhabitants of Mallorca between 1000 and 800 BC (see pages 28–29).

Some of the ruins are surprisingly well preserved, including an impressive portal and most of the perimeter walls which measure up to 3m in depth. Some blocks used in the settlement's construction weigh as much as 8 tonnes. It is not difficult to picture the halls and dwellings, and the lookout tower that would have warned of approaching ships.

It is believed that the settlement was abandoned after the 1st century BC and its inhabitants, together with those of neighbouring Talaiotic villages, settled at the foot of Puig Sant Salvador, forming the original nucleus of the present town of Artà. After exploring the Talaiotic remains at Ses Païsses, you can interpret them at Artà's Museu Regional (see page 135).

The winged lion of Sineu

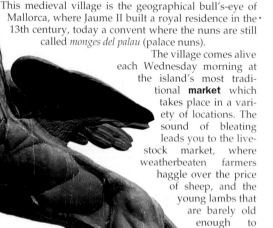

►► **Sineu**   *124A1*

This medieval village is the geographical bull's-eye of Mallorca, where Jaume II built a royal residence in the 13th century, today a convent where the nuns are still called *monges del palau* (palace nuns).

The village comes alive each Wednesday morning at the island's most traditional **market** which takes place in a variety of locations. The sound of bleating leads you to the livestock market, where weatherbeaten farmers haggle over the price of sheep, and the young lambs that are barely old enough to walk are carried off with their legs tied together, and protesting loudly. The narrow streets leading up to the church of San Marcos (passing the town's symbol, a winged lion) are packed with stalls that are designed to appeal to the growing number of foreign tourists, and selling lace, leather and pearls.

Eventually you reach Sa Plaça, thé church square, where the action is liveliest of all as local housewives turn out to buy the week's food. Buckets of olives, strings of sun-dried tomatoes, bags of squirming snails, cheeses, hams, whole salt cod – it's all here, along with plenty of fresh fruit, vegetables and flowers. Come early in the morning before the tour buses arrive if you want to catch the flavour of a traditional country market. Best buys include dried figs, apricots and pottery from Pòrtol.

With so much fresh produce, it is hardly surprising that Sineu is considered a gastronomic centre, known especially for its *celler* restaurants, **Ca'n Font** and **Es Crup** (see page 202) – join the local farmers after market to eat the local specialities of *frit* or *arròs brut* (see pages 90–91).

Local produce on display at Sineu market

▶ Vilafranca de Bonany   *124A1*

Most people's contact with Vilafranca usually involves shopping, for strings of garlic, red and green peppers, tomatoes, aubergines, gourds, sweetcorn and other home-grown produce that hangs temptingly outside the photogenic stalls and shops that line the Palma–Manacor road as it crosses the village. Try the melons – Vilafranca produces the best on the island. The village's most popular festivity is the **Festa des Meló** every September (see page 18). When summer ends, winter fruit and vegetables share shelf space with huge bowls of sweet, hot, bite-sized doughnuts, called *bunyols*, freshly made by the ladies of the village.

STATION MASTERPIECES
Sineu was once on the railway line between Inca and Artà, and the old station in the eastern outskirts has now been converted into an attractive modern art gallery, called **S'Estació** (tel: 971 520750. *Open* Mon–Fri 9:30–1:30, 4–7, Sat 9:30–1).

The South

▶▶▶ REGION HIGHLIGHTS

Cala Figuera *page 160*
Coves del Drac
page 167
Porto Colom *page 172*

The South

Map of The South region of Mallorca showing locations including:

- Sa Indioteria
- PALMA (CIUTAT DE MALLORCA)
- Son Ferriol
- Es Molinar
- Coll d'en Rabassa
- Can Pastilla
- Platja de Palma
- Les Meravelles
- S'Arenal
- Aquacity
- Cala Blava
- Cap Enderrocat
- Badia de Palma
- Sant Jordi
- S'Aranjassa
- Sant Francesc
- Casa Gordiola
- Son Gual Parc Prehistòric
- Pina
- Algaida
- Randa
- Santuari de Cura
- Puig de Randa 543m
- Santuari de Sant Honorat
- Es Marroig
- Son Cambeia
- Llucmajor
- Santuari de Monti-Sion
- Sant Joan
- Vilafranca de Bonany
- Montuïri
- Porreres
- El Dorado
- Sa Torre
- Es Pedregar
- Capocorb Vell
- Capocorb
- Vernissa
- Sa Sorda
- Campos del Port
- Ermita de Sant Blai
- Cap de Regana
- Vallgornera
- Cala Pi
- Cap Blanc
- Punta Plana
- S'Estanyol
- S'Ràpita
- Ses Covetes
- Platja es Trenc
- Salines de Llevant
- Botanicactus
- Ses Salines
- Sa Colònia de Sant Jordi
- Cap de ses Salines
- Torrent de son Catiar

0   5   10 km
0   5 miles

A   B   C

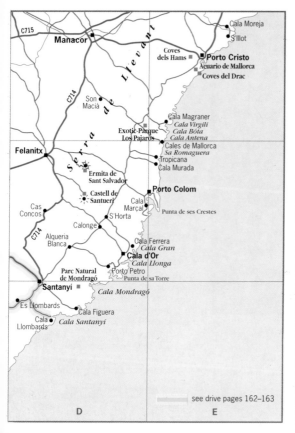

see drive pages 162–163

D   E

THE SOUTH Southern Mallorca is predominantly flat and agricultural, a beguiling landscape of dusty towns, windmills, salt pans and relatively undeveloped beaches. In the south-east, Es Plá, the inland plain, ends abruptly in the mountainous Serra de Llevant, capped with a castle and religious sanctuaries. Beyond this, the island's east coast is indented with *calas* (coves), now fringed with resorts.

Ca'n Gordiola glass at Algaida

COAST OF A HUNDRED BAYS Mallorca's south coast, from the rim of the Bay of Palma beyond S'Arenal, round the bleak Cap de ses Salines and up to Porto Cristo, is fretted with more than 100 deep inlets and pine-shaded coves, creating a fjord-like landscape. Many of these picturesque bays, with their white sandy beaches and unnaturally blue waters, are only accessible by boat. A few, like Cales de Mallorca and Cala d'Or, have been turned into brash holiday resorts, but most of the harbours of the south coast, such as Cala Figuera, Porto Colom and Porto Cristo, make good holiday centres for families with young children or for anyone seeking a quiet winter break.

Pages 152–153: Mending fishing nets at Cala Figuera

Cala Figuera must be the most photographed cove in all Mallorca – a tiny fishing harbour edged with white-washed fishermen's cottages, where fishermen can be seen unloading the daily catch or mending their nets. Other fishing villages, such as Porto Colom and Porto

Opposite: Quaint fishing harbour at Porto Colom

Ghostly formations in the Coves dels Hams

Petro, have also retained some of their old charm, by restricting the number of hotels and preserving their fishing harbours. Porto Cristo, once a fishing village, is now a quite sizeable resort, best known for its caves.

Every string of Mallorcan postcards that you buy, every tourist brochure that you peruse is sure to include shots of the island's caves, in particular the Coves del Drac and the Coves dels Hams at Porto Cristo. These huge caverns, cut into the limestone by the sea, have become major tourist attractions, justifiably famous for their forests of fancifully named, floodlit stalactites, stalagmites and underground lakes.

SERRA DE LLEVANT Another scenic highlight of this area is the Serra de Llevant mountain range, a slim band of grassy hills running parallel with the coast, several kilometres inshore. Although much lower than the Serra de Tramuntana in the north-west, they still provide spectacular views out to sea and over the plain, especially from their highest point, at the monastery of Sant Salvador (509m) near Felanitx. Another regional highpoint is the impressive Sanctuari de Cura at the summit of Puig Randa, founded

SALT SELLERS
In the days before refrigerators, salt was used to preserve meat and fish, and owners of salt flats were numbered among the wealthiest islanders. The methods of obtaining salt by the evaporation of sea water have changed little since those days, except that donkeys are no longer used to pull the wagons of salt to the refinery. Practically all the salt used in Mallorca comes from Campos del Port and Ses Salines. It is also exported as table salt, mostly to Scandinavia and Asia.

Safe swimming at Platja es Trenc

by Ramón Llull, the 13th-century missionary and one of Mallorca's most famous sons.

The principal towns in this region are Llucmajor, famous for its shoemakers, almonds and apricots; Felanitx, one of two main wine-producing areas; and Manacor, the largest town in Mallorca after Palma, and the centre of the island's lucrative artificial pearl industry.

"GARDEN" OF MALLORCA Further south, the landscape becomes more varied. Long drystone walls contain the well-tended fields of corn, capers and artichokes, while whitewashed *fincas*, drenched in geraniums, bougainvillaea and prickly pears, lie hidden amid sweetly scented orchards of citrus fruit. This is one of the most attractive and fertile regions on Mallorca, hence the names S'Horta (from *"hort"* meaning garden) and Cala d'Or (a derivative of Cala d'Hort).

SALINES DE LLEVANT By contrast the island's most southerly point, Cap de ses Salines, has hardly been developed at all. Villages are few and far between, and the coast is rocky and spartan. In the salt pans around Sa Colònia de Sant Jordi, tinged pink by the red soil, and at the Salines de Llevant, salt is produced by ancient methods introduced by the Phoenicians (see panel). The surrounding *garigue* scrub is good for spotting Marmora's warblers, Thekla larks and orchids while the salt pans and lagoons harbour breeding black-winged stilts, Kentish plovers and, in winter, small groups of flamingos. Near by, the Platja es Trenc may be the last undeveloped beach of any size on the island, but it is certainly not undiscovered.

THE NAKED MILE
"The naked mile" is an expression frequently applied to the extensive sandy beach that stretches 5km along the coast from Palma, embracing three of Mallorca's most popular seaside resorts – Can Pastilla, Las Maravillas and S'Arenal – where the shops sell "I love Mallorca" T-shirts and sombreros "Made in Taiwan", and where the discos, bars and strip joints stay open all night. In 1923, the beach was divided into three separate sections: one for men, one for women, and one for animals! It was English and American women who first challenged this segregation, placing themselves on the men-only stretch of beach and braving the surprised stares.

157

Stained glass at Ca'n Gordiola

▶ **Algaida**   *154B3*

Algaida is a typical Mallorcan town less than 20km from Palma – all green shutters, narrow streets without pavements, and a central square dominated by a sandstone church. It takes its name from the Arabic *"al gaida"*, meaning "the woods", although the woods have been replaced by almond orchards and olive groves.

During the last 20 years the town has developed a reputation as the island's gastronomic mecca. Along the main Palma–Manacor road, you can find some of Mallorca's most popular restaurants which serve mainly hearty, old-fashioned local cuisine (see pages 202–203).

Another good reason to visit Algaida is for its glass factory, housed in a mock-medieval castle – **Vidrios Gordiola▶** (Carreterra Palma–Manacor, km21, tel: 971 665046. *Open* May–Sep daily, 9–7; Oct–Apr, Mon–Sat 9–1:30, 3–7, Sun 9–1. *Admission* free). Here craftsmen can be seen blowing and fashioning glass, which has been made on the island by the Gordiola family since 1719. Next door to the workshop is a series of showrooms with a huge choice of glass, ceramics and souvenirs. Be sure to go upstairs to the museum, which has glass from various countries, and furniture and paintings belonging to the Gordiola family.

▶ **Botanicactus**   *154C1*

Tel: 971 649494
Open: daily 9–7 (winter 10:30–5). Admission: moderate
Botanicactus claims to be the largest botanical garden in Europe (15 hectares) with over 12,000 cacti ranging across some 400 different species. Stone walls have been built to protect the cacti from sea breezes. One-third of the gardens is given over to wetland plants (including a bamboo plantation, palms, pines, fruit trees and a Mallorcan-style garden). However, it is the cacti gardens which take your breath away – extraordinary shapes, sizes and exotic blooms, including a 300-year-old Carnegie Giant from Arizona. There is also a nursery selling tropical plants, while the artificial lake provides a welcome splash in the otherwise arid surroundings.

▶▶ **Cabrera**   *44B1*

The island of Cabrera (Goat Island) lies 18km off Mallorca's south coast, the largest in a small archipelago which also includes Conillera (Rabbit Island) and Foradada (Lighthouse Island). Roughly 7km by 5km, its coastline is indented and craggy and rises no higher than Na Picamosques (171m), the "Fly Bite". In 1991 Cabrera became a protected Parc Nacional Marítímo Terrestre (National Land-Sea Park), the first of its kind in Spain.

Although today virtually uninhabited, the island has been home to pirates, former fishermen and – most notoriously – to 9,000 French prisoners of war following the Spanish victory at Bailén in 1808. Left with little water and only meagre rations, the soldiers fell victim to disease and indiscipline – it is said that cannibalism was rife. Six years later, the 3,600 survivors were finally taken off. A monument on the hillside near the small port remembers the victims of this tragedy.

In 1916 Cabrera was taken over for military use, and a handful of soldiers are still stationed there. The island has a superb natural harbour, equipped with a tiny jetty, and it was often used as a stepping-stone for pirates raiding the Balearics. The shell of a 14th-century castle-cum-prison stands on a nearby hilltop, but is officially out of bounds.

The appeal of Cabrera today is its rarity: a wilderness island in the midst of the over-developed Mediterranean. Among the many birds it attracts are Eleonora's falcons, cormorants and a colony of rare Audouin's gulls. Wild goats also thrive here, with an exclusive sub-species of blue-bellied Lilford's wall lizard, and a rich marine life.

Boat excursions depart from the port at Sa Colònia de Sant Jordi daily between May and mid-October. You should allow a full day for the trip, which includes a visit to Cabrera's **Cova Blava** (Blue Grotto). There is no accommodation on the island and little for refreshment. Bring a picnic, swimming costume and snorkel.

Colourful blooms at Botanicactus

159

Giant cacti in Europe's largest botanical garden

Cala d'Or – a shady spot for a drink

▶▶ **Cala d'Or** 155D2

Tourist Office: Avda. Cala Llonga (tel: 971 657463)

This large, tourist-boom resort is built around a series of pretty bays: Cala Ferrera, Cala Esmeralda, Cala Gran, Cala d'Or and Cala Longa. Its centrepiece is an Ibizan pueblo-style complex, begun in 1932, with low whitewashed buildings, spacious courtyards and an appealing range of boutiques, craft shops, bars and restaurants. The narrow golden beaches of Cala Gran, Cala Longa and Platja d'Or are lined with pine trees, but are usually jam-packed in high season.

A tourist train runs from the town centre along to the marina. Brimming with luxury yachts and pleasure boats, this is a favourite spot for a waterfront meal. Cala d'Or is a popular venue for sporting holidays, with good facilities for sailing, diving and tennis.

▶▶▶ **Cala Figuera** 155D1

Mallorca's "Little Venice" is built round the sides of a beautiful narrow inlet with tiny, white-painted fishermen's houses built up to the water's edge. A path follows the miniscule harbour and onto the cliffs.

This truly picture-postcard village also manages to retain the atmosphere of a working fishing port more than anywhere else in Mallorca. Arrive early in the morning to avoid the crowds, and you might see the catch being unloaded from the brightly painted boats. Or in the early evening you can watch the fishermen sitting on the steps mending their vivid blue nets before you go for dinner in a seafront restaurant.

The calm, deep waters and fjord-like scenery make Cala Figuera a favoured anchorage for luxury yachts, and, although there is no beach, there are good ones near by at Cala Mondragó (see page 171) and Cala Santanyí.

▶ **Cales de Mallorca** 155E2

This large, carefully planned holiday settlement is located on a bare, indented stretch of coast between Cala Magraner and Cala Murada. The resort is dominated by a number of massive hotel eyesores, although the majority of the development has been restricted to single- or two-storey buildings. Most nightlife takes place in the hotels.

There are, however, around 20 small bays and coves here fringed by sandy beaches. Many are only accessible from the sea, and best explored on the memorable boat trip from Cala Murada to Porto Cristo. Other coves, including Calas Margraner, Virgili, Bota, Setri and

Antena, have tracks leading down to them. Sa Romaguera is probably the most appealing inlet, with bars and cafés close to the sea.

▶ Can Pastilla   154A3

Every summer the Badia de Palma to the east of Palma is invaded by tens of thousands of cut-price holiday-makers who pour straight off their coaches into the pubs, restaurants and pounding discos of Can Pastilla and S'Arenal (see page 176), two resorts which have merged to create one massive concrete jungle. Prices are rock-bottom and menus, all in English and German, are as likely to feature bratwurst or beans on toast as paella.

The resort is a mecca for fun-loving families and the young at heart looking for a beach holiday with plenty to do in the evenings. By day, the main attraction is the **Platja de Palma**, ideal for children with its 5km of clean, white sand, shallow water, sun umbrellas, ice-cream sellers and playgrounds. A palm-lined promenade follows the shore, particularly enjoyable at night.

▶ Capocorb Vell   154B2

Ctra Cap Blanc-Llucmajor tel: 971 180155
Open: Fri–Wed 10–5. Closed: Thu.
Admission: inexpensive
Capocorb Vell is the site of a Bronze Age settlement dating back to at least 1000 BC. The 28 ruined dwellings still have enough of their sturdy walls, doorways, pillars and winding passages to make a thought-provoking ghost town. Beyond the main group of buildings, lie the remains of five ancient towers or *talaiots* (see page 29), spread among the fields.

Cala Figuera – Mallorca's most photographed cove

Drive

The tranquil South

See map on pages 154–155.

This route leaves the frenzy of the Badia de Palma for an easygoing drive around the cliffs, coves and sandy beaches of Mallorca's southern coast. It then heads inland, returning through a fertile countryside of farms, windmills and historic towns.

The circular 123km drive takes around 5 hours, starting from Can Pastilla. Take the coastal dual carriageway eastwards. Drive through S'Arenal and uphill to a roundabout. Turn right following signs to Cap Blanc, passing **Aquacity** (see panel, page 176) on the left and Cala Blava to the right. Follow the coast south to **Cap Blanc▶**, a remote, rocky headland, punctuated only by a lighthouse, which offers spectacular sea views across to

Talaiotic remains and Bronze Age dwellings at Capocorb Vell

the island of Cabrera, and beautiful, bleak clifftop walks.

Continue north-east for 5km to **Capocorb Vell,** one of the most important prehistoric sites in Mallorca, with five *talaiots* and Bronze Age dwellings dating from around 1000 BC (see also page 161).

After visiting Capocorb Vell, drive south for 4km to reach **Cala Pi▶▶**. Once an island secret, this tiny cove lies tucked away beneath thick pine woods. Developers have built luxury villas and apartments around the inlet, but you can still enjoy the clear turquoise waters and sandy beach, reached by climbing down steep steps. Beside the restored watchtower is a viewpoint with parking and a bar-restaurant.

From here, follow the signs for Vallgornera, then drive inland and turn right in the direction of Campos and

Sa Colònia de Sant Jordi. Along the way rural roads lead south to the small resorts of S'Estanyol and Sa Ràpita, and the splendid beaches at Ses Covetes and Platja es Trenc (see page 172). After 14km turn right, passing salt lakes, the **Salines de Llevant**, on the right (see page 157).

The *garigue* scrub surrounding these salt pans is particularly noted for its wide variety of birdlife, including marsh harriers, kestrels, spotted cranes, fan-tailed warblers, hoopoes and, in spring, avocets, little-ringed plovers, little egrets, black-tailed godwits, collared pratincoles and black terns (see page 17).

Carry on to the resort of **Sa Colònia de Sant Jordi** (see page 176). A good range of bars and restaurants makes this a convenient place to stop for a drink or for lunch.

After lunch, continue east towards Santanyí, and 3km outside the town turn right, passing through low pines to reach the small resort of **Cala Llombards▶▶**. A steep road leads down to the sandy beach, hidden in a picturesque cove and sheltered by wooded cliffs. Its shallow waters make it particularly suitable for young children. A short rocky walk by the sea provides a good view.

Santanyí where yellow sandstone buildings offer welcome shade

Return to the main road and turn right for **Santanyí**. This old Mallorcan town, like Campos further on, is a world away from the island's brash tourist resorts. Sturdy buildings line its streets, constructed with the local warm-toned sandstone that graces many of Mallorca's finest buildings (see page 176). It was ransacked by pirates on more than one occasion, but one of the old town gates, Sa Porta, has survived together with sections of the medieval city walls. From Santanyí take the C717 west to **Campos del Port▶**.

Campos was founded by the Romans, but also has other claims to fame. It possesses the best pâtisserie on the island (Pastelería Pomar) and, in its mighty 16th-century church, a painting attributed to Murillo, *El Santo Cristo de la Paciencia* (The Christ of Patience). Since being restored, the Ajuntament (town hall) across the road, with its balustrades and coat of arms, is a monument to the town's civic pride.

To return to the starting point, follow the fast C717 through **Llucmajor** (see page 168) to Can Pastilla.

Among the most popular sightseeing attractions in Mallorca are its magnificent limestone caves, once refuges and now technicolour tourist attractions, with their bizarre formations enhanced by high-tech son et lumière. Incidentally, map-readers should take care not to confuse caves (coves) with the island's other big draw – coves (calas).

QUEEN OF PILLARS

One of the chambers in the Coves d'Artà is as large as the nave of Palma cathedral and contains "Queen of Pillars", a 22m-high stalagmite which grows upwards at a rate of 1cm a year. In another 5,000 years it will be joined to the ceiling.

164

Grand entrance to the Coves d'Artà

History of the caves The naturally formed caves found in Mallorca's limestone rocks provide a common thread through the island's social history. They provided shelter for the Pre-Talaiotic settlers (see page 28) who set up home here around 2000 BC, and made good hideaways from invaders. During the Christian conquest of 1229, Jaume I found 2,000 Arabs hiding in the Coves d'Artà (see pages 140–141) together with their livestock. Over the centuries, caves served as refuges from slave-raiders, lairs for pirates, dens for smugglers and sanctuaries for religious hermits. Rediscovered in the late 19th century, the largest now draw hordes of sightseers.

Mallorca's most impressive caverns can be found in the eastern part of the island, and most were first exploited by French geologist Édouard Martel in the late 19th century. Locals claim a visit to the Coves del Drac was one of Gaudí's greatest inspirations (reflected in the "stalagmite" spires of his most extravagant opus, the Sagrada Familia in Barcelona); the caves at Artà are said to have inspired Jules Verne's book *Journey to the Centre of the Earth*.

Speleology The caves on Mallorca's east coast were formed by waves reacting with the limestone cliffs, creating fissures in the rock which turned to caverns as the water-table dropped. It is hard to believe that the caves at Artà, generally considered the best on the island, are an example of a marine cave system. Today these extensive caverns stand 35m above sea level and burrow some 300m into the rockface, and they rise at some points to a height of 45m.

The inland caves were created by water acidified by dissolved carbon dioxide circulating through the joints and faults in the calcareous rock. In time, the passages and channels

that formed became caverns which were revealed when the water table dropped. Coves dels Hams were formed by an underground river.

Both marine and inland caves share common features, including stalagmites (spikes rising from the ground), stalactites (like icicles hanging from above), draperies (resembling curtains), knobbly clusters known as "cave coral", and other extraordinary deposits.

Special effects Five caves are open to the public: **Artà** (see pages 140–141), **Campanet** (see page 100), **Drac** (see page 167), **Gènova** (see page 79) and **Hams** (see page 167). Since the temperature inside is constant all year round (about 20°C), you don't need a coat, but do wear suitable shoes, as the ground can be wet and slippery. Visitors with limited mobility might find some of the paths and staircases difficult. If you are claustrophobic, it would be better not to go at all!

The caves of Artà, Drac and Hams are among the island's top tourist sights, with groups of several hundred at a time herded along the slippery paths by guides who tell you in four languages how to interpret the bizarre rock formations, encouraging your imagination to run riot at the suggestive shapes of the formations. Once likened to pious subjects like the Virgin, a cathedral, or grottoes fit for classical deities, nowadays they are more often seen to resemble human towers, monstrous hairy nostrils, leaning towers of Pisa, eggs and bacon, or even vegetables in a great subterranean supermarket.

Clever lighting and classical music enhance the effects, seen most flamboyantly at Coves del Drac, where the slick one-hour tour climaxes in a lavish, floodlit floating violin concert on Lake Martel, before returning by boat.

Lake Martel – Europe's largest underground lake

165

Stunning stalactite reflections in the Coves del Drac

▶▶ Castell de Santueri   *155D2*

Open: daily 10–7. Admission: inexpensive
Strategically sited at the summit of a 408m peak in the
Serra de Llevant, Castell de Santueri was built into the
cliffs in the 14th century on the site of a ruined Arab
fortress. The wild flowers and views make this
picturesque ruin a worthwhile excursion.

▶▶▶ Coves del Drac   *155E3*

Tel: 971 820753
Tours: summer, on the hour 10–5 (not 1 PM); winter, at 10:45,
12, 2 and 3:30. Admission: moderate
The Coves del Drac (Dragon Caves) were first explored in
1896 by a French geologist, Édouard Martel. The entrance
is down a steep flight of steps, followed by a walk along
narrow but well-lit underground passages.

   The vast labyrinth of tunnels and caves is estimated to
run for about 2km in total, and fanciful names have been
given to many of its physical features. The tour culminates in the vast Lago Martel (Lake Martel) and a
cavernous auditorium which can hold over a thousand
spectators. The show features a torchlit procession with
musicians and singers gliding across the water in boats.

▶▶ Coves dels Hams   *155E3*

Tel: 971 820988
Open: summer, daily 10–6; winter, daily 10:30–5:30.
Admission charge: expensive
The distinguishing feature of these caves is the large
number of stalactites that are amazingly white, suggest-
ing that the name "dels Hams" refers to white ceramic
tiles. However, the way these same stalactites curve
upwards brings to mind *"hams"*, a Mallorquín word for
fish-hooks, often cited as the origin of the name.

   Although they are not as extensive as the nearby Coves
del Drac (see above), their underground formations,
which were only discovered in 1906, are an impressive
natural sight, made accessible by a guided tour. Coloured
lights and a concert add sparkle to the occasion.

▶▶ Ermita de Sant Salvador   *155D2*

This magnificent 14th-century sanctuary marks a physical
and spiritual high point of the island: set atop a 509m
summit (Puig de Sant Salvador) at the highest point in the
Serra de Llevant, it has long been a magnet for both casual
visitors and religious pilgrims. This was the last monastic
house to lose its monks in 1992. The sanctuary still offers
simple accommodation to pilgrims (see page 194).

   On the snaking ascent to the hermitage, you will pass a
small chapel, the 12 Stations of the Cross, a 14m stone
cross, and a 37m-high statue of Christ holding out his
right hand as if to bless the sanctuary.

   Inside the huge gatehouse is a Gothic depiction of the
Last Supper and offerings left by pilgrims. In the 18th-
century church, note the much-revered Virgin figure and
look for the Bethlehem Grotto – a nativity scene viewed
through magnifying windows and showing Mallorcan-
style windmills among the desert scenery. A small room
near by, full of poignant mementoes and prayers to Our
Lady, testifies that the Ermita continues to represent a
crucial source of spiritual aid.

LAKE MARTEL
Named after the famous
French speleologist who
discovered it, Lake Martel
in Coves del Drac is 177m
long, 40m wide and 9m
deep and lies 29m under
the surface, making it the
largest underground lake
in Europe.

Opposite: Coves del Drac
Below: Ermita de Sant
Salvador

Llucmajor's popular market

▶ Felanitx 155D2

With its mellow stone streets and medieval houses, Felanitx is considered one of the best-kept towns in Mallorca. Its unusual name is thought to be derived, rather poetically, from "*fiel a nit*" ("faithful to the night").

Situated at the heart of one of the two main wine-producing areas, it is also the centre of the *azulejos* (blue tiles) industry and the export centre for Mallorca's capers, or "green pearls" (see panel, page 140), which are said to be among the finest in the world. You can buy them at the Sunday morning market, when local pottery and glassware is displayed on the steps leading up to the fine **church of Sant Miquel▶**. The church façade contains a memorial to 414 people who died when a wall collapsed in the town in 1844. Further up, beneath the rose window, you can see the Archangel Michael standing on the Devil's head. If you are lucky, you may even hear the 50-strong town band giving one of their regular open-air concerts.

Felanitx was the birthplace of 14th-century architect Guillem Sagrera – whose many masterpieces include La Llotja in Palma (see page 51) and the cathedral's Portal del Mirador (see page 58) . It is also the home town of Mallorca's most celebrated contemporary artist, Miquel Barceló (see panel), who still has a studio in the town.

▶ Llucmajor 154B2

This seemingly ordinary country town, the largest in southern Mallorca, has an important place in history as the site of the battle in which Pedro IV of Aragón killed his relative Jaume III in 1349 to end Mallorca's brief spell as an independent kingdom. Jaume's death is commemorated by a statue at the end of the Passeig de Jaume III. Near by, along Carrer Obispo Taxaquet, is another statue – in honour of Llucmajor's cobblers.

Most people here are employed by the shoe factories, or work in the dried fruit trade. Look out for figs, almonds and apricots, grown on the flat agricultural land surrounding the town. These are the best buys to be had at Llucmajor's market, which is held every Wednesday, Friday and Sunday around the Plaça d'Espanya.

Walk

Serra de Llevant

A comfortable 4km walk from historic Castell de Santueri to the Ermita de Sant Salvador, through fields of wild flowers to the summit of the Serra de Llevant with its sweeping views.

The walk requires sturdy shoes, food, water and a sense of direction. A car can be parked at either end. Allow 90 minutes one way.

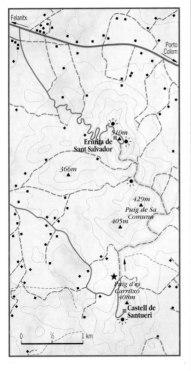

Statue of Christ, Ermita de Sant Salvador

Drive south from Felanitx towards Santanyí. Turn left after about 2km on to a country lane signposted to Castell de Santueri (see page 167). Continue until the road starts to climb in a sharp bend to the right. At the next bend, park on the rough ground to the left, where a track leads east.

The first part of the walk (variously marked by yellow and red paint marks on trees and stones) follows a gently undulating route. After about 50m turn left along a narrower path, crossing a boundary wall where the ground begins to rise. Join a forest track and continue until you reach an orchard with carob, almond and fig trees. Turn left and walk through the orchard to a gateway near a farmhouse.

Cross the next field with its colourful strawberry trees (*Arbutus unedo*), then continue over several other tracks, before skirting eastward round a hill, Puig de Sa Comuna.

As you start to climb, a huge statue of Christ comes into view. Continue up a narrow track, which rises to a small ridge with sight of the great buildings of the **Ermita de Sant Salvador** (see page 167). The route now follows a well-worn path, climbing to the hermitage and its views.

Retrace your steps to the start.

The numerous watchtowers and windmills that stud the countryside are often the first thing noticed by visitors flying into Mallorca. In fact windmills have become a Mallorcan symbol, their whirling blades often imitating the red and yellow bars of the island's flag.

WHAT'S IN A NAME?
The word for watchtower, "*atalaya*", comes from the Arabic "*atalayi*", meaning to "guard" or "watch".

Coastal defences On a map of Mallorca in 1683, (displayed in Palma's Museu Diocesà), the island is shown protected by over 40 watchtowers or *atalaya*, mostly along the north coast. Watchtowers have been a feature of the Mallorcan landscape since Talaiotic times, and several still punctuate the skyline, at the Mirador de Ses Animes near Banyalbufar and at Punta de n'Amer.

Most were constructed by the islanders as a defence measure during the 16th century, when Moorish corsairs increased the number and ferocity of their raids. Smoke signals during the day and torches at night were used to warn of approaching pirate raids.

Symbol of Mallorca More common today though – and sometimes similar in shape – are the windmills that are as much an essential aspect of the image of Mallorca as are *ensaimadas* (see page 91) or the Sóller railway line.

Originally, *molinos* (mills) were used for the grinding of corn. Others were specially constructed to suck the marshland dry in order to make the land available for agriculture. They all had cloth sails, which were later replaced by wooden slats or metal fans. Nowadays, the huge blades of the working mills draw up water from below ground to irrigate the fields.

By the end of the 19th century, Mallorca had over 4,000 working windmills. Just a few remain today, scattered about the flat, dusty plain east of Palma, with other clusters around Sa Pobla, Campos and Llucmajor. Some are still revolving, others stand dilapidated like old scarecrows. Thanks to the Asociación de Amigos de los Molinos (Association of Friends of the Windmills), founded in 1975, more and more of these classic national symbols are being restored.

UNIQUE WINDMILLS
"They have six sails instead of four, which gives them a strange and unfamiliar appearance. In addition to this, the mass of ropes and cordage makes the sails look as complicated and intricate as the rigging of a ship."
(*Letters from Majorca*, Charles Wood, 1886)

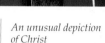

▶ Manacor   155D3

Manacor – "the metropolis of the East" – is Mallorca's second largest town and the centre of the island's artificial pearl industry. It has always been associated with crafts – in particular furniture and tiles – and the local shops bulge with dark Mallorcan pottery, painted ceramics and items carved from olive wood. The town is also known for its local sweets, called *sospiros* (sighs).

Despite the lack of obvious sights, the narrow streets of the old town behind the church make a pleasant place to stroll. The **Church of the Virgin of the Sorrows▶** (Plaça del Rector Rubi. *Open* Mon–Fri 9–1, 3–7, Sat 9–1. *Admission:* inexpensive) is built on the site of a mosque. Enter the mighty wooden doors to marvel at the huge domed ceiling and an extraordinary figure of Christ on the Cross with long, straggly hair and a skirt.

An unusual depiction of Christ

Artificial pearls have been made in Manacor since 1890. Today there are several factories that you can visit on an excursion or independently. Mallorca's artificial pearl industry produces 50 million pearls a year, using a secret method involving finely ground fish scales and resin. The pearls are said to be indistinguishable from the real thing and their lustre lasts forever.

▶▶ Parc Natural de Mondragó   155D1

Tel: 971 181022
Open: winter, daily 9–1; summer, daily 9–1, 2–5.
Admission free
Designated as a conservation area since 1990, the park is set amid attractive landscapes with small lakes and dunes and is rich in both flora and fauna. It borders the sea and contains several appealing coves, including Cala Mondragó, an unspoilt double bay with white sand.

SHOPPING MECCA
There is more to Manacor than pearls. Several giant factory shops grab your attention as you enter the city on the C715 from Palma. **OlivArt** sells artefacts carved out of olive wood, Further on, if you are interested in pottery look out for **Ceramica Mallorquina** and **Bar Cerámicas**. The various painstaking stages in the birth of an artificial pearl are demonstrated in several pearl factories. **Majorica**, the best known, is at Vía Roma 52 (tel: 971 550800. *Open* Mon–Fri 9:30–1, 2:30–7; Sat–Sun 10–1. *Admission* free).

Wild agapanthus add a splash of colour

The South

JAUME II

The present-day shape of Mallorca owes a lot to the enlightened King Jaume II, who reigned between 1276 and 1311. During this time, he strengthened coastal defences and established 11 new towns on the Plá (Algaida, Binissalem, Selva, Sant Joan, Sa Pobla, Llucmajor, Manacor, Porreres, Campos, Felanitx and Santuari), thereby encouraging a growth in commerce, agriculture and trade. The monarch also built new churches, bridges and reservoirs, minted a Mallorcan coinage and introduced a programme of weekly local markets.

THE MALLORCA AQUARIUM

From Porto Cristo it is just 20 minutes' walk southwards to the Acuario de Mallorca – a well-stocked freshwater and seawater aquarium which exhibits fierce and exotic fish from around the world, including sharks, electric eels and stinging fish. (Carrer de Vèlla, tel: 971 820971. *Open* daily 10:30–5:30 *Admission:* moderate.)

▶▶ Platja es Trenc   154C1

Many visitors consider this beach the finest in Mallorca: blissfully undeveloped, with low pines, wild flowers, dunes and a 5km white-sand shore. Platja es Trenc is a designated nature reserve, popular with nudists due to its remote location. Yet the arrival of sun umbrellas and the opening of a small bar are proof that the tide of tourism is relentless. The surrounding pine woods and the Salines de Llevant (see page 157) are a bird-watcher's heaven.

▶ Porreres   154C3

Embedded in the heart of the island, this quiet market town is known throughout Mallorca for its apricots and wine. It has a splendid 17th-century church, **Nostra Senyora de Consolació▶**, (Open Mon–Fri 9:30–12:30, 4:30–7, Sat 9:30–12:30) decorated with majolica pictures. Three kilometres south-west of Porreres a road climbs up to the **Santuari de Mont-Sión▶▶▶**, notable for its cloisters.

▶▶▶ Porto Colom   155E2

One of the many villages in the Mediterranean claiming to be the birthplace of Christopher Columbus, Porto Colom was the port for the nearby town of Felanitx and is now a burgeoning holiday resort. The modern marina at the south end of the bay is one of the east coast's most popular moorings. At the northern end, the tiny fishing harbour is truly delightful, having retained its ancient, colourful fishermen's houses and sheds, today complemented by a few souvenir shops, fish restaurants and a diving school. The sun-baked back streets contain quaint cottages with red, blue, green or yellow painted shutters, surrounding small pine-shaded squares.

▶▶ Porto Cristo   155E3

Tourist Office: Avinguda Gual 31 (tel: 971 820931)

One of Mallorca's most attractive ports, this is also a popular beach resort, with a bustling marina and an attractive fishing harbour at the end of a long, sheltered inlet. Once the port of Manacor, Porto Cristo was the only place in Mallorca involved in the Spanish Civil War, when it was briefly captured by Republican forces.

There is little to do here but swim, sunbathe and dine at the terrace restaurants which are perfectly placed to catch the lunchtime sun – or explore the nearby Coves del Drac and Coves dels Hams (see page 167), both visited in droves by day trippers.

▶▶ Porto Petro 155D2

In contrast to its lively neighbour, Cala d'Or, this simple small fishing port has retained its charm: typical white-washed cottages outnumber the high-rise developments, there are few hotels, and more fishing boats than luxury yachts sit in the palm-shaded harbour. On the waterfront, several unpretentious restaurants serve fresh fish. Although the resort lacks a good sandy beach, a regular bus service runs visitors to the magnificent sandy beaches of nearby Cala Mondragó (see page 171).

▶▶ Puig de Randa 154B3

A striking and revered island landmark, this table mountain rises abruptly 543m out of the agricultural plains of central Mallorca, and has been a traditional focus for pilgrims and religious festivals since Ramón Llull founded a hermitage here in 1275 (see page 50). On its slopes are three separate hermitages: the lowest, the 15th-century **Oratorio de Nostra Senyora de Gràcia** is perched on a ledge in the cliff above a 200m sheer drop; further up the corkscrewing lane is the 14th-century **Santuari de Sant Honorat**; finally, atop the summit is the **Santuari de Cura**, where Llull lived.

These days the pilgrims to Puig de Randa are as likely to be weekend cyclists in search of a challenge as seekers after religious truth. Nevertheless, despite the radio mast on the mountain top, the electric candles in the church, and the bar, the sacred aura of Santuari de Cura lives on – not least because of the magical views its terraces offer over most of Mallorca. In the church, stained-glass windows depict the story of the founder's life.

Picture postcard village of Porto Petro

SERRA DE LLEVANT
Should you tire of the seaside, keen walkers will enjoy trekking in the Serra de Llevant mountain range, running parallel with the coast several kilometres inshore, with its spectacular views out to sea and over the Plain of Mallorca. Its highest points are crowned by the 14th-century Ermita de Sant Salvador (Monastery of Saint Salvador) and the ancient Castel de Santueri (Castle of Sanctuary), built originally as a defence against pirates (see walk, page 169). To explore the area on horseback, contact Escola d'Equitació Son Menut near Felanitx (tel: 971 582920).

There are two ways of eating out in Mallorca: either a full meal in a restaurant or a succession of tapas – *Spanish-style* hors d'oeuvres – *at one or more bars. If you choose* tapas, *you have the advatage of being able to experiment.*

Some bars still serve free tapas *with your drinks*

Many places have food laid out on the counter so you can see what is available and order it simply by pointing. You can also sample several bars in an evening, following the Andalusian custom of the *tapeo*, moving from bar to bar and sampling just one dish in each.

ORIGINS

The term *tapas* is thought to come from the habit of having a few nibbles with a drink to *tapar el apetito* ("to put a lid on the appetite") before a meal, or from the little saucers (*tapas*) of snacks that bartenders used to place over drinks. Some bars still serve free *tapas* at the bar – perhaps a bowl of olives or some salted almonds.

A snack or a meal? *Tapas* consist of small portions of fish, meat or vegetables. *Raciones* are bigger portions, served with bread and usually enough for a light meal – half a dozen *tapas* dishes and a couple of *raciones* make a filling and varied meal for a small group. When ordering, remember to make it clear whether you want a *tapa* or a *racion* and, if you have trouble choosing, order a *tapa combinada* – a mouthful of everything.

Classic *tapas* dishes range from simple bowls of olives, crisps and nuts to *tortilla* (Spanish omelette filled with potato and onion and served cold in slices), mushrooms, olives, fried sardines, mussels, red peppers in olive oil, snails, meat balls, potato salad, prawns in garlic and *calamares* (tiny, marinated squid). Local specialities include *cocos* (small pizza-like snacks), *empanadas* (meat pies), *sobrasada*, *botifarró* and *llongarusa* (types of highly seasoned pork sausage), *callos* (tripe in a tomato and onion sauce) and *pa amb oli* (see panel opposite).

Tapas bars Most bars serve *tapas*, although many have a limited choice. They usually open from around 9 AM until early in the evening, and many stay open till late at night. In Palma, there is a particularly lively *tapas* scene, which ranges from chic modernist bars such as L'Angel Blau to simple cafés like Bar Pica-Pica where the atmosphere and snacks more than compensate for the décor.

The following is a selection of popular tapas bars around the island.

Palma

L'Angel Blau, Carrer Capiscolat (no phone). Chic, trendy *tapas* bar with classical music.

Bar Bosch, Plaça Rei Joan Carles I 6 (tel: 971 721131). One of Palma's most popular *tapas* bars.

La Boveda, Carrer Boteria 3 (tel: 971 714863). Jam-packed restaurant-bar lined with huge wine barrels.

Es Cantó de S'Arc , Carrer Morey 6 (no phone). Dark and cosy with *variado de tapas* (a mixed plate of *tapas*) for two at a good price including half a bottle of wine.

La Paloma, Carrer dels Apuntadors 16 (tel: 971 721745). Reasonably priced *tapas* by lamplight.

Pica-Pica, Carrer Pelaires 21 (tel: 971 210086). A real locals' bar, down a quiet alley behind the Born ("*pica-pica*" means "assorted nibbles").

El Pilón, Carrer Cifre (tel: 971 717590). Tiny bar with superb seafood specials.

Andratx

Bar Nuevo, Plaça Espanya 4 (tel: 971 136073). One of several bars lining a sunny, fountain-splashed square.

Capdepera

Bar Gabelins, Plaça de l'Orient 2 (tel: 971 818263). Locals' bar on the main square.

Inca

Bar Antonio, Carrer Mayor 52 (tel: 971 500005). Tasty *tapas* on a shaded terrace beside the parish church.

Port d'Andratx

Bar Central, Avenguda Mateo Bosch 30 (tel: 971 673692). Limited *tapas* but an idyllic waterfront venue for watching the setting sun.

Porto Petro

Blau i Blanc, Passeig del Porto 43 (tel: 971 658002). Smart tiled bar opposite the marina. Try the fried crab-meat and peppers, spinach and cheese and the plentiful vegetarian dishes.

Sa Colònia de Sant Jordi

Bar Maxim, Carrer Lonja 9 (tel: 971 655039). Atmospheric bar on the edge of a lively marina.

Santanyí

Bar Sa Plaça, Plaça Mayor 26 (tel: 971 653278). A good bet for *bocadillos* or *pa amb oli*.

Sóller

Bar Es Firo, Plaça Constitució 10 (tel: 971 630134). Real country *tapas*. Try lamb baked with peppers and aubergines, fish in chilli and garlic, snails and wild mushrooms.

PA AMB OLI

Pa amb oli is a traditional Mallorcan breakfast dish – a massive slice of brown bread drizzled in olive oil, rubbed with tomato and garlic and sprinkled with salt, sometimes with an additional slice of cheese or *jamón serrano* on top. Simple, tasty and delicious washed down with a flagon of wine, *pa amb oli* is served in most bars around the island.

Visitors and locals all enjoy tasty tapas

MALLORCAN SANDWICHES

Don't be misled by the word "sandwich" which always consists of toasted sliced bread. The Mallorcan equivalent of sandwich is *bocadillo*. Typical fillings include *chorizo* (spicy sausage), *jamón* (ham, either *serrano* or *York*, ie cured or cooked), *atún* (tuna), *lomo* (loin of pork), *queso* (cheese), *salami* or *tortilla* (omelette).

*Sunseekers will find
Mallorca has everything
they need*

▶ S'Arenal 154A3

*Tourist Office: Plaça de la Reina Maria Cristina (tel: 971
440414)*
If you are looking for peace and quiet, forget S'Arenal. But
if you are a fun-in-the-sun addict or hoping to enjoy
24-hour partying, this is definitely the best destination.
S'Arenal is the kind of resort that keeps charter airlines
and tour operators in business – a pulsating tourist mecca
of high-rise hotels, cheap, cheerful fast-food joints and
tourist-trash gift shops which, by night, erupts into a blaze
of neon lights, loud lively bars and pounding discos.

During the day, the beach is often packed, which is
how everyone likes it, and there are special *balnearios*
(bathing stations) and playgrounds for children. In the
summer a tourist train runs along the 7km seafront
between S'Arenal and Can Pastilla (see page 161).

▶▶ Sa Colònia de Sant Jordi 154C1

Tourist Office: Carrer de Doctor Barraquer 5 (tel: 971 656073)
This is one of Mallorca's quieter seaside resorts, its
sprawling modern buildings and chic hotels contrasting
sharply with the charms of its atmospheric harbour where
local fishermen repair their boats in the yard. Once the
haunt of smugglers from the North African coast, its
waters are now busy with pleasure boats and glass-
bottomed vessels offering excursions around the coast
and south to Cabrera. Several good-value cafés and
restaurants line the waterfront and, although there is only
a tiny beach, the resort is within easy reach of one of the
island's best beaches, Platja es Trenc (see page 172).

▶ Santanyí 155D1

This town, close to Mallorca's south-eastern tip, is the
source of the mellow, honey-coloured sandstone used in
Palma's cathedral and Castell de Bellver among other
buildings. The old gate, Sa Porta Murada, is a further
example of this warm-toned stone and a reminder that
Santanyí was once a walled town. The massive rococo
organ in the **church of Sant Andreu Apòstel** is rated one of
the most precious organs in Spain.

AQUACITY PARK
Aquacity Park, on the
outskirts of S'Arenal,
advertises itself as the
world's largest water
funfair. Among its many
thrills and attractions are
landscaped swimming-
pools, kamikaze water
slides, a Hawaiian wave
pool, a mini zoo and farm,
parrot shows, shops and
restaurants – a great day
out for all the family.
(Autopista PM19 exit 13,
tel: 971 440000. *Open*
May–Oct 10–5. *Closed*
Sun in October.
Admission: expensive.)

Arriving by air

Iberia, the Spanish national airline, is the main operator of scheduled flights to Palma from destinations in Spain and Europe. **British Midland** also operate daily scheduled services direct from Heathrow and **Air Europa** have three scheduled flights a week from Gatwick. The cheapest-price scheduled tickets often carry almost as many restrictions as charter flights. They usually need to be booked a minimum of 14 days in advance, require you to stay at least one Saturday night and do not allow for change or cancellation.

Scheduled services between North America and Mallorca via Madrid are provided by **Iberia** and **American Airlines**.

Other airlines, offering charter flights, include **Palmair** and **Britannia**. Alternatively, fly to Barcelona and take a local flight or a passenger ferry from there. For inter-island travel, there are several daily flights between Palma and Mahón in Menorca; the trip takes about 30 minutes.

Useful telephone numbers:
American Airlines: (USA) 0800/433 7300.
British Midland: (Palma) 971 453112; (UK) 0345-554554.
Air Europa: (UK) 0990 772233; (Palma) 971 178100/178190;
Iberia: (Palma) 971 262600; (Madrid) 902 400500; (UK) 020 7830 0011; (USA) 1800 772 4642.
Palmair: (Palma) 971 717940; (UK) 01202-299299.

Son Sant Joan airport (11km east of Palma) has two terminals that offer a full range of souvenir shops, car rental facilities, post office and hotel booking services, as well as a small tourist information office. For airport information, tel: 971 264624; for tourist information, tel: 971 260803.

On departure, there is a large duty-free shop which you can visit after passing passport and security controls. If travelling at peak times on charter flights, make sure you have some entertainment and pesetas on hand in case of delay ("Retrasado" on the flight information screen); "Embarcando" means "Boarding".

Transport to and from the airport

Bus 17 runs from the airport to Palma (Plaça d'Espanya) approximately every 30 minutes from 7 AM until midnight. The journey time is about 30 minutes. There is a 24-hour taxi service.

Arriving by sea

Trasmediterránea operate daily connections by car and passenger ferry from Barcelona and Valencia to Palma. Reservations can be made at Compañía Trasmediterránea, Estació Maritime no 2, Palma (tel: 971 707377). They also sail between Palma and Mahón (Menorca). For information tel: (Palma) 971 707377; (Mahón) 971 366050; (Ibiza) 971 315050; or Madrid, 902 454645, for mainland connections. **Balearia** operate a regular car and passenger hydrofoil/ferry service from Dénia (Alicante) to Palma via Ibiza, and between Port d'Alcúdia and Ciutadella (Menorca). For more information, tel: (Palma) 971 405360.

Arriving by train or bus

It can take as little as 15 hours to travel by train from London via the Channel Tunnel to Barcelona, from where there are regular ferries to

Mallorca. For information, tel: **Rail Europe** Information line on 0870 584 8848 or **Eurostar** on 01233-617575 (international calls), or 0870 518 6186 (UK calls).

The journey from London to Barcelona by cross-channel ferry and coach takes around 26 hours with stops every 4 or 5 hours. For more information, contact **Eurolines** on 01582 404511.

Arriving by car

The traditional route by car involves driving through France to Barcelona and then catching the ferry to Palma. Alternatively, the direct ferry services from Plymouth or Portsmouth to Santander or Bilbao take between 24 and 30 hours and greatly reduce the driving time. For information, tel: **Brittany Ferries** on 0990-360360.

Customs regulations

"Duty free" has now been phased out in Europe. In theory there is no limit on goods imported from one EU country to another, provided tax has been paid and they are for personal use. However, the authorities have issued "guidelines", as follows: 10 litres of spirits, 20 litres of fortified wines, 90 litres of wine, 110 litres of beer, 800 cigarettes, 400 cigarillos, 200 cigars, 1kg pipe tobacco, no limit on perfume.

Duty-free limits for visitors travelling from a non-EU country into Spain are: 200 cigarettes or 100 cigarillos or 50 cigars or 250g of tobacco; 1 litre of spirits or 2 litres of fortified wines or sparkling wine; 2 litres of still table wine; 60ml of perfume and 250ml of toilet water; gifts, souvenirs and other goods up to a value of 36,000ptas/EUR216.

The import of wildlife souvenirs sourced from rare or endangered species may be either illegal or require a special permit. Before purchase you should check your home country's customs regulations.

Visas

Citizens of EU countries, USA, Canada, New Zealand and Japan who hold valid passports do not require a visa to visit Spain for less than 90 days, provided they are not taking up paid employment. Other travellers should check with their nearest Spanish Consulate.

179

❏ When planning your holiday, you may wish to consider this old island saying which advises: "*Hasta el cuarenta de mayo no te quites el sayo*", meaning "Don't discard your coat until the 40th day of May", in other words, until 10 June – which is reckoned to be the first day of summer in Mallorca. ❏

When to go

The temperate climate of Mallorca makes it a pleasant holiday destination at any time of year. Winter holidays, which brought so many visitors to the island early in the 20th century prior to the big package-tourist boom, are very much back in vogue. The almond blossom of January and February makes an unforgettable sight, and Easter is another popular time, with mild spring days and an abundance of wildflowers. Most people visit Mallorca between April and September when the island is invariably warm and sunny. July and August are the hottest, driest and dustiest months. Autumn is generally regarded as the best time to visit, when the main tourist rush is over, but the sea remains warm enough for bathing. Rain is most likely between October and February, when it can be quite cold. At the height of winter, snow occasionally falls in the mountains.

Climate

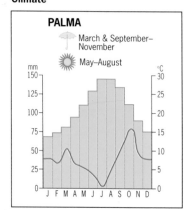

National holidays

Many Spanish national holidays are keenly observed in Mallorca:

  1 Jan **New Year's Day** (Año Nuevo)
  6 Jan **Epiphany** (Reyes Magos)
 19 March **St Joseph's Day** (San José)
 Easter **Good Friday** (Viernes Santo)/
    Easter Monday (Lunes de Pasqua)
  1 May **Labour Day** (Día del Trabajo)
 Early or mid-June **Corpus Christi**
 24 June **St John's Day** (San Juan) –
    the King's name-day
 29 June **St Peter and St Paul** (San
    Pedro y San Pablo)
 25 July **St James's Day** (Santiago)
 15 August **Assumption Day**
    (Asunción)
 12 October **Discovery of America
    Day** (Día de la Hispanidad)
  1 November **All Saints** (Todos los
    Santos)
  8 December **Immaculate
    Conception** (Inmaculada
    Concepción)
 25 December **Christmas Day**
    (Navidad)

The major resorts seem little affected by these holidays, but elsewhere public transport is reduced to a minimum. Most businesses and shops are closed and it can be difficult to find accommodation.

Time differences

The time in the Balearic Islands is the same as in mainland Spain. Spain is one hour ahead of Greenwich Mean Time (GMT). Spanish Summer Time, when the clocks are put forward an hour, is from the last Sunday of March to the last Sunday of September.

Travel insurance

It is advisable to take out fully comprehensive travel insurance, covering theft, loss of baggage, holiday cancellation and health care. If you are planning to drive a rented car, check whether you are covered under your existing insurance policy and remember to bring your driving licence with you.

Money matters

Spain has signed up to the European single currency. From 1 January 2002 Euro bank notes will be introduced, which come in denominations of 5,

10, 20, 50, 100, 200 and 500; coins will come in denominations of 1, 2, 5, 10, 20 and 50 centimes, 1 and 2 Euros. In July 2002, pesatas will be withdrawn. One Euro is equivalent to 166.386ptas. This is a fixed exchange rate.

Credit cards (especially American Express, Visa and MasterCard) can be widely used in Palma and the resorts, but take cash as a back-up if you are going to shops or restaurants off the beaten track. Most UK banks' cash cards can be used to obtain cash in local currency from automatic cash machines (ATMs).

Travellers' cheques Taking travellers' cheques avoids the hazard of carrying large amounts of cash, as they can be quickly refunded in the event of loss or theft. Cheques in local currency are recommended, but cheques in US dollars and pounds sterling are accepted. Many hotels, large restaurants and some shops will accept travellers' cheques. You will need your passport when using them.

Banks The most widespread Spanish banks on the island are Banco de Bilbao, Banco March, Banco de Crédito Balear and Banco de Santander. Sa Nostra and La Caixa are the largest savings banks. All handle travellers' cheques, and most give cash advances on credit cards.

Getting around by car

Car rental There are about 60 car rental companies and their prices vary considerably. Check whether the 12 per cent IVA (VAT) and car insurance are included in the price. It is advisable to take out fully comprehensive insurance and Collision Damage Waiver. Credit cards are generally accepted.

Avis, Passeig Marítim 19, Palma (tel: 971 730720); **Hertz**, Passeig Marítim 13, Palma (tel: 971 732374).

Some smaller car rental firms work with the large hotels to offer special terms for guests. If you intend to collect a car at the airport, or need a child seat, make arrangements before you leave home. Drivers normally have to be over 21 and to have held a licence for at least six months.

Accidents and breakdown If you are renting a car, be sure to check the company's conditions and procedures for breakdown before you set off. In the event of an accident or breakdown on a major road, summon help by dialling 009 (no coins required) at one of the SOS telephones. The police must be informed as soon as possible after an accident. For emergency services see page 186. Carry a spare set of bulbs and a red warning triangle.

Driving tips Drive on the right. Speed limits are 120kph on motorways, 100kph on main roads, 90kph on other roads except in urban areas, where it is 60kph or as signposted. Seat belts are compulsory in front seats and in the rear seats where fitted. Lights must be dipped for oncoming traffic; no hooting in urban areas unless in an emergency. Do not drink and drive as penalties are severe. If you are stopped for any violation, the police usually levy on-the-spot fines.

Mountain roads tend to be narrow and winding, with numerous sharp bends; if you meet a coach, you are obliged to reverse. Be vigilant.

Palma is by-passed by a ringroad known as Via Cintura. An *autopista* (motorway) runs west to Peguera, and another north-east almost as far as Inca. A third extends south past the airport to S'Arenal. The recent opening of the Coll de Sóller tunnel has made the north coast more accessible from Palma.

Documentation If you are bringing your own car to Mallorca, you will need your passport, current driving licence (EU or international), vehicle registration document and adequate insurance documents. A green card and a bail bond are also advised.

Parking Parking restrictions are enforced by a scheme known as ORA (Ordenación Regulación Aparcamiento). In town centres, parking lots marked in blue with Zona Blava (Blue Zone) signs can only be used with a ticket bought in advance from a newsagent or tobacconist. These are valid for 30–90

minutes and have to be marked and displayed before you leave the car. Failure to do this can result in fines, wheel-clamping or your vehicle being towed away. For information on ORA in Palma, see page 71.

In Palma there are car parks on the seafront and beneath Plaça Major.

Petrol Petrol is *gasolina*; unleaded is *sin plomo*. Petrol stations are normally open 6 AM–10 PM, closed Sundays and holidays, and most take credit cards. Addresses of 24-hour petrol stations are printed in the *Majorca Daily Bulletin*.

Getting around by public transport
Bus Services are cheap, regular and efficient. Timetables are posted at *paradas* (bus stops) or available free from tourist offices. Pay as you enter and keep hold of your ticket for the inspector. The island's central bus station is in Plaça d'Espanya in Palma, where an information kiosk and tourist office supply timetables. In the city, buses are run by **EMT** (tel 971 431024 for information).

183

Taxi You can hail the black and white taxis in the street in Palma (see page 71).

Horse-drawn carriage Sundays, when there is less traffic, is the best time to ride around the historic centre of Palma by horse and carriage (see page 71 and panel on page 59).

Train Mallorca has two narrow-gauge railway lines. Trains depart from adjacent stations in Plaça d'Espanya in Palma, one route running north to Sóller (55 minutes) five or six times daily, and the other travelling east to Inca (35 minutes) at approximately hourly intervals from 6 AM to 10 PM. For information, tel: (Palma–Sóller) 971 752051; (Palma–Inca) 971 752245. The Inca line will soon be extended as far as Artà and Sa Pobla.

Tram A historic tram line runs between Sóller and Port de Sóller (see page 109).

Smoking is not permitted on any public transport in Mallorca.

□ The *Majorca Daily Bulletin*, affectionately known as "The Daily Bee", is a venerable example of the outspoken, visitor-pleasing publications found in many holiday destinations, with serious reporting of world news, sport and local issues, spiced with a few sensational and quirky stories. Inexpensively priced, it would surely be churlish not to buy it! □

The media

British and other foreign-language newspapers and magazines can be bought from newsagents in the centre of Palma and also in the larger resorts, many on their day of publication.

The English-language *Majorca Daily Bulletin* includes useful local information and comment, as well as topical stories (see box above). The bi-monthly *Mallorca Tourist Info* is printed in English, German, Dutch and Swedish and contains reports and advertisements about what's on throughout the island. The *Reader* is an English-language weekly newspaper covering all the Balearics, while the glossy weekly lifestyle magazine *Balearic Leisure and Living* is published in Spanish and English.

The local newspapers are *Diario de Mallorca*, *Última Hora*, *Baleares* and *El Día 16 de Baleares*, all published in Castilian. The Barcelona editions of the liberal *El País* and its left-of-centre rival *El Mundo*, national Spanish newspapers with high international reputation, can also be found. Papers printed in Catalan include the nationalist *Avui* and the more liberal *El Diari de Barcelona*.

In the Balearic Islands there are television channels broadcasting in both Catalan and Castilian. Look for the two main national channels, TV1 and TV2, two Catalan channels TV3 and Canal 33, and the private Antena 3 channel. Satellite channels are received in some hotels and bars in the large resorts.

Keeping up with the news over coffee in Cala Figuera

hotel bedroom. Phonecards (Credifone) can be bought from post offices and *Tabacos*. A public telephone (*teléfono*) takes a variety of coins; local calls will be inexpensive although you will need to gather a pile of coins if you are calling abroad. The coins should be lined up in the slot before you dial. Rates are cheaper between 10 PM and 8 AM.

Many bars have a payphone and you can also make calls from the Locutori Public Telefónica booths in resorts – the call is metered and you pay a cashier afterwards. In Palma, a Telefónica is opposite the post office, at Carrer de Constitució 1.

Dialling codes All telephone numbers in Mallorca begin with 971. This is part of the phone number, so you dial all nine digits, even when calling from the island. To make an international call from Mallorca, dial 00, followed by the country code (eg Australia 61, Canada and USA 1, Irish Republic 353, New Zealand 64, UK 44).

185

Useful telephone numbers:
Operator: 002
Directory Enquiries Mallorca: 780303. Spain: 003
International Directory Enquiries: 025
Weather forecast: 094

Language guide
Since the creation of the autonomous government – the Gobern Balear – in 1983, both Mallorquín and Castilian Spanish have become the official languages of Mallorca. Mallorquín is a variant of Catalan, the language of the Spanish mainland from Catalunya to Valencia. All place and street names have reverted to their Mallorquín forms and Mallorquín is increasingly being used in education. Menus, newspapers and most books are still in Castilian. For this reason, all place and street names in this guide book have been given in their Mallorquín (Catalan) forms, whereas culinary dishes appear in the Castilian Spanish versions. For more on language, see pages 60–61.

Post offices
The main post office (*correos*) in Palma is just east of Passeig des Born at Carrer de Constitució 5 (tel: 902-197197). It is open Mon–Fri 8:30–8, Sat 9–2. There are post offices in every town and many villages, generally open Mon–Fri 9–1 and 4–7, and morning only on Sat. All post offices close on public holidays. Letters can be sent to a post office for collection (marked "Lista de Correos") followed by the surname of the addressee – take your passport when collecting.

Stamps (*sellos*) can be bought from tobacconists – look for a brown and yellow sign saying "Tabacos" – or at the post office. Some hotels and souvenir shops also stock stamps. Letter boxes are yellow.

Telephone
The Spanish telephone system is good and, with the availability of Credifone kiosks accepting phonecards, there is little need to pay the cost of international calls from a

Emergencies
Crime and police
Though you may be in holiday mood, commonsense precautions against petty crime are essential. Beware of pickpockets in markets, outside tourist sights and in crowded places. If you are harassed by persistent vendors of carnations, watches or tablecloths, keep moving and never get any money out as it will only make things worse. Bear in mind that thefts can be carried out by your fellow holiday-makers too – apartments are sometimes vulnerable in this respect. Never carry valuables or large amounts of cash, and always use safe deposit boxes in hotels. Leave nothing valuable in your car or unattended on a beach. If you are unhappy about carrying your passport, get a photocopy of it verified and stamped at a police station.

There are three types of police. The urban-based Policia Municipal wear blue and keep the traffic under control. The Policia Nacional wear brown and uphold law and order in towns and cities. The Guardia Civil wear green and control the highways and country areas. Some resorts have their own tourist-friendly police, the Policia Turistica. If you need a police station, ask for *la comisaría*.

Policia Municipal, Carrer de Sant Ferran, Palma (tel: 971 281600)
Policia Nacional, Carrer de Ruiz Alda 8, Palma (tel: 971 225200)
Guardia Civil, Carrer de Manuel Azaña 10, Palma (tel: 971 465112)
Consulates
Ireland: Sant Miquel 68, Palma (tel: 971 719244)

UK: Plaça Major 3A, Palma (tel: 971 712445)

US: Avinguda Jaume III 26, Palma (tel: 971 722660)

Emergency telephone numbers
Police: Policía Nacional (theft and burglary) 091; Policía Municipal (traffic accidents) 092
Fire: 085 (081 for Palma)
Ambulance: 061
Emergency 24-hour doctor/dentist: Urgencias Médicas 971 722222

Lost property
If you lose anything of value inform the police, if only for insurance purposes. The loss of a passport should be reported to your consulate. In theory, objects that are found and handed in make their way to the local Ajuntament (town hall). In Palma this is at Plaça Cort 1 (tel: 971 727744 ext 1165).

Health
Medical care British nationals, like all other EU citizens, are entitled to reciprocal medical care under the Spanish health services on the same basis as Spanish people, provided they have with them a completed E111 form (available from any British post office or DSS). However, not all doctors offer treatment under this scheme,

and you need first to contact the Instituto Nacional de la Seguridad Social (INSS) to obtain treatment vouchers. The central office in Palma is at La Rambla 18 (tel: 971 723100). Nor will an E111 exempt you from charges for prescribed medicines or for dental treatment. Adequate medical insurance is therefore highly recommended for all visitors – and is a pre-travel requirement with many package holidays.

If you need to consult a doctor (*médico*) or dentist (*dentista*), ask at your hotel reception. The state-run hospital in Palma is Clínica Son Dureta (tel: 971 289100). Clinic Balear (tel: 971 466262) offers 24-hour medical services from centres around the island. In most resorts, the medical centres (*Centros Médicos*) have staff who speak English. The Red Cross (tel: 971 202222) operate a number of first-aid stations on beaches.

Precautions Remember to pack a strong suntan cream, anti-diarrhoea pills, any prescription medicines you require and – particularly if you are staying in the Badia d'Alcúdia area – mosquito repellent.

Two of the biggest health hazards for visitors are sunstroke and alcoholic over-indulgence. Pace your exposure to the sun, use high-filter creams, wear a hat, drink alcohol in moderation and make sure you drink lots of bottled water (*agua mineral*).

Vaccinations There are no mandatory vaccination requirements for visitors entering Mallorca, but tetanus and

polio immunisation should be kept up to date. As in many parts of Europe, rabies is considered a threat and any animal bites should be seen by a doctor.

Pharmacies Chemists (*farmacias*) in Mallorca display a green cross outside. Unlike *droguerías*, which sell toiletries and perfume, they are devoted to dispensing medication and can be useful sources of advice and treatment for minor ailments. Most pharmacies open 9 AM–1 PM and 4–7 PM. A notice on the door of each pharmacy or in local newspapers (including the *Majorca Daily Bulletin*) give the address and opening times of the nearest on-duty chemist outside these hours.

Camping and self-catering accommodation

There is only one official campsite in Mallorca, and this gets extremely crowded in summer. The tourist authorities do not actively encourage visitors to bring caravans or motorhomes to Mallorca.

As on the Spanish mainland, you will find camping with a tent is only permitted outside official sites if you have obtained prior permission from the landowner. It is forbidden to sleep on the beaches or in mountain areas.

Camping Platja Blava, Platja del Muro (tel: 971 537863) is a large site which is open all year. It lies near a sandy beach and within walking distance of the S'Albufera nature reserve.

Self-catering accommodation can vary from apartment complexes attached to large hotels in busy resorts to luxury *fincas* (farmhouses) in idyllic rural settings. The Spanish authorities grade their *apartamentos turísticos* (AT) into 4 classes which are symbolised by keys.

medical attention are all positive reasons for visitors with disabilities to consider a visit to Mallorca.

Many new developments have wheelchair access and suitable toilets. Several package holiday operators cater for people with disabilities visiting Mallorca and can provide information on the facilities available at the hotels they use. For further details, contact the main association for people with disabilities – **ASPROM**, Carrer Pascual Ribot 6a, Palma (tel: 971 289052).

Local **transport** facilities for visitors with disabilities (*minusválido*) include: **EMT Bus Special Service** (tel: 971 295700), and there are two taxi companies catering to disabled needs contactable on 608 537194, and 608 839434.

189

Opening times
Shops: generally Mon–Fri from 9 or 10 AM until 1:30, reopening after a siesta around 4:30 or 5 until 8 PM. Hypermarkets and most department stores stay open all day. On Saturday, shops open in the morning only. In high season, shops in the major resorts may stay open later to take advantage of the tourist trade.
Businesses: normally 9–1:30 and 4:30–7.
Banks: Mon–Thu 8:30–4:30, Fri 8:30–2, Sat (main branches only) 8:30–1.
Post offices: generally Mon–Fri 9:30–1 and 4–7, Sat morning only. The main post office in Palma (Carrer de Constitució 5, tel: 971 721095) opens Mon–Fri 8:30 AM to 8:30 PM and Sat 9:30–2.
Museums: opening times vary considerably but most are open at least 10–1 and 4–6 (often longer), and most close for at least one day a week.

Places of worship
Mallorca is Roman Catholic. Visitors are free to attend Mass in local churches, some of which hold services in English. A comprehensive list of places of worship catering for different faiths and nationalities is available from tourist offices. The large hotels can often supply details

More comprehensive details about self-catering accommodation can be found in the annual guide *Hoteles, Campings, Apartamentos Baleares*, available from tourist offices.

Visitors with disabilities
Although facilities for people with disabilities are still insufficient, the island compares favourably with much of Europe. Access to many sights remains a problem, but a benign climate, long level seafronts and the proximity of qualified

CONVERSION CHARTS

FROM	TO	MULTIPLY BY
Inches	Centimetres	2.54
Centimetres	Inches	0.3937
Feet	Metres	0.3048
Metres	Feet	3.2810
Yards	Metres	0.9144
Metres	Yards	1.0940
Miles	Kilometres	1.6090
Kilometres	Miles	0.6214
Acres	Hectares	0.4047
Hectares	Acres	2.4710
Gallons	Litres	4.5460
Litres	Gallons	0.2200
Ounces	Grams	28.35
Grams	Ounces	0.0353
Pounds	Grams	453.6
Grams	Pounds	0.0022
Pounds	Kilograms	0.4536
Kilograms	Pounds	2.205
Tons	Tonnes	1.0160
Tonnes	Tons	0.9842

MEN'S SUITS

UK	36	38	40	42	44	46	48
Rest of Europe	46	48	50	52	54	56	58
US	36	38	40	42	44	46	48

DRESS SIZES

UK	8	10	12	14	16	18
France	36	38	40	42	44	46
Italy	38	40	42	44	46	48
Rest of Europe	34	36	38	40	42	44
US	6	8	10	12	14	16

MEN'S SHIRTS

UK	14	14.5	15	15.5	16	16.5	17
Rest of Europe	36	37	38	39/40	41	42	43
US	14	14.5	15	15.5	16	16.5	17

MEN'S SHOES

UK	7	7.5	8.5	9.5	10.5	11
Rest of Europe	41	42	43	44	45	46
US	8	8.5	9.5	10.5	11.5	12

WOMEN'S SHOES

UK	4.5	5	5.5	6	6.5	7
Rest of Europe	38	38	39	39	40	41
US	6	6.5	7	7.5	8	8.5

of local services. High Mass in Palma Cathedral is at 10.30 AM every Sunday and can be attended by non-Catholics.

Anglican Church, Carrer de Nunyez de Balboa 6, Palma (tel: 971 737279). Services on Sunday and Wednesday.

Catholic Church of San Fernando, Carretera S'Arenal 308, Las Maravillas, between S'Arenal and Can Pastilla (tel: 971 262893). Daily service in German, plus English and French on Sunday.

Toilets

Public toilets are few and far between and, if you do manage to find them, they are unlikely to have paper. You do not have to be a customer to use the services of a bar or restaurant, but it is considered polite to ask first.

❑ Toilets are variously described as *servicios* and *aseos* and heralded by entertaining pictograms: *señores*, *hombres* and *caballeros* are for pipe-smoking dudes while ladies with long, dark curls and dangerous-looking earrings should go for *señoras* and *damas*. ❑

Photography

Mallorca is very photogenic, with early morning and late afternoon as the best times for panoramic shots, avoiding midday haze. Make allowances for bright sunlight and glare and keep film and cameras out of the heat and away from sand and sea.

Photography (or use of a flashlight) is not allowed in some tourist attractions, and it is very unwise to attempt to photograph policemen, military personnel or military installations. Purchasing and developing film is generally more expensive in Spain than in other European countries.

Electricity

220–225 volts. Sockets take round two-pin style plugs, so an adaptor may be required.

Etiquette and local customs

The Mallorcan day Locals usually gather at mid-morning (which can be any time between 10 and 2), for a late breakfast (*churros* – dough-sticks – dunked in coffee or chocolate) or for pre-lunch *aperitivos* and *tapas* (see pages 174–175). Lunch, rarely eaten before 2 or even 3, is followed by a well-earned siesta. Nobody would ever dream of arriving at a restaurant for dinner before 9:30 or 10 PM. If you go to a bar before 10 PM, you'll find yourself alone, and it is not worth even contemplating a nightclub until around 1 AM.

Dress The Spanish are chic dressers, so make sure you are clothed appropriately. The convention is that beachwear and swimming costumes belong on the beach. You may be refused entry to Palma cathedral and other churches, as well as some banks, shops and restaurants, if you are considered to be improperly dressed. Topless sunbathing is common on many beaches, but nudism is confined to Platja es Trenc, Platja Mago and some remote coves.

Tipping

In restaurants a service charge is usually included in the price, but people often leave tips as well. Leave a few coins for bar staff or waiters; give a small tip to porters, maids, coach drivers and guides; consider 10 per cent for taxis.

Children

Nappies, baby food and formula milk can be bought in Mallorca but if you have a preferred brand take a supply. Not all hotels and restaurants have sufficient high chairs, so if you own the screw-on type, take it with you. If you need to hire a car seat for a child, double-check availability when making the booking.

Many hotel and apartment complexes operate an entertainment programme for children during the day and a room-listening service at night. Ask locally about *canguros* (professional baby-sitters) and *guarderías* (crèches).

Maps

Free maps are available at tourist offices. For more sophisticated maps try the bookshop Librería Fondevila, Costa de Sa Pols 18, Palma (tel: 971 725616), which offers a wide selection of general maps and walking maps, as well as an A–Z type pocket street atlas of Palma.

Complaints

Hotels, restaurants and petrol stations have to keep *hojas de reclamación* (complaints forms), should you wish officially to lodge a grievance. Once the form is completed, one copy is retained by you, one by the organisation and a third is sent to the tourism department of the regional government. This consumer protection facility should not be abused by using it for petty complaints.

Laundry

Most hotels offer laundry and dry-cleaning services although it is cheaper to go to a *lavandería* (laundry) or *tintorería* (dry cleaner) in town. They usually charge by weight and need 24 hours.

Tourist offices
Overseas

For information on Mallorca before you leave home, there are Spanish National Tourist Offices in many countries around the world.

Canada: Tourist Office of Spain, 34th Floor, 2 Bloor Street West, Toronto, Ontario M4W 3E2 (tel: 1416/961 3131)

UK: Spanish Tourist Office, 22–3 Manchester Square, London W1U 3PX (tel: 020 7486 8077 and 0891-669 920)

USA: Tourist Office of Spain, 35th Floor, 665 Fifth Avenue, New York, NY 10103 (tel: 212/265 8822)

In Mallorca

The *Oficinas de Turísme* (tourist offices) on the island provide city and island-wide information, help visitors to find accommodation, dispense free maps, bus schedules, ferry timetables, lists of car rental firms, details of recommended restaurants, boat trip information and all sorts of special interest leaflets, including the useful "Artesanía", which lists specialist and craft shops. In summer, tourist offices are generally open Monday to Friday 9 AM–8 PM and Saturday 9 AM–1:30 PM. Small offices may be open shorter hours.

The main tourist offices in **Palma** are:
Plaça de la Reina 2 (tel: 971 712216)
Carrer Santo Domingo 11 (tel: 971 724090)
Plaça d'Espanya (tel: 971 711527)

Tourist information is also available from the following towns and resorts (see individual entries for addresses):
West of Palma: Calvià, Magaluf, Palma Nova, Peguera, Santa Ponça
North-west: Sóller, Port de Sóller, Valldemossa
North-east: Cala Millor, Cala Ratjada, Can Picafort, Port d'Alcúdia, Port de Pollença
South: Cala d'Or, Porto Cristo, Sa Colònia de Sant Jordi

92

COCINA
MALLORQUINA

SOPAS MALLORQUINAS
ARROZ BRUT
LOMO CON COL
CARACOLES
SEPIA MALLORQUINA
FRITO MALLORQUIN
PA AMB OLI
(Jamón o Queso)

Menu Diario
de 13 h. a 16h.

1º Plato
2º Plato
Postre
Vino y Agua

800 Ptas.

HOTELS

Hotels are classified by government inspectors according to a star system that goes from basic 1-star to 5-star luxury. Star ratings do not always mean a great deal, but a room in a 3-star hotel will have at least a shower and a telephone. Prices are regulated by the tourist authorities according to their star rating, with tariffs shown at the reception desk and the rooms. Note that some prices include IVA (7 per cent VAT, rising to 15 per cent in 5-star hotels) in the total charge while others do not. This is specified on the rate card. Unless you are on a package holiday, breakfast is not normally included.

Mallorca has more than 1,000 hotels and 500 apartment blocks, over 250,000 tourist beds in total. Nevertheless, early booking is still essential if you plan to arrive in high season (June–September and the weeks around Easter). Most accommodation in the resorts is booked up by tour operators, and it is through them that you will find the best deals. The cheapest way of all is to chance your luck and book a holiday with "accommodation allocated on arrival". *Hoteles, Campings, Apartamentos Baleares* is published annually and is available from Spanish tourist offices. The listings may be confusing – H is a hotel (one to five stars), HR a *hotel residencia* (no dining room), HS is a *hostal* (1 to 3 stars), HSR a *hostal residencia*. *Hostales* are usually cheaper but often just as comfortable. Reservations can be made through a central booking system: **Central de Reservas de la Federación Empressaria Hotelera de Mallorca (FEHM)** (tel: 971 706007; www.fehm.es. Other hotel details can be found on www.mallorcaonline.com). For luxury accommodation, several of the island's top hotels, with an emphasis on architectural beauty and Mallorcan character, have grouped together under the title **Reis de Mallorca** (for information and reservations, tel: 971 430674; www.reisdemallorca.com).

The recommended accommodation below has been divided into three price categories:
- budget (£) under 13,500ptas/EUR80
- moderate (££) 13,500–27,000ptas/ EUR80–160
- expensive (£££) over 27,000ptas/EUR160

Fincas

For self-catering accommodation far from the crowds, consider staying in a *finca*, or country mansion, combining character (log fires, antiques, orchards) with modern amenities such as swimming-pools. Some are advertised privately through foreign newspapers; others can be booked through the **Asociación de Agroturisme Balear** (tel: 971 721508) who will send you a leaflet showing the main *fincas*.

Monasteries

An intriguing alternative is to stay in a former hermitage (*hosterías*). Even though the monks have now left, the religious orders continue to offer simple hospitality to pilgrims and travellers. Facilities are basic (you may not get a shower) but prices are very low and the experience is one to remember. By nature of the hilltop settings, the views are superb. The following monasteries all have "cells" available:

Ermita de Bonany (£)
Petra tel: 971 561101
Simple whitewashed "cells" with vaulted ceilings, washbasin and a cold shower.

Ermita de Sant Salvador (£)
Felanitx tel: 971 827282
Pilgrims here appreciate the basic accommodation and simple restaurant bar.

Hostal Santuari del Refugio (£)
Castell d'Alaró tel: 971 510480
Accommodation here is spartan (take a sleeping bag), with no shower, but worth tolerating for the astonishing views right across the island.

Monasteri Cura de Randa (£)
Puig de Randa tel: 971 120260
Comfortable, clean accommodation, and a bar serving hot and cold snacks.

Santuari de Lluc (£)
Lluc tel: 971 517025
Staying here is more like staying in a hotel than a hermitage, with en-suite bathrooms for every monk's cell. You do, however, have to make your own bed.

Santuari del Puig de Maria (£)
Pollença tel: 971 184132
The caretaker here will send a mule down for your luggage if you are on foot, and may rustle up an omelette to save you the long trek into town.

Youth Hostels

There are only two youth hostels (*albergues juveniles*) on Mallorca, one near Palma (see page 69, tel: 971 260892) and the other near Alcúdia. They only open in high season and they are frequently block-booked by school groups.

PALMA

Arabella Sheraton Golf Hotel (£££)
Carrer de la Vinagrella, Urbanización Son Vida, 5km north-west of Palma tel: 971 799999
Luxury hotel and health farm, with one of Mallorca's top golf courses and other top-class sporting facilities.

Born (££)
Carrer de Sant Jaume 3 tel: 971 712942
A 2-star hotel in a renovated 16th-century palace at the very heart of town. Excellent value.

Costa Azúl (££)
Passeig Marítim 7 tel: 971 731940
Don't be put off by the ugly exterior. Each room has its own balcony overlooking the Badia de Palma and, although a little noisy, this hotel is central.

Meliá Confort Palas Atenea (£££)
Passeig Marítim 29 tel: 971 281400
A highly commercial hotel on the promenade, combining top conference facilities with fantastic views over the Bay of Palma.

Meliá Victoria (£££)
Avinguda Joan Miró 21 tel: 971 732542; www.solmelia.es
A massive, old-fashioned 4-star hotel, overlooking the bay, yet set far enough back to avoid the noise of traffic rushing along Passeig Marítim.

194

Mirador (££)
Passeig Marítim 10 tel: 971 732046;
www.hotelmirador.es
Reasonably priced, old-fashioned 3-star hotel near
the centre of town, popular with business clientele.
Palacio Ca Sa Galesa (£££)
Carrer Miramar 8 tel: 971 715400;
www.palaciocasagalesa.com
This is a sumptuous 17th-century *palacio*, set in
the heart of medieval Palma near the cathedral.
Palladium (££)
Passeig de Mallorca 40 tel: 971 713945
Centrally located, comfortable and open all year.
A popular option for business travellers.
Pons (£)
Carrer del Vi 8 tel: 971 722658
Clean, simple rooms in a beautiful old house,
arranged around a courtyard in the old part of town.
Ritzi (£)
Carrer dels Apuntadors 6 tel: 971 714610
Cheap, basic rooms just off the Passeig des Born.
Excellent value.
San Lorenzo (£££)
Carrer de Sant Llorenç 14 tel: 971 728200
This small, cosy hotel in a converted 17th- century
mansion, has 12 beds, a picturesque garden and a
swimming-pool. Booking is essential however.
Saratoga (£££)
Passeig de Mallorca 6 tel: 971 727240
Recently refurbished, with a stunning rooftop
swimming-pool. There are balconies in most rooms.
Son Vida (£££)
Urbanización Son Vida, 5km north-west of Palma
tel: 971 790000; www.hsonvida.balears.net
Arguably Mallorca's top hotel, in an 18th-century
mansion, offering many first-class facilities.
Valparaiso Palace (£££)
Calle Francisco Vidal, Bonanova tel: 971 400411
Affords spectacular views over Palma and its bay.
Ideal for those on an expense account.

WEST OF PALMA

Banyalbufar
Barónia (££)
Carrer de General Goded 16, Banyalbufar
tel: 971 618156
Friendly, family-run *hostal*, in a 17th-century baronial
mansion, with its own watchtower and well, over-
looking the unspoilt north-west coast of Mallorca.
Mar y Vent (£££)
Carrer Major 49, Banyalbufar tel: 971 618000
Secluded 3-star hotel with a homely atmosphere,
superb views and an attractive swimming-pool.

Estellencs
Maristel (££)
Carrer Eusebi Pascual 10, Estellencs
tel: 971 618529
A homely hotel in an idyllic, wild valley in central
Mallorca.

Palma Nova
Son Caliu (£££)
Urbanización Son Caliu, Palma Nova
tel: 971 682300; www.baleares.com/
touristguidesoncaliu
It's pure self-indulgence to stay at this luxury hotel-
cum-health-farm.

Peguera
Cala Fornells (£)
Cala Fornells tel: 971 686950
Quaint, white, green-shuttered hotel just north
of Peguera.
Villamil Hesperia (£££)
Avinguda Peguera 66, Peguera tel: 971 686050
An old-fashioned, long-established hotel on the beach
at the centre of town, with magnificent gardens,
restaurants, swimming-pool and sports facilities.

Port d'Andratx
Villa Italia (£££)
Camí de Sant Carlos, Port d'Andratx tel: 971
674011; www.hotelvillaitalia.com
Elegant Florentine-style *belle époque* villa on the
exclusive Es Moll peninsula.

Portals Nous
Bendinat (£££)
Avinguda Bendinat 58, Portals Nous
tel: 971 675725
Sophisticated Mallorcan-style house, situated on the
seashore with generous gardens and sunny terraces.
Punta Negra (£££)
Carretera Andratx, Costa d'en Blanes
tel: 971 680762
Extravagant hotel with adjoining bungalows on a
headland overlooking the glamorous marina of
Porto Portals. Two private beaches.

Santa Ponça
Club Galatzó (£££)
Urbanización Ses Rotes Velles, Peguera
tel: 971 686270; www.galatzo.de
Ideal for sporty holiday-makers with its tennis courts
and golf. In a quiet location outside the main resort.

Ses Illetes
Bon Sol (£££)
Passeig de Illetes 30, Ses Illetes tel: 971
402111
Smart, comfortable, family-run hotel with sub-
tropical gardens, within easy reach of Palma.

THE NORTH-WEST

Binissalem
Scott's (£££)
Plaça de Iglesia, Binissalem tel: 971 870100;
www.scottshotel.com
This former merchant's house is now an exclusive,
English-run bed and breakfast. A jacuzzi and bistro
occupy the stables and servants' quarters.

Campanet
Monnaber Nou (£££)
Predio Monnaber Nou, Campanet tel: 971
877176
A medieval manor house, converted into a luxury
hotel, but maintaining the rural atmosphere.

Deià
Es Molí (£££)
Carretera Valldemossa–Deià, Deià tel: 971
639000
4-star luxury is combined with tradition. The freshly
squeezed orange and lemon juice served at breakfast comes from fruit picked in the gardens.

Hotels and Restaurants

La Residencia (£££)
Carrer Son Moragues, Deià tel: 971 639011;
www.hotel-laresidencia.com
Mallorca's top country hotel with four-poster beds
and teddy bears in every suite. Also excellent
cuisine (see page 200).
Villa Verde (£)
Carrer Ramón Llull 19, Deià tel: 971 639037
An affordable pension whose breakfast terrace is
brimming with flowers and overlooks the village.

Fornalutx
Fornalutx (££)
*Carretera Fornalutx–Sóller, Fornalutx tel: 971
631997*
Once a convent, then a school, and now the only
hostal in Mallorca's "most beautiful village".

Lluc-Alcari
Costa D'Or (££)
Lluc-Alcari tel: 971 639025
This charming traditional hotel is on the craggy north-
ern coast, in the smallest village on the island.

Orient
L'Hermitage (£££)
Carretera Sollerich, Orient tel: 971 613300;
www.hermitage-hotel.com
A former convent, transformed into a country hotel
– a haven of peace in the Tramuntana mountains.
Muntanya (£)
Orient tel: 971 615373
Rural *hostal*, popular with walkers and lovers of
roast pork.

Port de Sóller
Es Port (££)
Carrer Antonio Montis, Port de Sóller
tel: 971 631650; www.hotelsport.com
A 3-star *hostal* overlooking the port, based on a
15th-century mansion with a private chapel in the
courtyard. Rooms in the square tower have four-
poster beds.
Marbell (£)
Port de Sóller tel: 971 631300
Welcoming hotel, overlooking the harbour and a
lovely, sandy beach.

Sa Calobra
La Calobra (£)
Playa de la Calobra, Sa Calobra tel: 971 517016
Stay in this comfortable 2-star hotel to see the
Torrent de Pareis (see page 107) at its best, when
all the day trippers have left.

Santa Maria del Camí
Read's (£££)
Ca'n Moragues, Santa Maria del Camí
tel: 971 140261; www.readshotel.com
This beautiful *finca*, decorated in bold Mediterranean
colours, is set in lush gardens. .

Sóller
El Guia (£)
Carrer Castaner 2, Sóller tel: 971 630227
Traditional hotel with a highly reputed restaurant
near the old railway station. A good base for
exploring the region.

Finca Ca N'ai (£££)
Camí Son Sales, Sóller tel: 971 632494;
www.canai.com
Luxuriously converted manor house in a shady
orange grove in a silent valley just outside the town.

Valldemossa
Ca'n Mário (£)
*Carrer de Uetam 8, Valldemossa tel: 971
612122*
Plain, simple 1-star *hostal* with 2-star comfort.
Only 16 beds so book in advance. There is a
popular restaurant (see page 201).
Vistamar (£££)
Carretera Valldemossa–Banyalbufar
tel: 971 612300; www.vistamarhotel.es
This luxurious country house hotel has every imag-
inable home comfort and wonderful views.

THE NORTH-EAST

Cala Millor
Royal Mediterráneo (£££)
Sa Coma tel: 971 810105
A massive holiday complex set right on the beach.

Cala Ratjada
Dos Playas (££)
Carrer Mistral 2, Cala Ratjada tel: 971 563802
Open all year and conveniently situated near the
beaches of Cala Guya and Son Moll.
Marina (£)
Carrer Leonor Servera 94, Cala Ratjada
tel: 971 563491
Clean, cheap and quiet, this hotel is near Casa
March and the harbour.
Serrano Palace (£££)
Playa de Son Moll, Cala Ratjada tel: 971 563350
The luxurious interior justifies the 5-star rating,
despite the uncompromisingly modern exterior.
Ses Rotjes (£££)
Carrer Rafael Blanes 21, Cala Ratjada
tel: 971 563108; www.sesrotjes.com
A small, charming hotel built in Mallorcan style.
The owner is chef of the restaurant (see page 202).

Cala Sant Vicenç
Don Pedro (££)
Cala San Vicenç, Sant Vicenç tel: 971 530050
Although this vast modern hotel is a bit of an eye-
sore, it is well placed directly on the beach.
Molíns (£££)
Cala Molíns, Sant Vicenç tel: 971 530200
The most exclusive hotel in this small, seaside
resort, set back from the beach.

Can Picafort
Can Picafort (£)
Via Alemania/Avinguda Cervantes, Can Picafort
tel: 971 850109
A popular family choice, set right on the beach.

Cap de Formentor
Hotel Formentor (£££)
Platja de Formentor, Cap de Formentor
tel: 971 899100
Mallorca's first luxury hotel, opened in 1926. It
possesses one of Mallorca's finest beaches.

Pollença

Juma (££)
Plaça Major 9, Pollença tel: 971 535002
The seven rooms in this traditional hotel have
Mallorca antiques and overlook the main square.

Port d'Alcúdia

Bahía de Alcúdia (££)
*Avinguda de la Playa, Port d'Alcúdia
tel: 971 545800*
This popular family hotel is conveniently located
near Mallorca's longest sandy beach.

Parc Natural (£££)
*Carretera Alcúdia–Artà, Port d'Alcúdia
tel: 971 892017*
A palatial, modern 5-star hotel, ideal for naturalists,
opposite the entrance to Parc Natural de S'Albufera.

Playa de Muro (£££)
*Carretera Alcúdia–Artà, Port d'Alcúdia
tel: 971 890443; www.iberostar.es*
This beach-side hotel has a pool, marble interior
and lush gardens. It is popular with package tours.

Port de Pollença

Carotti (£)
Carrer La Gola, Port de Pollença tel: 971 865096
Friendly French-owned family hotel with swimming-
pool, bar, buffet breakfast. Good value.

Miramar (££)
*Passeig Anglada Camarasa 39, Port de
Pollença tel: 971 867211;
www.pollensanet.com/miramar*
Old-style, 3-star seaside hotel with marvellous sea
and mountain vistas.

Romantic (£)
*Carretera Port de Pollença–Alcúdia, Port de
Pollença tel: 971 865153*
Aptly named hotel with romantic views over the bay
from every seafront room.

Sis Pins (££)
*Avinguda Anglada Camarasa 77, Port de
Pollença tel: 971 867050*
Popular seafront hotel with excellent facilities for
guests with disabilities.

Sa Colònia de Sant Pere

Rocamar (£)
*Carrer Les Margueritas 14 Sa Colònia de Sant
Pere tel: 971 589347*
The only *hostal* in town, a whitewashed house with
blue shutters, a large terrace and shady garden.
Each room has its own balcony and shower.

THE SOUTH

Cala d'Or

Cala d'Or (£££)
Avinguda de Bélgica, Cala d'Or tel: 971 657252
The sea, sandy beaches and pine-fringed bay are
all part of the charm of the top hotel in the resort.

Oasis d'Or (££)
Carrer Es Revells 4, Cala d'Or tel: 971 657427
Cool, quiet *hostal* away from the main hubbub of the
resort but just 50m from the beach at Cala Gran.

Tucán (£££)
Carrer Bulevar, Cala d'Or tel: 971 657200
Large, purpose-built 4-star hotel, well placed for
shopping, restaurants and nightspots.

Cala Figuera

Cala Figuera (££)
*Carrer de Sant Pedro 28, Cala Figuera
tel: 971 645251*
Smart 2-star hotel, affording breathtaking views
over the cove from its upper floors.

Ventura (£)
*Carrer Bennaregi 17, Cala Figuera tel: 971
645102*
Family-run *hostal* at the heart of Cala Figuera with
an attractive swimming-pool and good cuisine.

Villa Serena (£)
Carrer Virgen del Carmen 37 tel: 971 645303
Clean and simple, this hotel overlooks the bay.

Felanitx

Villa Hermosa (£££)
*Carretera Felanitx–Porto Colom tel: 971
824960*
Magnificent country mansion with 10 beautifully
furnished rooms and a distinguished restaurant
(see page 203).

Llucmajor

Delta (£££)
*Carretera Cabo Blanco, Llucmajor tel: 971
741000*
This is the top hotel in Mallorca's fourth largest town.

197

Mondragó

Playa Mondragó (£)
Cala Mondragó tel: 971 657752
Comfortable flower-filled *hostal* with a relaxed,
family atmosphere, and canaries on the veranda.

Porto Petro

Nereida (£)
*Carrer Patrons Martina 34, Porto Petro
tel: 971 657223*
Cheap, cheerful *hostal*, with a large swimming-
pool, two bars and a spacious garden. Children
very welcome.

Randa

Es Reco de Randa (£££)
Carrer Fuente 13, Randa tel: 971 660997
Exclusive 3-star hotel serving top-quality (albeit
pricey) Mallorcan cuisine on its attractive
dining terrace.

Sa Colònia de Sant Jordi

Don Leon (£££)
*Carrer Sol, Sa Colònia de Sant Jordi
tel: 971 655561*
Traditional Mediterranean hospitality combined
with modern comfort. Good sporting and
children's facilities.

Santanyí

Cala Santanyí (££)
Cala Santanyí tel: 971 645425
Popular family hotel right on the edge of this
picturesque creek.

Pinos Playa (££)
*Costa d'en Nofre, Cala Santanyí tel: 971
165000; www.pinosplaya.com*
Modern hotel overhanging a cove of turquoise
water and white sand.

RESTAURANTS

The following recommended restaurants have been divided into three price categories.

£ = under 2,500ptas/EUR15

££ = 2,500–4,500ptas/EUR15–27

£££ = over 4,500ptas/EUR27

PALMA

Arroceria Sa Cranca (££)
Passeig Marítim 13 tel: 971 737447
The house specialities here are substantial rice dishes, including "convent rice" (vegetarian) and seven different paellas.

Asador Tierra Aranda (££)
Carrer de la Concepció 4 tel: 971 714256
Castilian delicatessen and meat dishes on the first floor of an old mansion. Try suckling pig, lamb or goat, roasted in a wood-burning oven. Dinner only.

Baisakhi (££)
Passeig Marítim 8 tel: 971 736806
Try this upmarket Indian restaurant with plenty of atmosphere for a change. Even the pavement outside is sprinkled with flower petals.

Bilbaína (££)
Carrer de Bonaire 19 tel: 971 713510
Delicious Basque cuisine.

Bon Lloc (£)
Carrer Sant Feliu 7 tel: 971 718617
One of Mallorca's few vegetarian restaurants. Try the creative and filling 4-course lunchtime menu.

Bosch (£)
Plaça Rei Joan Carles I tel: 971 721131
This café-bar is still the meeting place in the centre of town. Delicious *tapas* and filled rolls.

Caballito de Mar (£££)
Passeig Sagrera 5 tel: 971 721074
Palma's best-known seafront fish restaurant with an extensive terrace beside La Llotja. Monkfish dishes are a real delicacy.

Café dels Artes (£)
Carrer de S'Aigo no telephone
Mingle with Palma's artists and student population over a light snack.

Cala Nova Club de Vela (£)
Carrer Joan Miró tel: 971 402512
Enjoy grilled meat and imaginative desserts, on the sunny terrace of this sailing school.

Ca'n Carlos (£)
Carrer de S'Aigo 5 tel: 971 713869
One of few restaurants in Palma serving authentic *cuina mallorquina*. Enjoy *fava pelada* (a bean stew containing various kinds of sausages).

Ca'n Eduardo (££)
Industria Pesquera 4 tel: 971 721182
One of the leading seafood establishments in the fishing port. Their fish stew is delectable.

Ca'n Joan de S'Aigo (£)
Carrer de Sant Sanç 10 tel: 971 710759
Old-fashioned, classy *chocolatería* with tiled floor and marble tabletops. Surely the best almond ice-cream you've ever tasted.

Cappuccino (£)
Passeig Marítim 1 tel: 971 282162
The coolest café in town, great for people-watching. The salads are tasty too.

Casa Gallega (££)
Carrer Pueyo 6 tel: 971 714377
No-frills restaurant serving Galician cuisine. The vast all-you-can-eat seafood buffet is a must.

Celler Sa Premsa (££)
Plaça Bisbe Berenguer de Palou 8 tel: 971 723529
Typical Mallorcan *celler*, where wine comes out of a tap in the wall. Just the place to try classic peasant dishes like *tumbet* or *frit mallorquí*.

Dalt Murada (££)
Carrer Sant Roc 1/Carrer Almudaina 6a tel: 971 714464
A real find, hidden in a deserted back street off the tourist track, but popular with the locals. There are orange and lemon trees in the sunny courtyard.

Diplomatic (££)
Palau Reial 5 tel: 971 726482
Exceptional "black paella" and interesting lunchtime menu. Popular among politicians and businessmen.

El Patio (££)
Carrer dels Apuntadors 3 tel: 971 711768
The simple pasta dishes at this relaxed patio restaurant make a pleasant change from all the Mallorcan favourites.

El Pato (£££)
Son Vida Golf Club, Urbanización Son Vida tel: 971 791500
Duck and venison specialities are served, overlooking the golf course.

El Pilón (££)
Carrer de San Cayetano 12 tel: 971 717590
Well-known restaurant and *tapas* bar, with a more refined dining-room upstairs. Arrive early.

Es Parlament (££)
Carrer de Conquistador 11 tel: 971 726026
Quiet, dignified restaurant in the Balearic Parliament buildings, famed for its squid (cooked in its own ink) and *paella ciega* (blind paella – no bones).

Fora Vila (£££)
Hotel Arabella, Son Vida, 5km north-west of Palma: tel: 971 799999
Haute cuisine in a 5-star hotel with gardens, golf and impeccable service.

Fundació La Caixa (££)
Plaça Weyler 3 tel: 971 728077
The former Gran Hotel houses this elegant bar. Here you can enjoy tasty salads and bar snacks.

Giovanni's (£)
Carrer San Juan tel: 971 722879
One of Palma's best Italian restaurants. Always crowded and lively.

Gran Dragon (£££)
Ruiz de Alda tel: 971 280200
The only Chinese restaurant in Spain to be awarded 3 Forks in the Michelin Guide.

Koldo Royo (£££)
Passeig Marítim 3 tel: 971 732435
Owner-chef Koldo Royo uses only the freshest ingredients in his sublime Mediterranean menus.

La Bodeguilla (££)
Carrer de Sant Jaume tel: 971 718274
Classic Castilian dishes in an atmospheric restaurant, decorated with hanging wine bottles.

La Bodeguita del Medio (££)
Carrer de Vallseca 18 tel: 971 717832
An imitation of its Havana namesake with appropriate graffiti, Cuban food and salsa music. Go late.

La Bóveda (£)
Carrer de Botería 3 tel: 971 714863
One of Palma's liveliest restaurants. Tuck into the *tapas* dishes while waiting for a table.

La Casbah (££)
Carrer Pursiana 14 tel: 971 453840
Mainly North African cuisine, including unusual lamb dishes and excellent couscous.

La Casita (££)
Avinguda Joan Miró tel: 971 737557
Tiny but top quality. Try the liver and onions or the potato pancakes. Booking recommended.

La Lubina (££)
Muelle Viejo tel: 971 723350
Elegant dining right on the quayside. Specialities include *caldereta de langosta* (lobster stew).

Le Bistrot (££)
Teodoro Llorente 4 tel: 971 287175
Top-notch steak tartare and tarte tatin, in a Parisian-style bistro.

Mediterráneo 1930 (£££)
Passeig Marítim 33 tel: 971 458877
Expensive international cuisine on the seafront.

Na Bauçana (£)
Carrer de Santa Bàrbara 4 tel: 971 721886
Imaginative menu changes daily. Open only for lunch.

Orient Express (££)
Carrer Marina 6 tel: 971 711183
Journey through a menu of *tapas* and crêpes from within a carriage of the great Orient Express.

Payes (££)
Carrer Felip Bauza 2 tel: 971 726036
Popular for business lunches. Lovingly prepared traditional dishes – try the stuffed aubergines.

Porto Pi (£££)
Avinguda Joan Miró 174 tel: 971 400087
Stylish Mediterranean cuisine in a faded stately mansion, the holder of one of Mallorca's rare Michelin stars. The duck in a quince and sage sauce is delicious.

Reial Club Nautic (££)
Muelle San Pedro 1 tel: 971 726848
Fish and ships in the Royal Yacht Club.

Sa Taverna (£)
Carrer Pou 12 tel: 971 454826
Here is the place to try the delicious local delicacy, *pa amb oli* (see page 175).

Sa Volta (£)
Carrer dels Apuntadors 5 no telephone
An intimate restaurant, where hams hang from the ceiling.

Shogun (££)
Carrer Camilo José Cela 14 tel: 971 735748
Generous portions of first-rate Japanese food. Superb sushi. Very busy. Best to book.

S'Olivera (££)
Carrer Morey 5 tel: 971 712935
This popular Mediterranean restaurant is in the ancient Arab quarter. The *tapas* are especially good.

WEST OF PALMA

Andratx
El Patio (£££)
Carretera Andratx–Port d'Andratx tel: 971 672013
Nouvelle cuisine in a pretty shaded courtyard, surrounding an ancient wine-press.

Banyalbufar
Mar y Vent (££)
Carrer de Major 49, Banyalbufar tel: 971 618000
A family-run restaurant in a tranquil coastal village. There are spectacular sea views from the terrace.

Calvià
Méson Ca'n Torrat (££)
Carrer Major, Calvià tel: 971 670682
Small rustic restaurant-bar opposite the church serving wholesome country fare.

Gènova
Ca'n Pedro (££)
Carrer de Rector Vives 14, Gènova tel: 971 702162
Typical Mallorcan dishes in a favourite Sunday-lunch venue for local families. Snails are a speciality.

Samantha's (£££)
Carrer Francisco Vidal Sureda 115, Bonanova tel: 971 700000
Imaginative international menu and impeccable service in a lovely 18th-century house. Just the place for a night of sophistication and extravagance.

Ses Coves (£)
Carrer de Barranc 45, Gènova tel: 971 402387
Small restaurant by the caves serving hearty Catalan dishes.

Magaluf
Dauphine (£)
Playas de Magaluf tel: 971 680786
Friendly beach restaurant serving *tortilla*, sardines and other light meals.

Los Caracoles (££)
Galerias Toboso, Torrenova tel: 971 680267
Magaluf's best restaurant, famed for its fish casseroles and steak dishes on a wooden platter.

Palma Nova
Ciro's (££)
Passeig del Mar 3, Palma Nova tel: 971 681052
The Mallorcan and Italian cuisine here makes a refreshing change from burgers and chips.

Tabú (££)
Passeig del Mar 28, Palma Nova (no telephone)
Excellent-value Mallorcan cuisine in this lively restaurant that is extremely popular with locals.

Peguera
La Gran Tortuga (££)
Aldea Cala Fornells 1 tel: 971 686023
Delicious seafood specialities served on the terrace overlooking picturesque Cala Fornells. There's even a swimming-pool.

Port d'Andratx
Bar Bellavista (£)
Avinguda Mateo Bosch 31, Port d'Andratx tel: 971 672214
The pizzas and filled rolls here make a pleasant snack lunch beside the old fishing harbour.

Barlovento (£££)
Camí Vell des Far 1 tel: 971 671049
Customers enjoy fantastic views of the bay in this top-notch fish restaurant. The menu varies depending on the daily catch.

Hotels and Restaurants

La Consigna (£)
Avinguda Mateo Bosch 26, Port d'Andratx
tel: 971 671604
This comfortable café-cum-pâtisserie serves delicious filled croissants, meat pies and *gato almendra* (almond cake) to eat in or take away.

Miramar (£££)
Avinguda Mateo Bosch 22, Port d'Andratx
tel: 971 671617
Classic, expensive Mediterranean restaurant by the harbour. Even the *menu del dia* is pricey.

Portals Nous
Binnacle (£££)
Porto Portals, Portals Nous tel: 971 676977
Fashionable dining at the water's edge, where fresh fish is served by nautically uniformed waiters.

Diablito (££)
Porto Portals, Portals Nous tel: 971 676503
Popular pizzeria on the waterfront in the marina.Try the "Popeye" pizza or "The Sailor's Favourite".

Flanigan (££)
Porto Portals, Portals Nous tel: 971 676117
Ideal for a hearty breakfast, snack lunch or a more substantial evening meal. Try "just anything" (mixed *hors d'oeuvres*) and the house speciality, thin apple tart. Takeaway service also available.

Tristan (£££)
Porto Portals, Portals Nous tel: 971 675547
Prized for its Michelin star and renowned for its *nouvelle cuisine*, dining here is considered the height of decadence. **Bistro del Tristan** next door is marginally more affordable. Booking essential.

Wellies (££)
Porto Portals, Portals Nous tel: 971 676444
A Mallorcan institution serving international cuisine and delicious desserts, including English apple crumble and American-style cheesecake.

Puigpunyent
Sa Tafona (£££)
Carrer Galilea 24 tel: 971 614180
On offer is a sophisticated new Balearic cuisine. This restaurant is housed in an old olive press, attached to a country-house hotel.

The Rose (££)
Puigpunyent tel: 971 614180
One of Mallorca's oldest British-run restaurants, hiding in a mountain village. You will need to book in advance for Sunday lunch.

Sant Telm
Flexax (£)
Avinguda Rei Jaume I, Sant Telm (no telephone)
No-frills seafront fish restaurant overlooking a turquoise bay flecked with tiny white fishing boats. Try their grilled sardines and salad for lunch.

Na Carogala (££)
Avinguda Rei Jaume I, Sant Telm (no telephone)
Where better to enjoy a paella and a jug of *sangria* than on this breezy terrace overlooking the island of Sa Dragonera!

Santa Ponça
Sa Masia (££)
Carretera Santa Ponça–Andratx tel: 971 694217
Elegant dining in a sun-bleached old farmhouse.

THE NORTH-WEST

Alfàbia
Ses Porxeres (££)
Carretera de Sóller tel: 971 613762
A high-ceilinged barn beside the gardens of Alfàbia, renowned for its Catalan game dishes. Try the wild boar with lobster or lamb chops cooked on heated stones at your table. Booking essential.

Binissalem
El Suizo (££)
Carrer des Pou Bo 20, Binissalem (no telephone)
Swiss-owned restaurant serving international cuisine including fondues.

Castell d'Alaró
Es Ponet (££)
Castell d'Alaró tel: 971 182126
Popular with walkers, this isolated barn with a huge open fire offers speciality lamb roasted in a wood-burning clay oven (see page100).

Deià
Ca'n Quet (££)
Ctra Valldemossa-Deià tel: 971 639196
Good regional cooking is available here. Customers dine in an old farmhouse, with a cool shady terrace.

El Olivo (£££)
Carrer Son Moragues, Deià tel: 971 639011
One of Mallorca's best restaurants. Pricey *nouvelle cuisine* is served in a former oil-mill, attached to Hotel La Residencia (see page 196).

Sa Caleta (£)
Cala de Deià tel: 971 639137
Grilled swordfish, prawns and squid are the specialities in this ramshackle beach bar-restaurant, perched precariously on the rocks above the cove.

Fornalutx
Bellavista (£)
Carrer San Bartolomé 30, Fornalutx
tel: 971 631590
Enjoy the citrus groves and distant mountain peaks from the pretty terrace. Lunchtime only.

Peramunt (££)
Carrer Bellavista 1, Fornalutx tel: 971 631952
This brasserie-style restaurant serves excellent steak and lamb. The terrace overlooks the valley.

Inca
Ca'n Amer (££)
Carrer Pau 39, Inca tel: 971 501261
This busy *celler* restaurant was chosen to represent Balearic cuisine at the Expo 92 fair in Seville.

Ca'n Ripoli (££)
Carrer Armengol 4, Inca tel: 971 500024
Mallorcan dishes in a cavernous *celler*, with wine drawn straight from the huge vats lining the walls.

Sa Travessa (££)
Carrer Murte 6, Inca tel: 971 500049
Another picturesque *celler* restaurant near the market, serving typical Mallorcan fare.

Lluc
Es Guix (££)
Carretera Lluc–Escorca tel: 971 517092
Tiny restaurant offering traditional meat dishes.

Escorca (£)
Carretera Lluc–Sóller, Escorca tel: 971 517095
The cool terrace is pleasant for an *aperitivo*, before tucking into hearty cooking, in this jolly restaurant.

Sa Fonda (£)
Monestir de Lluc, Lluc tel: 971 517022
Inside the monastery, the monks' former refectory serves a simple fare of tasty *tortilla* (omelettes) and meat dishes.

Orient
L'Hermitage (£££)
Carretera Sollerich, Orient tel: 971 180303
Luxury hotel restaurant in a converted convent. Ideal for country lovers (see page 196).

Mandela (££)
Orient tel: 971 615285
Innovative French-Indian restaurant at the top of a steep hill beside the church, but well worth the climb.

Muntanya (££)
Orient tel: 971 615373
At the hub of the village, sit on the terrace and enjoy roast meat followed by locally grown strawberries.

Orient (££)
Orient tel: 971 510248
Mallorcan dishes at reasonable prices. Particularly crowded at weekends. Try peasant dishes such as *lomo con col* (pork with cabbage) and suckling pig.

Port de Sóller
Celler d'es Port (£)
Carrer d'Antoni Montis, Port de Sóller (no telephone)
A favourite with locals for its traditional Mallorcan dishes.

Es Canyis (££)
Passeig Platja, Port de Sóller tel: 971 631406
Casual seafront restaurant with Mallorcan and French food.

Es Faro (££)
Cap Gros de Moleta, Port de Sóller tel: 971 633752
The "lighthouse" restaurant offers fish dishes, with some of the finest views of the north coast.

Sa Llotja des Peix (£££)
Muelle Pesquero, Port de Sóller tel: 971 632954
Exotic fish dishes in a neat restaurant-bar overlooking the attractive fishing harbour.

Sa Calobra
Es Vergeret (£££)
Cala Tuente tel: 971 517105
Beautiful patio terrace shaded by pine trees, high above the picturesque bay. A real find.

Santa Maria del Camí
Ca'n Moragues (£££)
Ctra Santa Maria-Alaró tel: 971 140262
This beautiful country house restaurant is attached to Read's Hotel (see page 196). Traditional dishes are served with an inventive twist.

Sóller
El Guia (££)
Carrer Castaner 2, Sóller tel: 971 630227
Old-fashioned restaurant serving staple country dishes such as *tumbet* and *escaldums* (see pages 90–91).The *menu del día* is always excellent value.

Sa Cova d'en Jordi (££)
Plaça Constitució, Sóller tel: 971 633222
Neat, friendly restaurant on the main square, serving international cuisine.

Son Marroig
Ca'n Costa (££)
Carretera Valldemossa–Deià tel: 971 612263
Fine Mallorcan cooking in a sun-ripened old oil-mill.

Mirador de Na Foradada (£)
Son Marroig tel: 971 639026
Panoramic restaurant perched on the cliffs beside Son Marroig. Phone in advance to order the paella.

Valldemossa
Ca'n Mario (££)
Carrer de Uetam 8, Valldemossa tel: 971 612122
Simple Mallorcan menu and happy, beaming service on the first floor of an old-style *hostal* (see page 196).

Ca'n Pedro (££)
Carrer de Arxiduc Luis Salvador 6, Valldemossa tel: 971 612170
This is a quiet, friendly restaurant, after all the tourist coaches have left.

Es Port (££)
Port de Valldemossa tel: 971 616194
The freshest of fish or a copious paella is your reward after a helter-skelter drive down to this isolated fishermen's village.

Merienda (£)
Carrer Blanquera, Valldemossa (no telephone)
Café full of village atmosphere. Be sure to try their speciality, *coca de patates* (light, fluffy buns dusted in icing sugar) with *xocolate* (hot chocolate).

Sa Cartoixa (££)
Plaça Ramòn Llull 5 (tel: 971 616059)
Tumbet, rabbit stew and paella are the specialities in this bustling village café-restaurant.

THE NORTH-EAST

Port d'Alcúdia
Khum Phanit's (££)
Avinguda de la Platja 7, Port d'Alcúdia tel: 971 548141
This is a real surprise – authentic Thai cooking at very good value.

Artà
Na Creu (££)
Calle 31 de Marzo, Artà tel: 971 836350
Found on a side road heading towards Alcúdia. Sample the specials – lamb with vegetables, fish with aubergine or meat-filled cuttlefish.

Cala Millor
Sa Gruta Nova (££)
Carretera Porto Cristo–Cala Millor tel: 971 822623
Barbecue restaurant with a huge terrace garden and open-air rustic bar. Relish the Mallorcan-style squid, monkfish or king prawns as the sun goes down.

S'Era de Pula (£££)
Carretera Son Servera–Capdepera tel: 971 567940
High-class, farmhouse-style dining with Mallorcan and fish specialities.

201

Hotels and Restaurants

Cala Ratjada
El Cactus (£)
Carrer Leona Servera 83, Cala Ratjada
tel: 971 564609
Mexican restaurant near the harbour that
specialises in *tortillas* and *tacos* stuffed with
freshly caught local fish at reasonable prices.
Ses Rotjes (£££)
Carrer Rafael Blanes 21, Cala Ratjada
tel: 971 563108
One of only three restaurants outside Palma with a
Michelin star. Dinner is eaten in the courtyard.

Capdepera
Binicanella (££)
*Carretera Son Servera–Capdepera tel: 971
567270*
Island cuisine in a converted monastery, popular with
locals. The Mallorcan-style pork (baked with red
peppers, pine kernels and sultanas) is delectable.
Ca's Padri (£££)
Carrer Poniente 5, Capdepera tel: 971 565667
In this typical *bodega* grill restaurant you can enjoy
the char-grilled specialities. There is a long, shady
garden with tables beneath the vines.
La Fragua (££)
Carrer Es Pla den Cosset 3, Capdepera
tel: 971 565050
Celler restaurant embellished with tiles, terracotta
and dried flowers. Traditional Spanish cuisine.
Los Pablos (££)
Carrer de la Pau, Capdepera tel: 971 564566
Pretty little restaurant with cool stone, copper pans,
fresh flowers and sophisticated Mallorquín cooking.
Porxada de Sa Torre (££)
Carretera de Canyamel-Artà, Canyamel
tel: 971 563044
This spacious rancho-style bar serves some of the
best Mallorquín meat dishes in the region. Heaven
for dedicated carnivores.

Costitx
Ca'n Font (£)
Plaça Rafael Horrach, Costitx (no telephone)
Cool, breezy restaurant, ideal for a light, tasty lunch,
with sweeping views to the Tramuntana mountains.

Petra
Es Brollador (£)
Ramón Llull, Petra (no telephone)
Cheerful locals' bar, serving excellent *pa amb oli* and
other tasty snacks in a fountain-splashed square.
Es Celler (££)
Carrer de l'Hospital, Petra tel: 971 561056
Large, atmospheric *celler* restaurant serving
hearty regional fare such as pigeon with cabbage,
roast suckling pig, *arroz brut* (see page 91) and
grilled rabbit.

Pollença
Ca'n Pacienci (£££)
Carretera Pollença–Port de Pollença
tel: 971 530787
This pretty *finca* is smothered in bougainvillaea. A
very popular restaurant, especially with local expats.
Clivia (££)
Avinguda Pollentia, Pollença tel: 971 533635
Locals consider this the top eatery in town.

La Font del Gall (££)
Carrer Montesion 4, Plaça Almoina, Pollença
tel: 971 530396
Small and chintzy, this French-run restaurant with
good food, good wine and proper puds.

Port de Pollença
Ca'n Pep (£)
Carrer Virgen del Carmen, Port de Pollença
tel: 971 530010
A good-value daily *menu de la casa*. On the à la
carte menu, the *caragols a la Mallorquína* (snail stew
with bacon, mint and garlic) and the almond ice-
cream smothered in fig sauce are all exceptional.
La Fortalesa (££)
Carretera Port de Pollença–Formentor
tel: 971 531059
This popular bar, restaurant and cafeteria has a
wide selection of *tapas* and local dishes.
La Lonja del Pescado (£££)
Port de Pollença tel: 971 866504
A top-quality seafood restaurant right on the wharf.
The Ivy Garden (££)
*Calle Llevant 64, Port de Pollença tel: 971
866271*
Savour the delicious deep-fried goat's cheese with
red pepper and cumin compote, and the home-made
cod and smoked haddock fishcakes in a chive sauce.

Sa Colònia de Sant Pere
Blau Mari (£££)
Passeig del Mar, Sa Colònia de Sant Pere
tel: 971 589407
An exclusive seafood restaurant on the fringe of a
tiny golden beach. Sample their fish lasagne, lobster stew or mixed grilled fish.

Sineu
Ca'n Font (££)
Plaça Espanya 18, Sineu tel: 971 520313
One of the island's best *celler* restaurants. By
10am on market day it is full of farmers tucking
into the traditional village dish, *frit de porcella*
(potatoes, vegetables, offal and pork).
Es Crup (££)
Carrer Major 18, Sineu tel: 971 520187
Cosy, welcoming *celler* in the main street, offering
roast lamb, *frit mallorquí*, *tumbet* and other
Mallorquín fare in steaming hot earthenware dishes.

THE SOUTH

Algaida
Ca'l Dimoni (££)
*Carretera Palma–Manacor, Algaida tel: 971
665035*
Specialists in meats and sausages which hang from
the ceiling waiting to be roasted over an open fire.
Es 4 Vents (££)
*Carretera Palma–Manacor, Algaida tel: 971
665173*
Classic Mallorcan cuisines served in a venue
popular with the residents of Palma.
Hostal d'Algaida (££)
*Carretera Palma–Manacor, Algaida tel: 971
665109*
Traditional-style restaurant in an ancient *finca*.
Also a shop selling pies, bread and preserves.

Cala d'Or
Bistro (££)
Carrer Andres Roig 17 tel: 971 658110
Charcoal grills and international menu for that special night out.
Cala Llonga (££)
Avinguda Cala Llonga, Cala d'Or tel: 971 658036
Smart terrace restaurant beside the marina, specialising in lobster and grilled seafood dishes.
Ca'n Trompé (£)
Avinguda de Bélgica 12, Cala d'Or tel: 971 657341
Classic Mallorcan restaurant, always full and serving an excellent-value 3-course menu with wine. Alternatively, try the *zarzuela* (seafood casserole) .

Cala Figuera
Casa de la Pasta (£)
Carrer de Bernaregi 20, Cala Figuera (no telephone)
If you are tired of fish restaurants, you won't be able to resist the pasta here.
La Marina (£)
Carrer Virgen del Carmen 64, Cala Figuera tel: 971 645052
One of several tempting fish restaurants serving the day's catch here on the waterfront. For dessert, try almond tart, piled high with nuts and cream.

Can Pastilla
El Rancho Picadero (££)
Carrer de Flamenco 1, Can Pastilla tel: 971 261002
Roast meats are barbequed on an attractive terrace for *alfresco* dining.

Es Llombards
La Pergola (££)
Carrer Major 13, Es Llombards tel: 971 163359
In this candlelit restaurant specials include venison in a nut coat and quail wrapped in cabbage leaves.

Felanitx
Vista Hermosa (£££)
Carretera Felanitx–Porto Colom tel: 971 824960
Galician cuisine, served on a wide stone terrace, with views of mountains, the valley and the sea.

Platja Es Trenc
Ca'n Pep Rapita (££)
Carrer Miramar 16, Sa Rapita tel: 971 640102
Classic Spanish restaurant serving generous portions of fish and seafood near Platja Es Trenc.
S'Escar (£)
Ses Covetes, Platja Es Trenc (no telephone)
Beach bar-café serving filling *bocadillos* and simple fish dishes.

Porto Colom
Celler Ses Portadores (£££)
Ronda del Creuer Baleares 59 (tel: 971 825271)
Fresh fish and lobster are the specialities here. The hake with asparagus and clams and the sea bass in fennel and onions are especially recommended.
Es Pamboliet (££)
Carrer Churruca 16 (tel: 971 824453)
This atmospheric barbecue-grill restaurant serves giant juicy steaks. It's a must for all carnivores.

Sa Sinia (££)
Porto Colom tel: 971 824323
Lively quayside restaurant and bar. The fresh fish menu varies according to the local daily catch.

Porto Cristo
Club Náutico (££)
Carrer Vela 29, Porto Cristo tel: 971 820880
Mouth-watering rice, pizza and pasta dishes as well as fresh fish and paella, overlooking the port.

Porto Petro
Bar Burvila (££)
Far 12, Porto Petro tel: 971 657809
Locals favour this waterfront *tapas* bar and fish restaurant. Try spicy prawns or spare ribs with honey.
Ca'n Martina (££)
Passeig d'es Port 56, Porto Petro tel: 971 657517
This top restaurant in a prime waterfront location beside the harbour, offers locally caught fresh fish, paellas and delicious home-made cakes and tarts.
Ca'n Xina (£)
Carrer Cristobal Colón 52/Passeig d'es Port, Porto Petro tel: 971 659559
Enjoy all your traditional Mallorcan favourites on the lovely shady terrace of this *celler* restaurant.
Porto Petro (££)
Passeig d'es Port 49, Porto Petro tel: 971 657704
One of the port's top fish restaurants, with specialities including sardines, cuttlefish and clams.

Puig de Randa
Puig de Randa (£)
Carrer Tanqueta 1, Randa tel: 971 120300
Small, unpretentious *celler* restaurant with a small garden terrace, presenting wholesome peasant fare – rabbit with snails, lamb in wild mushroom sauce.

Sa Colònia de Sant Jordi
Bar Maxim (£)
Carrer Lonja, Sa Colònia de Sant Jordi (no telephone)
Rather than a formal meal, fill yourself up with a variety of tasty seafood *tapas* treats.
El Puerto (££)
Carrer Lonja 2, Sa Colònia de Sant Jordi tel: 971 656047
This attractive fish restaurant is on the harbour front.
Els Pescadors (££)
Carrer de Sant Joan 58, Port Colònia de Sant Jordi tel: 971 656604
Atmospheric restaurant inside the old marina, serving fresh fish caught from the owner's boat.

Santanyí
Es Vinyet (£)
Carrer des Llombards 16, Santanyí tel: 971 163019
Tasty home cooking. For value, it's hard to beat the 2-course lunch menu here which includes wine.

Ses Salines
Casa Manolo (£)
Plaça San Bartolomé 2, Ses Salines tel: 971 649130
This small family restaurant is an ideal place for lunch.

203

Index

Principal references are
shown in **bold**

A

accidents and
breakdowns 182
accommodation 194–197
camping 188
central booking system
194
fincas 138–139, 143,
194
hotel rating system
194
hotels 194–197
luxury accommodation
194
monastic accommo
dation 194
the north-east 196–197
the north-west 195–196
Palma 68–69, 194–195
rural accommodation
143
self-catering 143,
186–187, 194
the south 197
west of Palma 195
youth hostels 69, 194
Acuario de Mallorca 172
agriculture 127, 143
agrotourism 143
airport and air services
178
Ajuntament 48
Alcúdia 21, 125,
130–131
Alfàbia **98–99**, 138
Alfonso III 100
Algaida 18, 104, 158
almond trees 14, 125
Anchorage The 139
Andratx 78
animal parks 83, 148,
161
Aquacity Park 83, 176
Aqualandia 83
Aquaparc 83
aquarium 172
Arab Baths 48
Arc de la Drassana Reial
54
Archduke's Bridlepath
115
architecture 36–37,
138–139
art galleries 21, 36, 51,
62
arts scene 20–21
Artà 20, 125–126, 132,
134–135
Artà Caves 126,
140–141, 164
arts festivals 20
atalaya 170
azulejos 168

B

baby-changing facilities
83
baby-sitters and crèches
191
Badia d'Alcúdia 12, 22,
132–133
Badia de Palma 12, 22,
75
Badia de Pollença 22

Badia de Sóller 112–113
Baetic Cordillera 13
Balearics 10–11
Banco de Sóller 37
banks 181, 189
Banyalbufar 77, **85**
Banys Arabs 48
Barceló Miquel 168
bars and pubs 21, 66–67
Basílica de Sant Francesc
48–49
basketball 128
basketmaking 137
Bassa, Guillermo 100
beaches 22
family beaches 82
Bendinat 75
Biniaraix 102
Binissalem **99**, 143
bird migration 16
birdlife **16–17**, 127, 146,
148, 157, 158,
159, 163
Blue Grotto 12, 159
boat excursions 12, 22,
51, 159
bocadillos 175
Bonany 142
Bóquer Valley 146
bordados 104
Botanicactus 158
Botanical Gardens 111
Boyd, Mary Stuart 38
Branson, Richard 26
Búger 99
bullfighting **129**, 142
Bunyola 20, **99**, 109
bus services 183
business hours 189
butterflies and moths 15
Byzantines 30–31

C

Cabrera 12, 15, **158–159**
Cabrit, Guillermo 100
caças a coll 16, 115
cacti gardens 158
cafés 66
Caimari 121
Cairats valley 115
Cala Agulla 23, 135
Cala Antena 161
Cala Bona 22, 135
Cala Bóquer 146
Cala Bota 160
Cala de Deià 23, 100
Cala Egos 23
Cala El Mago 77
Cala Esmeralda 160
Cala Felcó 77
Cala Ferrera 160
Cala Figuera 155, **160**
Cala Fornells 84, 139
Cala Gran 160
Cala Guya 135
Cala Llombards 23, 82,
163
Cala Longa 160
Cala Major 22, 75, **78–79**
Cala Margraner 160
Cala Mesquida 23, 135
Cala Millor 22, 82, 126,
135
Cala Mondragó 160, 171
Cala Murada 160
Cala d'Or 22, 155, **160**
Cala Pi 23, 82, **162**
Cala Portals Vells 77, 86
Cala Ratjada 126, 132,
135
Cala Sant Vicenç 136

Cala Santanyí 23, 82,
160
Cala Setri 160
Cala Tuent 23
Cala Virgili 160
calas 12, **23**
Cales de Mallorca 11,
155, **160–161**
Calvià 75, **79**
Calvià coast 75
Camí de S'Arxiduc 115
Camp de Mar 75, **79**
Campanet 100
camping 188
Campos del Port 163
Can Casasayas 37
Can Oleza 54, 139
Can Oleo 54
Can Pastilla 22, 39, 82,
157, **161**
Can Picafort 125, **136**,
137
Can Prunera 37, 111
Can Rei 37
Can Solleric 51
Can Vivot 139
Cap Blanc 13, 162
Cap de Formentor 13,
125, **136–137**
Cap des Pinar 131, 135
Cap de ses Salines 17,
156, 157
Capdepera 137
capers **140**, 141, 168
Capocorb Vell **161**, 162
car and passenger ferries
178–179
car rental 182
caravans and
motorhomes 188–189
carob tree 14
Carro de la Beata 19,
150
Carthaginians 30
Casa Gordiola 104
Casa March 135
Casa de Sa Fauna
Ibero-Balera 140
casino 84
Castell d'Alaró 100
Castell de Bellver 49
Castell de Bendinat 86
Castell de Capdepera 137
Castell de Santueri 167
Castilian 60, 185
Castillo Comte Mal 83
Castillo de Sant Telm 88
Catalan 60, 185
Catholicism 11
Cavellet fiesta 18
caves 164–165
see also Coves
celebrities 26
cemetery, Sóller 111
Chapel of Santa Ana 55
charcoal ovens 115
child seats 83
children's entertainment
82–83
children's facilities 83,
191
Chopin, Frédéric 12, 34,
85, 96, 116, 117,
118–119
Chopin Festival 117
Christie, Agatha 144
Church of Sant Andreu
Apòstel 176
Church of Sant Jaume
131
Church of Sant Joan 79
Church of Sant Joan
Baptista 142

Church of Sant Miquel,
Campanet 100
Church of Sant Miquel,
Felanitx 168
Church of Santa Eulalia
53
Church of Santa Maria,
Andratx 78
Church of Santa Maria,
Santa Maria del Camí
107
Church of the Virgin of the
Sorrows 171
cinemas 21, 66
circuses 82
clay whistles 104, 105
climate and seasons 11,
180
coach, arriving by 179
coastline 12
Col de Sóller 12
Colònia de Sant Pere 23
Columbus, Christopher
172
complaints procedure 191
Conillera 158
Consulat del Mar 45, 56
consulates 186
Convent dels Mínims 107
Convent of Santa Ana 142
conversion charts 190
Copa del Rey 24
Cossier dances 18
Costitx 140
Cova Blava 12, 159
Cove de la Mare de Déu
86
coves 12, **23**
see also Cala
Coves d'Artà 126,
140–141, 164
Coves de Campanet
100–101
Coves del Drac 156, 164,
165, **167**
Coves de Gènova 79
Coves dels Hams 156,
165, **167**
crafts 104–105
basketmaking 137
crochet 104
credit cards 181
crime and personal safety
71, **186**
crochet 104
Cúber 13, 121
currency 180–181
customs regulations 179
cycle rental 71
cycling 25, 71

D

dance festivals 18
dance, traditional 18, 20
Deià 20, 36, 96, **101**
dental treatment 187
dimonis 18–19
Diocesan Museum 59
disabilities, visitors with
189
discos 21, 84
domestic air services 178
Douglas, Michael 26
Dragon Caves 156, 164,
165, **167**
dress code 70, 191
drives
Badia d'Alcúdia
132–133
Serra de Tramuntana
120–121

the South 162–163
west of Palma 85
driving
in Mallorca 182–183
to Mallorca 179
driving documents 183
driving tips and
regulations 182–183

E

El Calvari 145
electricity 190
Eleonora's falcon
158
Els Blavets 103
Els Calderers 138, **141**
Embalse de Cúber 13,
121
Embalse del Gorg Blau
13, 121
emergencies 186–187
En Fumat 125
ensaimadas 91
entertainment 20–21
Ermita de Betlem 141
Ermita de Bonany 142
Ermita de Sant Salvador
156, **167**, 169
Ermita de Santa
Magdalena 102
Ermita de la Victoria 131
Es Colomer 146
Es Comu 148
Es Plá de Mallorca 13,
125, 127, **143**
Esporles 85
Establiments 85, 118
Estació Marítimo 56
Estellencs 85
etiquette and local
customs 191
Eurocheques 181
Exchange, Palma 51
Exotic-Parque Los Pajaros
161

F

Faro de Punta Grossa 113
Felanitx 18, 104, 157,
168
Festa d'es Botifarró o de
sa Torrada
18, 149
Festa des Meló 151
Festa d'es Verema 99
festivals and events
18–19
Carro de la Beata 19,
150
Cavellet fiesta 18
Chopin Festival 117
Festa d'es Botifarró o
de sa Torrada 18,
149
Festa des Meló 151
Festa d'es Verema 99
Grape Harvest
Festival 99
Los Moros i Los
Cristianos
18, 144
Revelta de Sant
Antoni 19
Sa Rúa 43
Sant Antoni de Juny
fiesta 135
Sant Bartholomew
fiesta 18

Sant Honorat fiesta 18
Sant Sebastià fiesta
20
Santa Barbara's Day
18
Sausage or Roast
Feast 18, 149
fincas **138–139**, 143,
194
flamenco 66
flea market 63
Flik Flak 82
floorshows 21
flora and fauna 14–15
food and drink
bocadillos 175
ensaimadas 91
festivals 18, 149
gourmet shopping
62–63
Mallorcan cuisine
90–91
pa amb oli 175
restaurants 198–203
tapas 174–175
wines, beers and
spirits 65, 99, 141
football 128
Foradada 158
Formentera 10
Fornalutx 36, 95, **102**
forns de calç 113, 115
frogs and toads 15
Fundació La Caixa
36, 51
Fundació Pilar i Joan Miró
80
Fundació J March 51
funparks 83

G

Galilea 80
garigue 13, 14, 157, 163
Gaudí, Antonio **37**, 59,
164
Gènova 79
Ginard, Father Rafel 149
glass-bottomed boat
excursions 12, 83
glass factory 158
glassware 104, 105
go-karting 83
Goat Island 12, 15,
158–159
golf 25
Golf Fantasia 83
Gorg Blau 13, 121
Grand Canyon 107
Grape Harvest Festival 99
Graves, Robert 12, **34–35**,
38, 96, 101, 119
Graves, William 101
Greeks 30
green tourism 39

H

Hannibal 30
health 186–187
health hazards 187
Herrara, Francesc 58
Hidroparc 83
historic houses 54,
138–139
history of Mallorca 28–39
cultural history 34–37
invasions 30–31
seafaring and piracy
32–33

Talaiotic culture 28–29
tourism, growth of
38–39
honderos 30, 54
horse-drawn carriages 59,
71, 183
horse-racing 128–129
horse-riding 25
Hort de Palma 80
hotels 194–197
Huertas de la Puebla 127,
133, 143
hunting 16
hypermarkets 63

I

Ibiza (Eivissa) 10, 21
Illetas 139
Illot des Colomer 136
Inca **102**, 105, 131
inter-island travel 178

J

Jardí Botànic 111
Jaume I 31, 32, 58, 75,
86, 88, 137, 141
Jaume II 150, 172
Jaume III 99, 168
Jaume IV 99

K

King Sancho's Palace 117
King's Cup 24
King's Gardens 54
Knights Templar 144
Krekovic, Kristian 54

L

La Granja 20, 77, **80–81**,
85, 138, 139
La Llotja 51
La Moreneta 96, 103
la oltra Mallorca 8, 76
La Reial Cartoixa
116–117, 118–119
La Reserva 77, **81**
La Seu 37, 45, **58–59**
Lago Martel 165, 167
Lake Martel 165, 167
language **60–61**, 185
Las Maravillas 157
laundry and dry cleaning
services 191
leather goods 105
Lennox, Annie 26
Lighthouse Island
158
lighthouses 56, 113
Lilford's wall lizard 15,
159
limekilns 113, 115
live music 67
Llobera, Miquel Costa I
150
Llubí **141**, 143
Lluc 37, 96, **103**
Lluc-Alcari 113
Llucmajor 143, 157,
168
Llull, Ramón 48–49, **50**,
60, 157, 173
local taxes 69, 194

Los Moros i Los
Cristianos
18, 144
lost property 186

M

Magaluf 22, 75, 82, **84**
Majorca Daily Bulletin 184
*Mallorca – Isla de la
Calma* (Rusinyol) 8
Mallorca Tourist Info
184
Mallorcan character 11
Mallorquín 60, 185
Manacor 157, **171**
maps 191
maquis 13, 14
March, Joan 36, 51, 52
Mare de Déu del Rufugi
100
Marineland 83, **84**
Marivent 78
markets 53, 63, 131,
150–151
marshland 15, 127, 148
Martel, Édouard
140–141, 164, 167
Maura, Antoni 57
mealtimes 191
measurements and sizes
190
media 184
medical treatment
186–187
medieval evenings 83
Menorca 10
Mercat Olivar 53, 63
Mirador d'es Colomer
136
Mirador del Pujol d'en
Banya 109
Mirador de Ses Animes
170
Mirador de Ses Barques
121
Miró Joan **34**, 36, **80**,
104
Modernism 36–37
Monastery of Santo
Domingo 145
monastic accommodation
194
money 180–181
Montuïri 18, 19, **141**
Moors 31, 32
moped rental 71
mountain climbing 25
mountains 13, 95
Muro 133, **142**, 143
Museu d'Art Espanyol
Contemporani
36, **51**
Museu Balear de Ciencias
Naturales 111
Museu and Casa Junípero
Serra 142
Museu Diocesà 52
Museu Etnològic de
Mallorca 142
Museu Krekovic 54
Museu de Mallorca 52
Museu Monogràfic de
Pollentia 131
Museu Municipal,
Pollença 145
Museu Regional d'Artà
135
Museu de Sóller 111
museum opening hours
189
music festivals 20, 117

Index

N

Na Picamosques 158
"the naked mile" 157
nappies, baby food and
formula milk 83, 191
national holidays 180
Natural Science Museum
111
navetas 28
Nemo Submarines
83
newspapers and
magazines 184
nightclubs 21, 67
nightlife 21, 66–67
Nin, Anaïs 101
The North-East 122–151
accommodation
196–197
restaurants 201–202
sightseeing 130–151
The North-West 92–121
accommodation
195–196
restaurants 200–201
sightseeing 98–121
Nostra Senyora de
Consolació 172
Nostra Senyora dels
Angels 144
nude sunbathing 22, 77,
86, 172, 191
Nus de la Corbeta 107

O

Old Town, Palma 45–46,
54
olive trees 14
olivewood carvings 104,
105, 171
opening times 189
Oratori de Sant Anna 131
Oratorio de Nostra
Senyora de Gràcia
173
Orient 106

P

pa amb oli 175
Palau de l'Almudaina
54–55
Palau de Desbruill 52
Palau de Justicia 57
Palau March 52
Palau Marivent 78–79
Palau del Rei Sanç 117
Palau Sollerich 139
Palma 20, 21, 37, **40–71**,
108, 120, 131
accommodation
68–69, 194–195
eating out 64–65,
198–199
festivals 43
nightlife 66–67
Old Town 45–46, 54
orientation 70
parking 71
paseo 45
post office
practical information
70
public transport 70,
71
shopping 62–63

sightseeing 48–59
tourist offices 70, 192
walks and walking
tours 53, 56, 70
Palma Cathedral 37, 45,
58–59
Palma Historical Museum
49
Palma Nova 22, 75, **84**
Palma–Sóller railway line
108–109, 111
Parc de la Mar 55
Parc Natural de Mondragó
13, **171**
Parc Natural de S'Albufera
127, 148
parking 183
paseo 45
Passeig des Born 57
Passeig Marítim 56
pearls, artificial 171
Peguera 75, **84**
Pensió Menorquina 37
people and culture archi-
tecture 36–37, 138–139
etiquette and local
customs 191
language **60–61**, 185
Mallorcan character
11
population 11
religion 11
Talaiotic culture **28–29**,
150
writers, musicians
and artists 34–37
see also history of
Mallorca
Petra 142
petrol 183
pharmacies 187
Phoenicians 30
photographic film 190
photography 190
Picasso, Pablo 101
Pirate Adventure 83
Plaça del Mercat 57
places of worship
189–190
Platja Blava 147
Platja de Canyamel 132
Platja es Trenc 22, 157,
163, **172**
Platja de Formentor 137
Platja Mago 22, 86
Platja de Muro 82, 136
Platja d'Or 160
Platja de Palma 161
Platja de Palmire 84
Platja de Tora 84
Platja Formentor 23
Poble Espanyol 57
police 186
Pollença 18, 19, 20, 21,
105, 144–145
Pollentia 131
Pont Romá 144
population 11
Porreres 18, **172**
Port d'Alcúdia 82, 125,
147
Port d'Andratx 75–76, 77,
86
Port de Pesca, Palma 56
Port de Pollença 82, 125,
146, **147**
Port de Sóller 82,
106–107, 109 .
Port de Valldemossa 117
Portals Nous 75, **86**
Portals Vells 86
Porto Colom 155, **172**
Porto Cristo 155, 156,
172

Porto Petro 155–156,
173, 175
Porto Portals 86
Pórtol 104
post offices and postal
services 185, 189
pottery 104, 105
prehistoric sites 150,
161, 162
Princess Elena Horse
Jumping Trophy 98
public transport 183
Palma 70, 71
Puig d'Inca 102
Puig Major 13, 25, 121
Puig de Maria 145
Puig de Randa 20, 173
Puig de Sa Comuna 169
Puig de Sant Salvador 13,
167
Puig Teix 115
Puig Tomir 144
Puigpunyent 86
Punta de n'Amer 13, 170
Punta de Capdepera 135
Punta de Covas 136
Punta Grossa 109, 113

R

Rabbit Island 158
La Rambla 58
reading list 35
Rei, Lluis Forteza 37
Reial Club Nautic 56
religion 11
religious festivals 18
reptiles 15
Reserva Africana 83, **148**
reservoirs 13
restaurants 198–203
the north-east 201–202
the north-west
200–201
Palma 64–5, 198–199
the south 202–203
west of Palma
199–200
Revelta de Sant Antoni 19
Ripoll, Luis 28, 29
roba de llengües 105
Roman theatre 131
Romans 30
royal family, Spanish 26,
55, 56, 78–79
Royal Palace 54
Royal Yacht Club 56
Rubió, Joan 37, 111
Ruines Romanes 131
Rusinyol, Santiago 8, 66,
101

S

Sa Calobra 23, **107**
Sa Colònia de Sant Jordi
157, 163, **176**
Sa Colònia de Sant Pere
141, **149**
Sa Coma 22, 82, 135
Sa Dragonera 12, 75, **86**
Sa Foradada 114
Sa Pobla 19, 133, 143
Sa Ràpita 163
Sa Romaguera 161
Sa Rúa 43
Sa Torre 139
Sa Trapa 88, **89**
Sagrera, Guillem 51, 58,
168

sailing 24
S'Albufera 15, 16–17,
148
S'Albufereta 17, 127
Salines de Llevant 17,
157
salt pans 156, 157
Salvador, Archduke Luis
33, 35, **114**, 115, 117
Sanctuari de Cura
156–157
Sand, George 10, 11, 34,
43, 85, 96, 116,
117, **118–119**
Sant Agustí 79
Sant Antoni 135
Sant Antoni de Juny fiesta
135
Sant Bartholomew fiesta
18
Sant Honorat fiesta 18
Sant Joan 18, 143, **149**
Sant Llorenç des Cardassar
132
Sant Miquel, Palma 58
Sant Sebastià fiesta 20
Sant Telm 75, **88**
Santa Barbara's Day 18
Santa Catalina Thomàs
116
Santa Margalida 19, **150**
Santa Maria del Camí
105, **107**
Santa Ponça 75, 82, **88**
Santanyí 163, **176**
Santuari de Cura 20, 173
Santuari de Mont-Sïon
172
Santuari de Sant Honorat
173
Santuari de Sant Salvador
132, **134–135**
S'Arenal 22, 39, 82, 157,
176
Sausage or Roast Feast
18, 149
scenery 12–13
scuba-diving 24
seat belts 182
Second World War 33
self-catering 143,
188–189, 194
Selva 121
Sencelles 143
Serra del Cavall Bernat
146
Serra, Juníper 48, **50**,
142
Serra de Llevant 13, 155,
156–157, 169
Serra de Tramuntana 11,
13, 15, 95, **120–121**,
125
Ses Covetes 163
Ses Illetas 79
Ses Païsses 150
Ses Voltes 51
S'Estació 21, 151
S'Estanyol 163
shopping 62–63, 189
S'Hort del Rei 54
S'Horta 157
Sineu 131, **150–151**
sitjas 115
siurells 104, 105
slingshot 30, 54, 128
smoking etiquette 183
snow pits 115
Sóller 18, 20, 37, 82, 95,
109, **110–111**, 112,
120
Son Berga 80
Son Forteza 86
Son Forteza Vell 138

Son Gual Parc Prehistòric
    83
Son Marroig **114**, 138
Son Sant Joan airport 178
Son Servera 132
Son Vida 69, 80
The South 152–176
    accommodation 197
    restaurants 202–203
    sightseeing 158–176
Spanish Civil War 33
Spanish Village 57
speed limits 182
sports **24–25**, **128–129**
    basketball 128
    cycling 25, 71
    football 128
    golf 25
    horse-racing 128–129
    horse-riding 25
    hunting 16
    mountain climbing
        25
    sailing 24
    scuba-diving 24
    tennis 25
    waterskiing 24
    windsurfing 24
stamps 185
supermarkets 63

T

Talaiotic culture **28–29**,
    150
talaiots 28, 29, 161
tapas 174–175
taulas 28
taxis 71, 183
Teatre Romà 131
telephone dialling codes
    185
telephone numbers
    emergency 186
    useful 185
telephones, public 185
television 184
tennis 25
textiles 105
theatre 66
thrush nets 16, 115
tiles 168
time differences 180
tipping 191
tiro con honda 128
toilets 190
topless sunbathing 191
Torre de Canyamel 132
Torre Major 131
Torre Paraires 56
Torre Picada 121
Torrent de Pareis 25, 107
Torrente Sa Riera 86
tourism 11, 33, **38–39**,
    75
tourist offices 70, **192**
Town Hall, Palma 48
train, arriving by 178–179
train journeys 82,
    108–109
train services 111, 183
tram line 109, 111, 183
travel insurance 180
travel and insurance docu-
    ments 179
travellers' cheques 181
travelling to Mallorca
    178–179
Tunel factory 109
Tunel Major 109

V

vaccinations 187
Valldemossa 20, 21, 96,
    116–117, 118, 119
Valle de los Naranjos 110
Vandals 30
vegetation 13, 14
Verne, Jules 164
Via Cintura 183
Victory Cross 88
Vidrios Gordiola 158
Vilafranca de Bonany 18,
    143, **151**
Villa Francisca 99
visas 179

W

walking 25, 95, 107, 136
walks
    Badia de Sóller,
        112–113
    The Bóquer Valley 146
    Camí de S'Arxiduc
        115
    Palma 53, 56
    Sa Trapa 89
    Serra de Llevant 169
watchtowers 33, 170
waterskiing 24
watersports 24
wax museum 83
West, Gordon 35, 58,
    145
West of Palma 72–92
    accommodation 195
    restaurants 199–200
    sightseeing 78–89
wetland birds 16–17
wild flowers 14
wildlife 15
windmills 56, 127, **170**
windsurfing 24
wine making 99
wines, beers and spirits
    65, 99, 141
A Winter in Majorca
    (Sand) 11, 35, 43,
    117, **119**
Wood, Charles 170
words and phrases, use-
    ful 61
writers, musicians and
    artists 34–37

Y

youth hostels 69, 194

207

Acknowledgements

Picture credits

The Automobile Association would like to thank the following photographers, libraries and associations for their assistance in the preparation of this book.

AKG LONDON 119b
THE BRIDGEMAN ART LIBRARY 32b Saint Jordi Altarpiece, detail showing the conquest of the City of Majorca by the army of James I, 1229 by Pedro Nisart (15th century) (Museu Diocesano de Mallorca); 33b Doblenc Diner (Catalan currency) from the reign of James I (1213-76), minted in Barcelona (recto) (Instituto Municipal de Historia, Barcelona); 33c Doblenc Diner (Catalan currency) from the reign of James I (1213- 76), minted in Barcelona (verso) (Instituto Municipal de Historia, Barcelona; 34/5 The Treasure and Mother Ubu: From 'Ubu Roi' a play by Alfred Jarry (gouache) by Joan Miro (1893-1983) (Private Collection) (© ADAGP, Paris and DACS, London 1998); 36a Harlequin's Carnival, 1924-25 by Joan Miro (1893-1983) (Albright Knox Art Gallery, Buffalo, New York) (© ADAGP, Paris and DACS, London 1998); 36b The hands play a big part (snail, woman, flower, star), design for a carpet, 1934 by Joan Miro (189301983) (Prado, Madrid) (© ADAGP, Paris and DACS, London 1998),
JAMES DAVIS TRAVEL PHOTOGRAPHY 116/7
EMPICS SPORT PHOTO AGENCY 128
MARY EVANS PICTURE LIBRARY 32a
FUNDACIÓ PILAR I JOAN MIRO a MALLORCA 80 L'Oiseau De Proi Fonce Sur Nous 1954 (© ADAGP, Paris and DACS, London 1998)
FUNDACIÓN JUAN MARCH 51 3 (5 x 5 - 1), 1981. Luis Gordillo. Oil and enamel on paper and on wood (© DACS 1998)
IMAGES COLOUR LIBRARY LTD 156, 165b
INSTITUTO BALEAR DE PROMOCIAN DEL TURISMO 19b, 19c
NATURE PHOTOGRAPHERS LTD 15a (Lea McNally), 15b (S C Bisserott), 15c (K Carlson), 16a (R Tidman), 16b (P R Sterry), 17a (D Smith), 17b M Bolton), 148b (P R Sterry)
PICTURES COLOUR LIBRARY LTD 122/3, 191
POPPERFOTO 35
SPECTRUM COLOUR LIBRARY 78/9, 130
THE STOCK MARKET PHOTO AGENCY INC. 138a, 138b
WORLD PICTURES 6/7, 68/69, 74, 176

All remaining pictures are held in the Association's own library (AA PHOTOLIBRARY) and were taken by KEN PATERSON with the exception of the following pages:
A BAKER 12a; P BAKER 2, 4b, 6, 11b, 24a, 25a, 29a, 29b, 30b, 31b, 39a, 39b, 50a, 57b, 71, 83a, 90b, 95, 100, 104b, 105, 118a, 119a, 126, 127a, 143a, 143b, 143c, 145, 148a, 148/9, 159b, 169, 170a, 171a, 172, 174b; S DAY 60b, 174a; E MEACHER 65; D MITIDERI 26a; C SAWYER 175; J A TIMS 129a, W VOYSEY 115, 116b

Acknowledgements

Teresa Fisher wishes to thank Palmair, 2GL, Cdr and Mrs Penfold and Ray Hugill for their assistance in the preparation of this book. The author and the Automobile Association would like to acknowledge the contribution of Nigel Tisdall, author of *Thomas Cook Mallorca,* and Tony Kelly, author of *Essential Mallorca.*

Contributors

Revision copy editor: Lodestone Publishing Ltd **Original copy editor**: Audrey Horne
Indexer: Marie Lorimer